learning about DANCE

DANCE AS AN ART FORM & ENTERTAINMENT

Kendall Hunt
publishing company

Eighth Edition
NORA AMBROSIO
Slippery Rock University

Cover and title page images contributed by Ben Viatori. ©Kendall Hunt Publishing Company.

Kendall Hunt
publishing company

www.kendallhunt.com
Send all inquiries to:
4050 Westmark Drive
Dubuque, IA 52004-1840

Previously titled: *Learning about Dance: An Introduction to Dance as an Art Form and Entertainment*

Copyright © 2003, 2006, 2008, 2010, 2016, 2018 by Kendall Hunt Publishing Company

Copyright © 1994, 1997 by Nora Ambrosio

ISBN 978-1-5249-2212-2

Printed in the United States of America

Brief Contents

Contents

During my years as a dance educator, it has always thrilled and fascinated me to witness the transformation that first-time dance students undergo during the course of a semester. The feelings of confusion, boredom, apathy, indifference, and nervousness dissipate with each passing class, until it is obvious that the student begins to feel that he or she is part of something very special—something not "ordinary." It would be wonderful if this experience could be given to every student across campus. Although dance technique, composition, and performance classes draw in many students, not every student will readily don leotards and tights and plunge into "the unknown."

The most successful introductory dance courses that I have taught have been the ones where the students vowed (at my encouragement) to *keep an open mind*. Making this vow helped them to delve into what, for most of them, was uncharted and unfamiliar territory. Making this vow also gave them room to have a positive learning experience, one that will remain with them the rest of their lives.

My hope is that people will use *Learning about Dance: Dance as an Art Form and Entertainment* as a springboard to further exploration of dance, leading them to become enthusiastic members of the dance audience (or possibly even dancers and choreographers themselves!). The world of dance is exciting, daring, ever-changing and dynamic—and is there for all to view, appreciate, participate in, and learn from.

Learning about Dance: Dance as an Art Form and Entertainment was created for use in introductory level courses: dance introduction courses; survey courses; courses that are a prerequisite for dance history; and technique or composition classes that have an introductory, lecture/discussion, or history component. This book is intended for students who require information regarding different aspects of the dance world, including dance as an art form; the choreographer; the dancer; the audience; the different dance genres (ballet, modern, jazz, world dance, etc.); dance production; dance in education; and careers in dance.

This textbook covers all the diverse elements that make up the world of dance. Beginning with a broad historic overview of the art form, the book moves into an engaging discussion of the respective roles of the dancer, choreographer, and audience, and then into more detailed considerations of the origins and evolution of the major genres: ballet, jazz, modern, post-modern dance, dance in world cultures, and jazz, tap, and musical theatre.

Wide-ranging in its scope, *Learning about Dance* also features sections on social dance, improvisation, creative movement, dance/theatre, dance production, dance in education and careers in dance.

Features of this Book

- Dramatic photos illustrate text information. Included are photos of *Fred Astaire and Ginger Rogers, Vernon and Irene Castle, Jack Cole, Merce Cunningham, Isadora Duncan, Loie Fuller, Doris Humphrey, Gene Kelly and Cyd Charisse, Anna Pavlova, Bill "Bojangles" Robinson and Shirley Temple, Ruth St. Denis, Anna Sokolow, Paul Taylor, Trisha Brown, Bill T. Jones,* and *Mark Morris,* among others.
- User-friendly writing style includes chapter introductions, text callouts, and chapter summaries.
- Discussion questions elicit the critical and creative thinking needed for group discussions.
- Creative projects apply text concepts to promote hands-on, experiential learning.
- Major Figures sections feature biographical statements, photos, and descriptions of renowned artists in ballet, modern dance, post-modern dance, jazz, tap, and musical theatre.
- Chronological timelines detail the events that made dance what it is today.
- Tables outline and compare characteristics of major dance genres.
- Additional resources include:
  - Suggested Readings
    - Ballet: History and Criticism
    - Ballroom and Social Dance
    - Biographies and Autobiographies
    - Choreography
    - Dance Education/Dance Pedagogy
    - Dance in World Cultures
    - Jazz Dance, Musical Theatre, and Tap Dance
    - Modern and Contemporary Dance: History and Criticism
    - Philosophy and Aesthetics
    - Related Topics
  - Magazines, Periodicals and Newspapers
  - Dance DVD and Digital Video Distributors
  - Dance on the Internet
  - Suggested Videos and DVDs (listed by chapter)

Acknowledgments

A heartfelt thank you to photographers Debra Brunken, Rhyme Wan Chang, Terry Clark, Bruce Davis, Johan Elbers, Dave Garson, Lois Greenfield, Candice Kaminski, Jack Mitchell, Eduardo Patino, Robert Ruschak, Ron Seymour, Ben Viatori, and Frank Ward for the use of their beautiful photographs.

Thanks also to Gina Ambrosio for her help and assistance.

Thanks to Catrionia Higgs, Gordon Phetteplace, and Teena Custer for their suggestions and comments. Special thanks and gratitude to David Skeele. Without his help, this book would have never come to fruition.

Also, special thanks to Judy Morris.

Nora Ambrosio is a Professor in the Department of Dance at Slippery Rock University of Pennsylvania, where she has taught since 1988. Ms. Ambrosio has been instrumental in developing their highly acclaimed and nationally accredited dance program, and served as department chairperson from 1998–2011. Ms. Ambrosio currently teaches Dance History, Dance Composition, Teaching of Dance, and Senior Synthesis. She has also served as the Artistic Director of Slippery Rock University Dance Theatre. In 1989, she developed *Learning about Dance: Dance as an Art Form and Entertainment* for Slippery Rock University's general education program. Other publications include *The Excellent Instructor and the Teaching of Dance Technique*, 3rd Edition, published by Kendall Hunt Publishing Company, 2018. She received her M.F.A. in Dance from Smith College in Massachusetts.

Contributed by Ben Viatori. ©Kendall Hunt Publishing Company.

Ms. Ambrosio is an active choreographer, working in the jazz dance, modern dance, and dance/theatre genres.

part one

THE ART OF DANCE

From the ritual dances of early cultures to the most sophisticated work of contemporary artists, dance has had a long, rich history. This chapter discusses dance as an art form and gives information on the historical, societal, and individual aesthestics that helped shape the world of dance.

Dance as an Art Form

Dance is an art form that is displayed through the human body using the medium of movement. Although there are many definitions, most people involved in dance would agree that dance is a "projection of inner thought and feeling into movement . . ."[1] Dance has the power to communicate and evoke responses. It provides a means for self-expression and enables the participants and viewers to feel and experience the joy of moving.

Contributed by dgarson.com.
©Kendall Hunt Publishing Company.

Dance is an art form that is displayed through the human body using the medium of movement.

Throughout history and all around the world, dance has been significant in the lives of many people: from the tribal leader enacting a sacred ritual to the professional dancer who has dedicated his or her life to dance, to the person who takes a dance class just for fun. Take, for example, the role that dance plays in the life of the average college student. In talking with college students and asking the question "What is your idea of a fun night out?," many enthusiastically reply "Going out dancing with friends!" It is interesting to note that although this activity seems to be exciting to many college-age students (as well as other age groups), most of them have never actually seen a "professional" dance concert and are also not aware of the rich and lengthy history of dance.

Dance and Society

Dance has the power to communicate and evoke responses.

Imagine a city block anywhere in the nation. Cars and buses fill the streets, the sidewalks are jammed with people and the rattle of the subway trains can be felt underfoot as the crowds pass on top of the grates. A variety of noises fill the air—horns honking, police car sirens, people yelling, a loud radio.

Here in this city dance can be found in many different places. At one corner on the fifth floor of a tall building is a dance studio, where couples are learning how to ballroom dance. Among the participants are members of different age groups, including older couples reliving the dances of their youth, gliding effortlessly across the floor. There are also younger couples experiencing ballroom dance for the first time, struggling with the elegance and precision demanded of this dance form. Across the street, in another studio, is a group of professional dancers taking a ballet class. Nervous energy abounds in the room as an artistic director of a major ballet company looks on, picking out the lucky few who will be invited to audition for the company. Down the street, a billboard advertises the opening of one of the world's most popular modern dance companies. The bold picture of a dancer caught in midair is striking and catches the attention of everyone who passes by. And on the other corner, a group of teenagers practice the latest hip-hop moves, their exuberant athleticism and lightning-fast footwork awing an audience of out-of-towners.

Forty miles outside the city is a rural community, where rolling hills, tall trees and green grass can be seen for miles. There is a peaceful calm and an almost lazy quality about the place. But all over this community there is plenty of dance activity. Today, the local senior center provides instruction in square dancing and each group cheers as the caller successfully navigates them through an intricate series of do-si-dos and promenades. At the elementary school, a guest teacher conducts a creative movement workshop with the students. At first the boys and girls are shy and apprehensive about dancing in front of each other, but they abandon all shyness when the teacher asks them to move like their favorite cartoon character. In the evening, the local high school will perform their annual musical theatre performance, filled with several show-stopping song and dance numbers. And in a neighboring town, the local performing arts council sponsors a dance concert, which will be performed by an African dance company. The concert will be filled with beautifully decorated, authentic African costumes, dynamic and powerfully charged movements and rhythmic drumming (see Figure 1.1).

In between the city and the countryside is a suburb. Neat houses line the streets and the voices and laughter of children can be heard. The neighborhood

Figure 1.1

African dancer and drummers.
©testing/Shutterstock, Inc.

park is crowded with children who jump, run, skip, leap, roll, hop, and crawl. Although they are not actually dancing, one can clearly see the dancelike quality of their movements and how easily these movements present the opportunity for uninhibited self-expression. During the morning church service liturgical dancers will perform as part of the mass. They will dance in the processional and will also interpret the day's reading through movement. In the afternoon, a family will gather to celebrate a Bar Mitzvah. They will perform traditional Hebrew dances that have been done for centuries at such occasions. The local dance studio down the street is giving lessons in the latest country and western line dances and hoots and hollers can be heard above the country music. And a world-renowned jazz and tap ensemble will perform tonight at the newly renovated performing arts center, where the syncopated rhythms of the taps will be a perfect complement to the rhythmic jazz music.

Dance can be found in many places, from the most populated to the most rural areas. From the earliest, most primitive cultures to today, every age has had its dance. Dance is recognized as being one of the oldest art forms known to the world and as dance writer and teacher Margaret H'Doubler pointed out, the fact that dance has lived on for thousands of years shows evidence of its value.[2] In order to fully understand the value of dance in society and to understand why it has lived on for so many years, it would be beneficial to look back at what we know to be the beginnings of dance—that of indigenous cultures—and to examine the cultures that followed.

> *Dance is recognized as being one of the oldest art forms known to the world . . .*

Upper Paleolithic (30000–10000 B.C.E.)– Neolithic (7000–3000 B.C.E.) Periods

One of the strongest pieces of evidence proving that dance existed in early cultures was discovered in a series of rock paintings depicting dance. People created these paintings hundreds of thousands of years ago (most likely during the Paleolithic Age) in France.[3] Wall paintings found in the Magura cave of Bulgaria also depict dance (see Figure 1.2). These paintings are considered significant to the understanding of dance in the Paleolithic era. These cave drawings point to the fact that movement played a role in early societies. Since the discovery of these rock paintings, several other drawings and carvings have been found that depict dance. For example, archaeologists discovered a wall painting in a tomb from the fifth dynasty of Giza (created circa 2700 B.C.E.), which depicted a harvest dance.[4] Also, "Paleolithic cave drawings near Palermo

Figure 1.2

Prehistoric wall paintings depicting dance found in the Magura cave of Bulgaria.
©Anton.Daskalov/Shutterstock.com

in Sicily depict human figures performing what appears to be ritualistic dance, an observation that implies dance must have been taught and learned."[5] Through much research by leading historians and by studying current uses of dance in several early cultures, we know that in these cultures people used dance as a means of communication and as a way of life.

In the absence of a common verbal language, people used their bodies to express thoughts and feelings. Movements and gestures became an essential part of all facets of people's lives. Life's daily rhythms, to which these people had a strong connection (internal rhythms, such as breathing, walking and the beat of one's heart, and external rhythms, such as the cycle of day and night and the change of the seasons), were a natural precursor to dancing and singing.

People used rituals to worship and appease the gods and believed that these rituals held magical and spiritual powers.

One of the most important aspects of their lives—where dance was used as the ultimate means of expression—was during dance rituals. People used rituals to worship and appease the gods and believed that these rituals held magical and spiritual powers. The occasion of a birth, marriage or death required that a dance ritual be performed in conjunction with the event. These rituals held great meaning for the participants and the viewers. For example, in some societies, a dance ritual held at birth would ensure a long, healthy life for the infant. A marriage ritual would celebrate the transition from single to married life (much like our own traditional wedding ceremony). A ritual at someone's death would ensure that the deceased's spirit would rest peacefully. Probably the most important rituals that occurred in these societies were those that revolved around fertility (for food and children). Many fertility rituals were done to ask the gods for rain, sunshine, an abundant harvest and healthy children.

It is sometimes hard for contemporary society to understand the magnitude of dance rituals and to see how much early humans' lives revolved around them. It is also difficult to visualize what these dances looked like. Many writers, such as Margaret H'Doubler, state that the movements were most likely very basic; such as running, hopping, swaying, stomping, and clapping. The movements were also imitative, devoted to the mimicry of animals, forces of nature and of the gods.[6] The length of the rituals varied, depending on their function. Some lasted only hours, whereas others were conducted over a period of several days.

Although much of what these rituals looked like and how they factored into early human's lives has been based on speculation, research continues to point to artifacts and discoveries that do depict prehistoric dancing cultures. More than 400 examples of carved stone and painted scenes on pottery from 140 sites in the Balkans and the Middle East illustrate a record of dancing from 9000 to 5000 years ago. This record coincides with the place and time of hunters and gatherers who first settled into villages. "Some artifacts show only stick figures with triangular heads, and some headless, in highly schematic scenes that appear to be dances. Others include figures in a dynamic posture, usually with bent arms and legs. Several scenes depict people in a line or completely circling an illustrated vessel, their hands linked."[7]

There are still cultures that have a strong connection to their ancestors and continue to incorporate dance in their daily lives. One example of such people are the Yanomami in the northern part of South America. The Yanomami, mostly found in parts of Venezuela, Brazil, Guyana, and Colombia, incorporate many dancing rituals into their lives. According to anthropologist Napoleon Chagnon, one such ritual is called *amoamo* and is performed before a hunt.[8] The men in the tribe do this ritual of song and dance to ensure good luck in capturing and killing animals for food and in anticipation of a feast. The movements of this ritual is high powered and dynamically charged:

> *Two at a time, the . . . dancers entered, pranced around the village periphery, wildly showing off their decorations and weapons and then returning to the group. Each dancer had unique decorations and a unique dance step, something personal that he could exhibit. He would burst into the village screaming a memorized phrase, wheel and spin, stop in his tracks, dance in place, throw his weapons down, pick them up again, aim them at the line of [people] with a wild expression on his face, prance ahead a few steps, repeat his performance and continue on around the village in this manner, while the [people] cheered wildly.*[9]

Although this description depicts a frantic dance display, the Yanomami are also known for their quiet and lovely dance rituals. For example, the Sanema are a branch of the Yanomami tribe living in the rain forest on either side of the border between Venezuela and Brazil. They continue to preserve ancient traditions, including making skirts from banana leaves for simple, repetitive dances that have been performed for more than 3,000 years. "The typical dance of the Yanomami is always performed at sunset, and its simple choreography is complemented by the cheerful character of the tribe . . ."[10]

It is fascinating to examine indigenous societies today and to analyze how they have continued performing the dance rituals that their ancestors did thousands of years ago (obviously not in the exact same way, but probably with the same ritualistic significance). Why did the cultures continue performing these dances? Why did they keep the dance rituals? Why do they still hold so much importance today? For cultures so steeped in tradition, ritual, and spirituality, negating these dances would not even be a consideration.

Dance and movement were prevalent in early cultures, and today it remains important to those indigenous cultures still in existence. But, obviously, other cultures developed throughout the ages. For this discussion, we will focus on the broad categories of Ancient, Medieval, Renaissance, and Contemporary, although the reader should realize that there are periods within these ages (such as the Baroque period during the Renaissance) in which different styles and dance aesthetics were developed. The reader should also realize that the titles of these periods are Western terms, and that other countries label these time periods differently. For example, what is known as the Medieval era in the West would coincide with the periods that fall between the Northern and Southern Dynasties and the Ming Dynasty in China, and the Yamato and Ashikaga periods in Japan.

In this brief overview, it is important to examine how dance continued throughout the ages and to see how dance developed. For example, when did it take on shape and form, and begin to hold artistic significance? As cultures became more advanced (such as those of Mesopotamia, Egypt, and Asia, who began to make significant developments in writing, government, and agriculture), people began to become more aware of how dance was presented. In other words, people began to pay attention to technique (form, content, and style), and also to the appearance of dance. Although rituals remained important, many were replaced by ceremonies.[11] Ceremonies were more highly structured and stylized than the spontaneous expression of the ritual, and the dance, whether serving a spiritual function or done for entertainment, was now seen more as an artistic product.

When referring to the different ages, it is important to remember that there are not specific moments in time when one age stopped existing and another one began. There were long periods of overlap between them, and the aesthetic sensibilities of each age permeated the next. These were also complex societies, with long, rich histories. What follows are brief descriptions of each age, highlighting the primary aesthetic and value placed on dance in the societies.

The Ancient Period: About 3000 B.C.E. to 400 C.E.

The dances of the Ancient civilizations were described as "thought . . . combined with dramatic intent, and aesthetic elements were consciously sought."[12] In other words, conscious decisions began to be made with regard to dance. How the dance *looked* and what the dance was to *represent* dictated what movement choices were made. In some areas, dance was still used as part of traditional rituals, as documented in seven bronze tablets inscribed between the end of the third and beginning of the first century B.C.E. These tablets, discovered in 1444 in Gubbio, Italy, document and give directions for certain rituals, many of which require the participants to "dance in ternary rhythm" at specified points, as well as perform circular patterns, turns, and stops for a specified duration.[13] Known as the Tables of Iguvium (or the Tables of Gubbio), these ancient relics give insight into the importance of dance to certain rituals and ceremonies. In this age, however, development of vocal language, as well as the invention of writing, agricultural advancements, centralized government, organized religion, and class distinctions all helped to shape aesthetic decisions. It would be difficult in this brief description to discuss the dance aesthetics of all the societies of Ancient times (including those in the Middle East, Asia, Africa, the Mediterranean, Greece, and Rome). Therefore, a few descriptions of dance in ancient times will be included.

India has one of the longest and richest traditions of dance. Archaeologists have found a wealth of evidence that proves that dance was a part of the lives of India's earliest civilizations (2300–1750 B.C.E.), most likely in the form of religious celebrations.[14] The dance and theatre that was developed in India in ancient times had a great impact on the dance developed throughout all of Asia. One of the places that dance appeared was in the Sanskrit dramas that flourished between the first and tenth centuries. These dramas were religious

Figure 1.3

in nature and reinforced the beliefs and practices of the ancient culture. Around 500–300 B.C.E., a dance technique was developed called *Bharata Natyam*. Bharata Natyam was a temple dance that required skill, grace, and stamina. It is still practiced today (see Figure 1.3) and is known for its flowing arm movements, exact head and eye gestures and complex rhythms that are stamped out by quickly moving feet. There are also records of many types of religious dances, court dances, and folk dances, some that lasted well past ancient times and some (like Bharata Natyam) that are still practiced today. There are eight recognized classical Indian dance forms. They include Bharata Natyam, Kathak, Kathakali (see Figure 1.4), Kuchipudi, Manipuri, Mohinattyam, Odissi and Sattriya. Each form represents the culture of a specific region.

China also has records of early dance. A wall painting from the Central Henan Province, dating back to about 200 C.E., depicts a large-scale banquet with dance, juggling, and musical performances taking place between the two rows of guests.[15] Today, much of what is known about China's dance comes from the Beijing Opera (formally Peking Opera, which can be traced back to the eighth century), but it is also known that dance was part of many theatrical performances of ancient times (see Figure 1.5). Dance dramas were also performed, with many of the lead characters portraying the gods and heroes found in Chinese myths.

Classical Indian dancer.
©Eduard Derule/Shutterstock, Inc.

Figure 1.4

Kathakali performers in South India. Kathakali is an ancient classical dance form.
©Alexandra Lande/Shutterstock, Inc.

Figure 1.5

Actors of the Beijing Opera Troupe perform the famous story *White Snake*.
©Hung Chung Chih/Shutterstock, Inc.

In much of Ancient Greece, the ideas of beauty and knowledge dominated the age, and dance, poetry, and education were part of daily life. The artistic high point of the Greek period (and perhaps of Ancient times in general) was the fifth century B.C.E., when the Greek sense of art and beauty provided artistic and spiritual satisfaction for society. This period (along with the later Roman period) is sometimes referred to in other art forms as the "Classical" period.

Figure 1.6

Neo attic relief—dancing maidens.
© Darryl Brooks/Shutterstock.com

The development of most Greek dances can be traced back to religious rituals. These dances combined movement, music, and poetry, and were often participatory group dances, where people were linked together by holding arms or hands. There were also animal dances, which were probably carried over from early history when the mimicry of animals was part of sacred rituals. Dance was also found in the popular Greek theatre, where it was used to emphasize the tragic or comedic aspect of the performance. Today, references to dancing in Ancient Greece can be found in Greek myths, literature, musical notations and on many art objects, such as carvings, sculptures and statues (see Figure 1.6).

The Medieval Period: About 400 C.E. to 1400 C.E.

During the Medieval era (also referred to as the Middle Ages), we again see many different examples of dance. Some of the most interesting dances during this time are those of the Islamic cultures. The Islamic lands flourished during the Medieval era, and dance was part of both rituals and daily life. There was a traditional form of dance that may have been developed during the ninth and tenth centuries, when Baghdad was the cultural center of Islam.[16] This type of dancing is still performed today, and is characterized by an undulating torso, swaying and rocking hips and other rhythmic full-body and arm movements. In Islamic countries, this dance has many different names, and Westerners usually refer to it as "belly dancing," although it would never be called that by the people of the Middle East. Many folk dances were also part of Medieval Islamic cultures, some of which are still performed today.

After the fall of the Roman Empire, the idea and importance of art, beauty, and aesthetics that was seen in Greece and throughout much of Europe eventually changed under the rule of the Christian church (again, because of the complexity of this era, a broad leap has been taken regarding much of the historical aspects of this period). Although many of the common people took part in folk dance activities, such as the Maypole dance, these dances were seen by the church as pagan activities. The creation of almost *any* art was frowned upon and even banned, unless it was created specifically for the purpose of glorifying the church (for example, the *Mystery Plays,* which are still performed every four years in York, England). While in the past, the development of the intellect was the main focus, now the enhancement of spirituality was the priority. "Dance, both because it was pleasurable and because it was physical, was frowned upon and all but suppressed in secular life, and was permitted to exist only in the staid form as a part of . . . worship."[17] Any non-religious dances (such as folk dances, which were at that time performed as rituals and for entertainment) were generally performed covertly.

The church dictated much of what happened in society. The church placed a great emphasis on the idea that the body was evil, and that the purity of the soul was the only thing that mattered. This idea, along with the outbreak of the Black (bubonic) Plague (around 1347), led to a preoccupation with death and dying, superstitions and witchcraft. Margaret H'Doubler noted that this side of medievalism tended to be fanatical and unbalanced, and in extreme cases led to a dancing frenzy:

> The dancing mania that swept over Europe during and immediately after the Black Death [a disease that killed as much as half the population of Europe] was no new disease, but a phenomenon well known to the Middle Ages . . . Men, women, and young boys and girls would dance in wild delirium, seemingly possessed and without any will of their own.[18]

Many historians have written about this dancing mania, commonly referred to as the Dance of Death or *Danse Macabre*. There are different theories

Figure 1.7

Artwork depicting the Dance of Death.
Image Copyright: © The Metropolitan Museum of Art.
Image source: Art Resource, NY.

The revival of dance as an art form was an important part of the general rebirth of the arts that is associated with the Renaissance period.

as to why this dancing mania occurred. Some speculate that these outbursts were truly part of a physical disorder caused by the plague, while others feel these dancing manias were in direct response to an extreme feeling of dread and to the overwhelming control that the church placed upon the society. Others believe they were due to a mental disorder that afflicted people across Europe, or possibly a reaction to widespread famine, while still others believe that it was due to a combination of the above. Whatever the reason, the idea of death obsessed many people, and much of the art created during this time centered on the death figure, usually portrayed as a skeleton or a group of skeletons (see Figure 1.7).

In spite of the church and the Black Plague, dance did continue, and by the end of the Middle Ages was beginning to be seen in theatrical performances and at balls. The revival of dance as an art form was an important part of the general rebirth of the arts that is associated with the Renaissance period.

The Renaissance Period: About 1400 C.E. to 1700 C.E.

Dance held much importance in the Renaissance period. In the West, this period was ". . . an expression of renewed interest in the culture of the ancient world . . . art became less and less a group activity and more and more the creative product of individual artists."[19] Court ballets were developed in this age, beginning in the fifteenth and sixteenth centuries, and folk dancing continued to be a popular means of expression for the working classes (court ballets, as well as Romantic ballet and folk dance, will be discussed in greater detail in *Part Three: Dance Genres*). Instrumental music became the accompaniment for many social dances, such as the minuet, pavan, allemande, and sara band, to name a few (see Figure 1.8). These dances, also known as preclassic dances, were performed in the courts, and were a combination of "common" folk dances and the aristocratic steps of the nobility.

The Renaissance period saw the rise of ballet as a professional art form, one that continued to develop throughout the seventeenth and eighteenth centuries. The birth of the Romantic ballet occurred during the nineteenth century. This ballet style followed the aesthetic that was already occurring in music, literature, painting, and sculpture (see *Chapter Five: Ballet*). Also during

Figure 1.8

Couples dancing the minuet, 18th C.E., engraving.
Bettmann/Getty Images

this time, some of the world's most captivating dance traditions were developed, many of which are still in existence today (some of these genres are discussed in *Chapter Eight: Dance in World Cultures*).

The Contemporary Period: 1700 C.E. to the Present

While Eastern countries continued to perform traditional dances and create new dances based on traditional elements, contemporary times have seen the development of many dance genres (particularly in the West). The early part of the twentieth century introduced classical and contemporary ballet, as well as modern and contemporary dance (since the majority of this book covers these major developments, no further discussion of specific dance genres is needed here). The twentieth century presented society with many advancements. Just as technology and science became more sophisticated, so did art; so did dance. As discussed throughout this book, the twentieth century presented the world with some of the greatest dance artists and dances ever known. And as we are finding in the twenty-first century, there is no shortage of creative and innovative dance artists.

From the earliest times to today, dance has remained relevant in most societies.

Although entertainment is a part of dance, it is not its most essential reason for being. Therefore, in order to understand the true meaning of dance, we must first understand dance as an art form.

Throughout the Ancient, Medieval, Renaissance, and Contemporary ages, dance underwent many changes: from being an intellectual endeavor to being banned as a pagan activity; from being the cultural undertaking of the nobility to being the artistic voice of the working class; and from being a spectacle of beautiful poses, costumes, and grace, to being a forum for social and political messages.

From the earliest times to today, dance has remained relevant in most societies. The importance that dance held in these societies, however, has differed from age to age and culture to culture. Today, while many people view dance as merely something to do or watch for entertainment purposes, others see dance as a viable and important art form. Although entertainment is a part of dance, it is not its most essential reason for being. Therefore, in order to understand the true meaning of dance, we must first understand dance as an art form.

Art and the Aesthetic Experience

When an artist creates (in dance, the creator is the choreographer), he or she usually creates in order to present something before an audience. More specifically, the artist wants to *communicate* something to the audience. Regardless of whether the created work is literal or abstract, the desire and need for self-expression propels the artist to create. Therefore, many times when viewing a work of art (whether it is a dance, painting, sculpture, poem, etc.), the audience is being challenged by the creator of the work to *think* about what the work of art represents or evokes. Choreographer and writer Agnes de Mille stated that works of art are "symbols through which people communicate what lies beyond ordinary speech . . . art is communication on the deepest and most lasting level."[20] Often, people will view art and quickly say "I like it," or "I don't like it," without ever knowing why. It is everyone's right and privilege to be critical of a work or to not like it, but "knee-jerk" reactions to art, whether they be positive or negative, are not expressing an informed opinion. If the viewer will take the time, however, to examine an artist's work with objectivity and with an open mind, they might connect with what the artist is trying to communicate or represent. This "connection" can be a very rewarding and satisfying experience, but can also be a thought-provoking or sometimes uncomfortable one. For example, if a person views a dance that the choreographer intended to be about love between two people and the viewer is also in love, then this dance might produce a very pleasurable feeling. But what if the viewer has just ended a long-term relationship? For that person, this dance might be very sad and even hard to watch. If de Mille is accurate in saying that "art is communication on the deepest and most lasting level," then one of the purposes of art is to illuminate for the viewer those things in life that touch us at the deepest core of our being. We relate to what we see in a work of art by using our aesthetic sense—perceiving something through feelings. Similarly, the feelings evoked from viewing a work of art can be said to produce an "aesthetic experience."

When viewing a work of art, an individual may have an aesthetic experience. A work can be said to be aesthetically moving when it evokes responses from the viewer with little conscious reasoning. These responses are not limited to things that make people feel happy, or to things that people consider to be beautiful, as we discovered in the example of the dance choreographed about two people in love. We now know that a dance that has a dark and dramatic theme, such as death, can have a strong aesthetic appeal to an audience, even though it may make them feel uncomfortable. It is important to remember that the interaction with the work of art must *do something to the viewer.* This "something" may be either a physical reaction (such as a "nervous" feeling in one's stomach), or an emotional reaction (such as happiness or sadness). The work of art must move the viewer in some way, either positively or negatively.[21]

Obviously, what one person considers to be aesthetically pleasing, another may not. How do people view art and what makes them decide what is aesthetically pleasing or moving? Many human characteristics and traits are factors in determining this answer. For example, a person's moral, religious, and ethical values may be a key factor in determining what might evoke an aesthetic response. Also, an individual's intellect, imagination, tastes and personal experiences may play a role, as may the amount of education a person has had. The socioeconomic background of a person may be another factor, as well as his or her emotional state (in general and at the time of viewing the work of art).

To illustrate this point more clearly, it might be beneficial to look at some hypothetical situations. For example, do you think a person from a conservative background might view a work of art (let's say a painting) that contained nudity differently than a person with a liberal background? Maybe, maybe not. What if a live dance that they were watching contained nudity? What if the dance contained references to alternative lifestyles? As in life, the more controversial or foreign things are to what we know, the more we question it, accept it, or push it aside. It is not possible, nor particularly desirable, for people to put aside the characteristics that comprise their emotional makeup when viewing a work of art. It is important, however, that people view art with an open mind and provide time for themselves to react to the work in an intelligent manner.

In addition to individual people having their own aesthetic sense, society (as a whole or as different groups) can also have particular aesthetic opinions. As people and times change, so will values and tastes. For example, many in their respective societies shunned several of our most treasured works of art. In 1913, composer Igor Stravinsky's *Le Sacre Du Printemps (The Rite of Spring)* caused a commotion the first time it was performed before an audience. With choreography by Vaslav Nijinsky, the ballet, performed in Paris, received boos and hisses from the time the music started until the final curtain (in addition to a near riot almost breaking out in the theatre). People reacted this way because the music and dance were different from *anything* that they had ever heard or seen before. The music had harsh and uneven rhythms and the choreography played upon those rhythms with movements that pounded and stamped the floor, employed turned-in legs and used sharp, angular gestures. The audience saw it as outrageous and unacceptable. Today, both the music and choreography of *Le Sacre Du Printemps* are regarded as outstanding works

. . . remember that the interaction with the work of art must do something to the viewer.

It is important, however, that people view art with an open mind and provide time for themselves to react to the work in an intelligent manner.

Figure 1.9

Le Sacre Du Printemps (The Rite of Spring), with music by Igor Stravinsky, choreographed by Kenneth MacMillan and performed by The Royal Ballet. Like many choreographers, MacMillan was inspired by Vaslaz Nijinsky's choreography to create his own version of *Le Sacre Du Printemps.*

Robbie Jack/Corbis Entertainment/Getty Images

of art, and have been the inspiration for and interpreted by many different dance companies (see Figure 1.9).

Another example are the plays of Henrik Ibsen that were produced in the late 1800s and were, for the most part, disliked by the European community because of the content and the style in which they were written. Ibsen dealt frankly with issues (such as moral hypocrisy and the oppression of women) that a complacent society preferred to keep hidden. Today, the plays of Ibsen are produced throughout the world, and he is considered one of the outstanding playwrights in the history of dramatic literature. It is important to remember that works of art do not become better or worse over time, they simply look different and have a different value as society changes.

. . . works of art do not become better or worse over time, they simply look different and have a different value as society changes.

Summary

From the earliest ritual dances of indigenous cultures to the most sophisticated work of contemporary artists, dance has had a long, rich history. Philosopher Susanne Langer described dance in this way:

> *. . . dance, like any other work of art, is a perceptible form that expresses the nature of human feeling—the rhythms and connections, crises and*

breaks, the complexity and richness of what is sometimes called [humanity's] "inner life," the stream of direct experience, life as it feels to the living.[22]

Though today many tend to view dance simply as a form of entertainment, it has the potential to significantly raise an audience's awareness, inviting them to think and feel in new and different ways. Of course, each individual's reaction to a dance will be determined, to an extent, by what that individual brings to the dance—an audience's response to a dance says as much about the audience as it does the dance. Table 1.1 outlines dance through the ages.

Figure 1.10

Table 1.1 *Dance through the Ages*

Dance in the Upper Paleolithic–Neolithic Periods	Dance in the Ancient Period	Dance in the Medieval Period	Dance in the Renaissance Period
■ Dance was used as a means of communication. ■ Dance rituals were done to worship and appease the gods. ■ Dance rituals were done at special occasions, such as a birth, marriage, or death. ■ Many dance rituals focused on fertility and having an abundant harvest. ■ Movements were most likely imitative (of nature and animals) and very basic.	■ Aesthetic elements were consciously sought. ■ Developments and advancements in writing, agriculture, and government helped to shape the dance aesthetic. ■ Movement choices were made in order to represent certain themes. ■ The height of the Ancient period was the Greek period, fifth century B.C.E., when the quest for art and beauty was the priority. ■ Many Greek dances developed out of religious rituals. ■ Dances combined movement, music, and poetry and were often participatory. ■ Dance was often found in the popular Greek Theatre. ■ Many dances of India were religious dances. *Bharata Natyam* developed as a temple dance. ■ Evidence of dance in China dates back to 200 C.E. The dances performed in eighth-century China influenced all of the dance that was to follow.	■ In most of Europe, the church saw dance as a pagan activity. ■ Dance was banned unless it glorified the church. ■ The Black Plague killed as much as half the population of Europe and led to a preoccupation with death and dying, superstitions, and witchcraft. The Dance of Death emerged at this time. ■ In Islamic lands dance flourished during this time and was done for rituals and for entertainment purposes.	■ A renewed interest in the arts developed. ■ Dance became less of a group activity and more about the individual artist. ■ Court ballets flourished and folk dancing remained popular with the working class. ■ Ballet emerged as a professional art form (see *Chapter Five: Ballet*).

Discussion Questions

Discuss in class or provide written answers.

1. Discuss your experiences with dance. For example, have you ever taken dance lessons? Was dancing a big part of your childhood, such as at family gatherings? How does dancing fit into your life now?

2. Do you see any similarities between the rituals of indigenous societies and rituals that we have in today's society?

3. How might people's moral, religious, and ethical values influence their thoughts and opinions on art? Discuss specific examples in relation to this question.

4. Did you ever have an aesthetic experience when viewing a work of art? If so, what were you viewing? Describe your reaction.

5. Can you think of any works of art, in addition to the ones mentioned, that were not readily accepted by the society in which they were created, but held in high regard years later?

6. What do you think is meant by the statement ". . . an audience's response to a dance says as much about the audience as it does the dance," and do you agree or disagree with this statement?

part two

THE PARTICIPANTS

The following chapters discuss the
choreographer, dancer, and audience—
the necessary participants in the world of
dance. Information is given on the role and
responsibility of each person and how each
participant is related to the other.

The Choreographer

This chapter describes the role, artistic vision, and the creative process of the choreographer. In certain cases, differences are found when describing specific dance genres, forms, and styles. What follows, however, is information relative to every choreographer.

Contributed by dgarson.com.
©Kendall Hunt Publishing Company.

The Choreographer as Artist

A choreographer is a person who utilizes the medium of dance (movement) to make his or her art. Through the use of movement and by manipulating the elements of space, time, and energy, the choreographer creates a work of art in the form of a dance.

Many people would agree that one of the primary reasons that choreographers (or any artists) create a work is because they want to communicate something to their audience. This "something" can be a very specific thought, feeling, emotion, or a story to which the choreographer wishes the audience to connect with and respond. Giving an audience a literal or specific message, however, is not the main motivation for all choreographers. Therefore, it is important to realize that not every dance has to mean something or be about

. . . one of the primary reasons that choreographers . . . create a work is because they want to communicate something to their audience.

23

something. "When [a dance] is good enough to involve and stimulate the senses, it is senseless to ask, 'What sense does it make?'"[1] Choreographers can choose abstract concepts to work with that do not necessarily have specific themes or storylines. These dances are commonly referred to as being "movement for movement's sake," and the importance of the creation is based on movement rather than on theme or storyline. Whatever the motivation to create, one thing is for certain: "Choreography means more than assembling movements. The artist is concerned with what results from the organization of movement rather than with the mere arrangement."[2] The choreographer must pay close attention to the form, look, shape, and feel of the dance. Dances should appear "seamless," with each phrase of movement flowing into the next.

How does a person become a choreographer? Many people feel that years of study and training in dance and composition can give the choreographer the tools that he or she will need in order to successfully create dances. Others feel that choreographers are born, not made, and that training will enhance an already-present instinctive ability that cannot be learned. The answer to this question may never be known or fully understood. There are certain characteristics and traits, however, that many choreographers seem to have in common and are important for all choreographers to possess.

Certain characteristics and traits must be part of the makeup of a choreographer, regardless of the dance genre in which he or she chooses to work. One of the most important attributes for a choreographer to possess is *passion*. The choreographer must have a passion and a love for dance, for without it they would not be able to create. The choreographer must also be *dedicated* and *committed* to his or her work. Most choreographers spend long hours in rehearsals, so *patience* is a requisite, especially when having to work with a diverse group of dancers, all of whom may learn, work, and behave differently from one another. The choreographer must be *sensitive* to the needs of the dancers as individuals and also as members of a group.

It is important for the choreographer and dancers to have *respect* for each other. This understanding is necessary for a comfortable and productive working environment. If the choreographer shows genuine appreciation, concern, and respect for the dancers, it will pay off immensely. This statement is not meant to imply that dancers have to be "babied." On the contrary, dancers are usually hard workers who need little motivation. Common courtesy, however, as well as common sense, tells us that in most work situations, people will give back what is given to them.

Because choreographers are always creating, many of them constantly look for new inspirations and new themes and ideas about which to choreograph. Therefore, choreographers are usually *observant* and *perceptive* people. They also have a great *thirst for knowledge* and are *inquisitive*. Could you imagine a choreographer who did not have these characteristics? Since a person's life experiences and knowledge are the basis for his or her creations, it is imperative that the choreographer remain a constant learner; a lifelong student.

One of the most important attributes for a choreographer to possess is passion. *The choreographer must have a passion and a love for dance, for without it they would not be able to create.*

A choreographer should possess *practical knowledge of dance technique.* Because he or she works with dancers and is ultimately responsible for their safety, it is desirable that the choreographer has an understanding of how the body works (i.e., anatomy and kinesiology). All too often, dancers receive injuries from executing movements incorrectly. A choreographer should make sure that the dancers are executing movements correctly and are working within the range of their bodies' abilities and their level of experience.

The Creative Process

For the choreographer, dance is a language. Movements are used as words to "say" something to the viewers. For most choreographers, using movement to convey a thought or message is easier than speaking about the subject. Although some choreographers find it easy to speak about their work, most would prefer to let the work speak for itself. "It is difficult to talk or write about a dance, to reconstruct in words what has been designed in action, through movement sensation, idea, feeling, kinetic memory and a host of connotations intermingled in the movement itself."[3] Sometimes, however, it is beneficial for audience members to hear the choreographer's perspective on the dance. Choreographers should learn how to speak about their work and the processes inherent in the creation of the work, as a method to help educate viewers.

Choreographers are usually very much aware of the world around them and of the many facets that make up their lives. For example, their own life experiences, the experiences of others, current events, their view of the world, and the human condition are just a few subjects with which choreographers may be concerned. These ideas and issues make up the subjective life of the choreographer, wherein creative decisions are determined by the thoughts, feelings, and state of mind of the artist. Therefore, "[t]he creative process is the process of change, of development, of evolution, in the organization of subjective life."[4]

The creative process is also thought to be directly linked to the choreographer's subconscious mind. This concept has been debated by some, particularly those in the field of psychology. Many others, however, believe that the subconscious plays a major role in the creative process. "Everyone uses from time to time such expressions as, 'a thought pops up,' an idea comes 'from [out of] the blue,' or 'dawns,' or 'comes as though out of a dream,' or 'it suddenly hit me.' These are various ways of describing a common experience: the breakthrough of ideas from some depth below the level of awareness."[5] Many believe that because an artist has a heightened sense of aesthetic sensibilities and is generally more "in-tune" with feelings and perceptions, that they are also receptive to ideas that may form in the subconscious mind.

Each choreographer has his or her own methods and ways of choreographing a dance. The creative process that each choreographer goes through differs. For example, some choreographers can create dances very quickly. This type of choreographer uses ideas that come in fast flashes and then translates

For the choreographer, dance is a language. Movements are used as words to "say" something to the viewers.

Each choreographer has his or her own methods and ways of choreographing a dance. The creative process that each choreographer goes through differs.

these ideas into movement in a limited number of rehearsals. Other choreographers need time to think, ponder and plan, and require a longer rehearsal time in order to complete a dance. Some choreographers, if they are creating a dance to music, will work very closely with the music, studying it to learn the phrasing, rhythmic structure, etc., before they create the movement. Other choreographers will create the movement first and then bring music in to fit the dance. Some choreographers have a specific plan of action (in terms of the movements that the dancers will learn) before the dancers come into rehearsal, while other choreographers prefer to create the movements on the spur of the moment as the dancers are with them in rehearsal.

Another way to generate choreography is through a collaborative means whereby the choreographer acts as a director and structures the movements developed by the dancers. Often times, this movement is developed through improvisation sessions. For example, the choreographer/director may give the dancers a specific problem to solve or theme to use as the impetus to create movement. The choreographer then helps the dancers to set the movement, or structures the movement to suit the dance. A dance can also include a combination of elements, where parts of the dance are created and taught by the choreographer, while other parts are created collaboratively with the dancers.

There are many different ways that people approach the act of choreography, but many would agree that "[t]he intimate act of choreography is an inner process, begun in a creative encounter with movement and pursued and refined with aesthetic sensibility."[6] In whatever way the choreographer chooses to work through the process, there comes a time when the choreographer has to "give" the dance to the dancers. This time is never an easy one for many choreographers. If the dancers are well-rehearsed and prepared, however, the choreographer must trust them and show that he or she has confidence in their abilities as performing artists. As stated earlier, a choreographer creates to communicate something, and the only way a dance can communicate is if it is performed before an audience. Ultimately, the dancers are the ones that are in control of the dance when they are on stage and the choreographer can only observe, the same way the audience does.

...all choreographers manipulate the elements of space, time, and energy to create and enhance the quality of their dances.

Choreographic Elements of Dance

Regardless of the genre the choreographer is working in, all choreographers manipulate the elements of space, time, and energy to create and enhance the quality of their dances. The following is a discussion of these elements.

Space

Space design and dance structure evolve together through the use of the space elements.

Movements mold the spatial aspects of dance and make the stage space come alive as an aesthetic element. Space design and dance structure evolve together through the use of the space elements.[7] Under the category of space are the elements of shape/line, level, direction, focus, points on the stage, floor pattern(s), depth/width, phrases, transitions and repetition.

Shape/Line: This element can be looked at from two different perspectives: in terms of the overall shape of the entire dance, and the shapes of specific movements. The choreographer can consider the overall shape of the dance. For example, will the majority of the dance appear to be curved, angular, linear, or a combination of spatial aspects? On a more specific level, a choreographer must pay attention to the specific shapes (single shapes as well as shapes that are part of a phrase) that are found within the dance (see Figure 2.1).

Figure 2.1

A dancer executing two shapes that have a strong, sharp, and angular appearance.
Copyright © 2001 by Bruce Davis.

A choreographer might shape his or her dance according to the theme of the dance. For example, if a dance is concerned with the military, the overall shape of the dance, as well as the specific shapes found in the dance, might be sharp and angular. On the other hand, if a dance is about happiness and joy, the shapes might be soft and curved. Be aware, however, that the previous statements are merely given as *examples* and not hard and fast rules. A choreographer can use *any* type of spatial designs to depict *any* type of mood or feeling.

Sometimes, a choreographer works with the concept of "positive" and "negative" space. These terms describe specific shapes and movements and their

A choreographer can use any type of spatial designs to depict any type of mood or feeling.

Figure 2.2

A dancer executing a movement that clearly shows the "positive" space, or the shapes the body makes, and the "negative" space, the areas around the body.
Copyright © 2001 by Bruce Davis.

Dancers demonstrating two different levels—high and low.
Copyright © 2001 by Bruce Davis.

Figure 2.3

relationship to the space around them. Positive space refers to the shapes formed by the body of the dancer, and negative space refers to the shapes formed by the empty area surrounding the dancer (see Figure 2.2).

Some choreographers, particularly those who work in the ballet genre, often refer to the "line" of the movement, which is in direct relation to shape. The term "line" is usually found in ballet choreography, referring to the movements in ballet that must be executed in a specific way in order for the dancers to achieve the desired/classic ballet shape.

Level: Changing levels in a dance can provide a way for the choreographer to make dances more interesting. For example, a choreographer may use the floor (low level) and the space above the dancer's heads (high level, see Figures 2.3 and 2.4) instead of constantly having the dancers perform upright (medium level), to produce a more visually interesting dance. The use of levels also provides informa-

Figure 2.4

Dancers demonstrating use of high level.
Contributed by Ben Viatori. ©Kendall Hunt Publishing Company.

tion to the audience as to the content or meaning of the dance. For example, if a choreographer was creating a dance about underwater sea creatures, crawling, rolling, or slithering at a low level might be used to create the effect of moving along the sea floor. Why might the use of high levels be incorporated into a dance? Themes focusing on joy, the concept of heaven, or using the image of floating in the clouds might require movements that are at a high level.

Direction: The directions that dancers move in and face (see Figure 2.5) are also factors in choreography. Having the dancers face front (toward the audience) for an entire dance might be uninteresting and predictable. It may be more interesting for the dancers to move in different directions (forward, backward, diagonally, etc.) and face different directions on the stage throughout the duration of the dance.

Figure 2.5

Dancer using eyes and body, particularly the arm gesture, to call attention to a specific direction.
Copyright © 2004 by Bruce Davis.

The dancer's use of focus, or where and how they are using their eyes and body, can greatly enhance the quality of the performance.

Figure 2.6

Dancers using strong outward focus toward the audience.
Courtesy of Rhyme Wan Chang.

Focus: The dancer's use of focus, or where and how they are using their eyes and body, can greatly enhance the quality of the performance. Often, when a dancer is very focused, the audience members are drawn into what the dancer is doing. If a dancer performs movement without total concentration and connection between the body, face, and eyes, the movement will appear unimportant and lack performance quality. Using focus not only shows commitment to the movement, but also makes the overall performance more exciting (see Figures 2.6 and 2.7). The dancer may use an "outward" focus, such as looking directly at the audience or looking out beyond the horizon for a lost love, or an "inward" focus, which shows the concentration more on the self. It is the choreographer's choice as to what type of focus is used, but using it effectively is important. It is imperative that the choreographer gives directions to dancers regarding focus, because it is an extension of the movements being performed.

Points on the stage: Before discussing the importance of using the points on the stage, it might be helpful to discuss the stage space in which the choreographer creates. The most powerful point on the stage, or the place that draws the most focus, is called "center stage." Any space in front of center stage (toward the audience) is called "downstage." Any space behind center stage (away from the audience) is called "upstage." From the *dancer's* perspective (as opposed to the audience's), any space on the right is called "stage right," and any space on the left is called "stage left." Therefore, if a dancer comes on to the stage from the farthest point upstage and also from the right side, that dancer would be upstage right. Examine the diagram of a stage in Figure 2.8. The wavy pattern in the upstage area represents a curtain, scrim, or cyclorama. The smaller wavy lines represent legs or flats and make the wing space in which dancers make entrances and exits.

It is evident that there are many places on the stage where dancers could be placed. The choreographer decides where to put the dancers in relation to the feeling or idea that he or she wants to portray. For example, if a choreographer wanted a dancer to appear strong and confident, then he or she might begin the dance either center stage or downstage center, with the dancer performing an appropriate shape or movement(s) to show strength. On the other hand, if the choreographer wanted the dancer to appear scared and fearful, the dancer could possibly start in one of the upstage corners, performing a shape or movement(s) that portray those emotions. Again, these statements are only *examples*, not hard and

Figure 2.7

A dancer using focus to place emphasis on a specific area within the stage space (in this case, behind the dancer, in the upstage right corner).

Figure 2.8

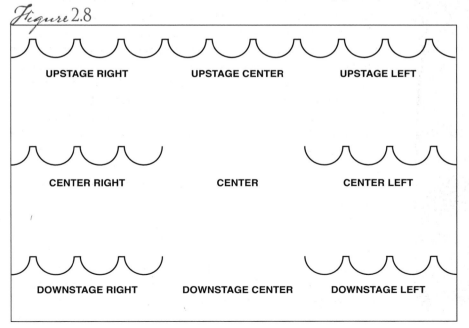

Stage diagram.

fast rules. Many dances do not start on stage at all; some begin by making an entrance from one of the wings.

Floor Pattern(s): Similar to using several of the other elements, the choreographer could use floor patterns (or pathways) to enhance the visual appeal of his or her dance. Use of floor patterns is the method by which the choreographer moves the dancers around the stage space. For example, in a modern dance, if a dance depicted a tornado, the floor pattern might be a circular, whirling pattern. Also, a choreographer might use a floor pattern(s) that is based on a specific shape or design. For example, the choreographer could have the dancers follow an imaginary zigzag or figure eight pattern along the floor (see Figure 2.9).

Figure 2.9

Dancers following a figure eight (curved) pattern along the floor.
Courtesy of Frank Ward.

Depth/Width: Choreographers should use the depth and width of the stage space to create specific designs, show symmetry, asymmetry, distance, and closeness. For example, in a modern dance, if there were two couples dancing on the stage at the same time, the choreographer might choose to put one couple downstage of the other in order to draw more focus to either or both of the couples (rather than having them dance side by side).

Phrases: All dances are made up of phrases that are linked together (often, phrases are made into different dance sections, and these sections are put together to comprise the whole dance). A phrase of movement can be thought of as being like a sentence, with a beginning, middle, and end. Just as a sentence has to be logical, so does a movement phrase. Additionally, linking together several movement phrases to make a dance is similar to linking sentences together to make a paragraph; paragraphs together to make a story; and so on. Movement phrases can be short or lengthy, but must not be movements simply thrown together haphazardly. There has to be shape and form to all phrases, with high points, low points, and dynamic changes. Movement phrases may stay on the same dynamic level, however, dynamic changes throughout the phrases may aid the choreographer in communicating a specific message or highlighting specific imagery. Dynamics may also be used to create varied and exciting moments within the dance (see also "Breath/Emotional Phrasing" under "Time").

Transitions: Transitions are what link one movement phrase to another, allowing a dance to flow smoothly from section to section. Clear, direct transitions are crucial to the overall look and feel of a dance. Without them, a dance will appear choppy and probably will not make much sense to the viewers. A transition can be a big movement, like a leap or jump, or a small movement, like a turn of a head or wave of an arm. Whatever the transition, it must appear seamless. In other words, it should not call attention to itself or appear out of place, but have a natural feel in relation to the movement that it precedes and follows. For example, if dancers were performing a phrase of movement that was very fast and dynamically charged, and the choreographer wanted them to then perform a phrase that was slow and controlled, the choreographer might have the dancers come to a sudden stop at the end of the fast phrase, and slowly melt into the beginning of the next. There are a number of different ways that the choreographer could connect those two phrases—the important thing is that the transitions should make sense within the context of the dance.

Repetition: The use of *repetition* in choreography can be a powerful tool. Often, when a viewer has the opportunity to see movements more than once, the specific idea, image, or feeling that the choreographer is trying to call attention to may become clearer. As with all of the dance elements, repetition must be used carefully and skillfully, and in a way that makes sense within the dance. Used wisely, movement repetition can greatly enhance a dance, whereas poor or perfunctory use tends to make a dance boring.

Time

All dances happen in a given time frame. Unlike some of the other arts, such as painting and sculpture, dance is ephemeral and can only be seen in its previous state if it was captured on video (this is not to say that dance on video is in any way the same as a live dance performance). Movements cause something to happen and thus a change occurs, which is sensed as having a duration and is perceived in terms of time.[8] Under the category of time are the elements of speed/tempo, pulse/underlying beat, rhythmic pattern, time signature/meter, no counts at all, breath/emotional phrasing, stillness, and words/text/sounds/silence.

The use of repetition in choreography can be a powerful tool. . . . the specific idea, image, or feeling that the choreographer is trying to call attention to may become clearer.

Speed/Tempo: The speed or tempo relates to how fast or slow the dancers are moving. This element of time might have to do with the music that the choreographer is using, although not all dances are performed to music. The choreographer decides how fast the dancers should move throughout the entire dance. For example, a choreographer might want the dancers to move very slowly for the entire dance, or very quickly. A combination of timing elements can also be used in order to produce a specific effect, mood, or feeling.

Pulse/Underlying Beat: This element usually has a direct relationship to music. The pulse is the steady beat that underlies the rhythm and the melody of some musical pieces. Because of its constant repetition, it can be very powerful, and the choreographer must decide whether to go with or against the pulse. Many novice choreographers choose to work with the pulse, and this decision sometimes can result in choreography that appears too symmetrical and elementary. An advanced choreographer may come up with a more sophisticated rhythmic structure for the dance (such as using syncopated rhythms), instead of only going with the underlying pulse or beat.

Rhythmic Pattern: This element concerns the rhythm that dancers follow when they perform movements. Music can influence the rhythmic pattern, but as stated earlier, not all dances are choreographed to music. Therefore, the choreographer must provide the rhythm (regular, irregular, simple, complex, syncopated, etc.) for the dancers, just as they provide the movements.

Time Signature/Meter: The time signature or the meter reflects the number of beats to a measure. For example, the time signature of a piece of music could be 2/4, which would have a marching quality to it, or 3/4, which would have a "round" quality to it, as does a waltz. Again, the choreographer makes the decision to work with the meter, against it, or use a combination of both methods.

No Counts at All: When a dancer learns a dance, the choreographer usually teaches the dance so that each movement has a specific count. The choreographer, however, might choose to choreograph the dance without using specific counts, therefore the dancers might rely on musical cues, using visual connections if it is a group dance, or breath or emotional phrasing to perform the movements.

Breath/Emotional Phrasing: In order for it to be executed properly, this element usually requires the experience of advanced dancers. In a sense, the choreographer asks the dancer to "feel" the movements. Instead of being given specific counts, the dancer might instead be given different images, dynamics, or qualities that pertain to how the movements should be performed. This method is usually difficult for a beginning dancer, as it requires much ability and experience on the dancer's part. The dancer might use his or her breath phrasing to give certain emotional qualities to the specific movements, and to remember how to perform them the way the choreographer desires.

Stillness: Stillness in dance can be beautiful and powerful, and provide a wonderful contrast to constant motion. Stillness, however, does not mean inactivity. When a dancer is in a still position on stage, his or her whole body and mind must stay charged and focused or else the audience may lose interest. This task is difficult to accomplish (particularly for beginning dancers), and requires much thought, effort, and energy on the part of the dancers (though they are not even moving!).

Words/Text/Sounds/Silence: In addition to dances that are choreographed to music, dances can be choreographed to words, text, and sounds, or performed in silence. Particularly with the advent of dance/theatre (which is discussed in *Part Three: Dance Genres*), it is not atypical for dances to be performed to this kind of accompaniment.

Energy

When a movement is executed, a certain amount of energy is used to accomplish the movement. The duration, intensity, and speed of each movement is determined by the amount of energy and the degree of force used.[9] The elements in this category include dynamics and qualities.

Using dynamics in a dance is probably one of the most important choreographic "tools" that can be used to enhance the dance and make it appear more exciting.

Dynamics: Dynamics are created when energy is used with time. For example, if a dancer exerts a lot of energy and performs a movement very quickly, the dynamic will be "sharp" (see Figure 2.10). If a dancer takes the same movement and performs it very slowly, the dynamic would be "sustained." Using dynamics in a dance is probably one of the most important choreographic "tools" that can be used to enhance the dance and make it appear more exciting. Without the use of dynamics, a dance may appear flat and uninteresting. Sometimes, watching a dance that does not change dynamics is comparable to listening to someone at a lecture who is only speaking in a monotone voice, never changing their inflection throughout the speech.

Qualities: "Movement qualities are the distinctly observable attributes or characteristics produced by dynamics and made manifest in movement."[10] Some movement qualities are *percussive, swinging, sustained, vibrating,* and *suspending.* Like dynamics,

Figure 2.10

The dancer has to use a great amount of energy and speed to attain the desired height of this jump.

qualities are used to enhance the dance, make the movements more interesting, and give insight into what the dance is about.

A choreographer may also utilize specific images to evoke the kind of qualities they want the dancer to demonstrate. For example, if the dancers were told to "move as if you are wearing the finest silk fabric," they may perform the movements in a luxurious way. If on the other hand the dancers were asked to "move as if you were wearing an itchy wool sweater," then the results would be markedly different. Using descriptive words such as silky, wooly, lightly, heavily, and so on, will allow choreographers to be specific about the qualities of movements.

Summary

All choreographers use the elements of space, time, and energy whenever they create a dance. Some choreographers make conscious decisions in manipulating these elements in a dance, while others allow instinct to dictate what the work will look like.

For many choreographers, the creative process is ongoing. Most choreographers would suggest that their dances are never really finished, although the audience might not realize it. There are many choreographers who continue to make refinements and enhancements to their dances even after they have been performed before a live audience. Most choreographers feel that there is always room for improvement and take advantage of rehearsal times between performances to better their work. There is a time, however, when choreographers have to release the dance and let it stand alone as a work of art. Then it is up to the audience (and sometimes the critics) to decide the failure or success of the work. It is important to remember that choreographers never set out to make a "bad" dance and also that every dance created will not necessarily be a masterpiece. Although the success of a piece of choreography can never be predetermined, there are certain pitfalls that choreographers should avoid at all costs: for example, filling the space with just *any* movement; having too much or not enough contrast; having too much symmetry for no reason; lacking exploration and wandering from the subject; having awkward or stereotyped rhythmic or space patterns; giving movement to the dancers that is beyond their technical or performance abilities; keeping the dance going on and on, long after its point had been made; relying too much on accompaniment, costuming, staging, narration, or a title to boost the artistic level of the dance; and being unreceptive to qualified criticism.[11]

The art of choreography is a demanding and difficult task for even the most advanced artists. Although choreographing may be natural for some people, it is certainly never easy. Through the creative exploration of the subconscious, to the making of conscious artistic choices, choreographers must always be aware of the world around them and remain open-minded to all possibilities.

The art of choreography is a demanding and difficult task for even the most advanced artists.

Discussion Questions

Discuss in class or provide written answers.

1. In addition to the characteristics already mentioned, what characteristics do you think a choreographer should possess?

2. What are some "abstract" concepts about which a choreographer might create a dance? Also, what are some current themes, issues, and ideas that a choreographer could work with in order to create a dance that is based more in reality or that has a storyline?

3. What do you think the choreographer/dancer relationship should be?

4. Out of all the elements of dance, which do you believe are the most important for a choreographer to utilize? Explain your choices.

Figure 2.11

Contributed by Candice Kaminski, clikstudiosonline.com. ©Kendall Hunt Publishing Company.

The Dancer

All artists use tools to create their works of art; the painter uses paints, brushes and canvas, the musician uses instruments. The "tool" of the choreographer is the dancer. Through the use of movement, the choreographer molds and shapes what the dancer will perform, just as a sculptor molds and shapes clay.

Contributed by dgarson.com. ©Kendall Hunt Publishing Company.

The Dancer as Artist

Dancers are a special group of people. The work that they do takes much discipline, dedication, and determination. Throughout the history of dance there have been outstanding artists, all of whom had to work daily to perfect their art. Some of these artists are very popular and known throughout the world. Most, however, are known in certain dance "circles," but will probably never become famous on a worldwide or even national scale. Still, this fact is not enough to deter people who love the art of dance. The sacrifices that they have to make (including financial and personal ones) are almost an accepted part of the territory and most people who dance probably would not be happy doing many other things.

It is fascinating and thrilling to watch an outstanding dancer perform. Take, for example, Mikhail Baryshnikov (b. 1948). He is said to be one of the world's greatest dancers and has thrilled audiences worldwide. What makes Baryshnikov so special? As a ballet dancer, was it his amazing ability to leap into the air and reach incredible heights? Or was it his perfection in performing multiple turns? What about his sensitivity to musical phrasing? All these fac-

chapter three

All artists use tools to create their works of art . . . The "tool" of the choreographer is the dancer.

39

tors contribute to his undeniable talent, but there is another reason why he is so unique. Baryshnikov is not only a dynamic technician, but also a *performer*, and one who has spent years perfecting the art of bringing movements to life on stage. He credits his teacher, Alexander Pushkin, with teaching him the most important lesson regarding dance:

> [Pushkin] taught me the difference between technique—dancing in the classroom—and real dancing. Real dancing happens on the space of a stage and to be aware of that space—its flexibility, its rules, its relationship to the audience—was what he stressed. As I work now, I still am always aware of those early lessons. One goes out on stage with a well-prepared technique, a knowledge of how to present that technique in its most refined form. But beyond that, what counts is the ability to be free on the stage, to dance. When I prepare a role, I naturally learn the steps first; however, I try to find the appropriate style from the beginning and then rehearse the steps in it. As a young dancer I had a quite developed, secure technique, but my sense of style was often appalling. I know now that style is what gives blood and color to the bones of the piece, the technique. It is of utmost importance to work very hard to make style and technique one.[1]

Baryshnikov, who began as a ballet dancer in Russia, has broadened his career to include dancing with modern dance choreographers and companies. He has also served as artistic director of a major ballet company (American Ballet Theatre), starred in a leading role on Broadway, and made several movies including *The Turning Point* (1978) and *White Nights* (1985). From 1990–2002, he performed with the White Oak Dance Project, a modern dance repertory company, which he began with choreographer Mark Morris. In 2005, Baryshnikov established the Baryshnikov Arts Center in New York. He is still an active performer.

The Dancer's Training

As seen in the above quote by Baryshnikov, a dancer must be an outstanding performer as well as an outstanding technician. When discussing the "technique" of a dancer, what is being referred to is the correct placement and alignment of the dancer's body and how that dancer executes the movements. (The term "technique" can also refer to a specific style of movement that a certain person developed, such as the "Graham technique," developed by Martha Graham. This use of the term "technique" is referred to in *Chapter Six: Modern and Contemporary Dance*).

Although there are dancers who don't regularly practice formal technique, such as ballet, modern, and jazz, good technique is necessary for those who aspire to be in most professional companies. Some dancers choose to practice other forms of movement, such as yoga, in order to hone their dance skills. Regardless of how dancers prepare, to be an outstanding technician, dancers

...a dancer must be an outstanding performer as well as an outstanding technician.

must have strength, flexibility, and excellent alignment of the body (see Figure 3.1). *Some* alignment issues that dancers have to be concerned with include: engaging the abdominal muscles and having a strong "center" so that the pelvis does not tilt (sway) back or tuck under when executing movements; having a strong connection between the top of the pelvis and the bottom of the ribcage; correctly rotating the legs out from the hip sockets; using the arms and upper body without displacing the ribcage; knowing how to take off and land from a jump with consideration to the alignment of the pelvis, knees, and feet; and making sure that tension is not held in certain parts of the body, such as the shoulders. Believe it or not, this list is far from complete. Dancers have much to concentrate and work on to perfect their instruments. They learn all this information by taking dance classes or other movement classes and working long, hard hours. Because dancers need specific, quality feedback, training under qualified teachers is essential. Also, it is important to remember that a person does not become a professional dancer by taking one or two classes a week. Ideally, dancers should dance five to six days a week, so that their muscles stay strong and their bodies remain flexible.

Dancers can take many different dance classes to advance their technical ability. They can study different dance genres such as modern, ballet, jazz, tap, and

Contributed by Ben Viatori. ©Kendall Hunt Publishing Company.

Dancers need a great amount of strength, flexibility, and excellent alignment to correctly execute these movements.

Figure 3.1

Contributed by dgarson.com. ©Kendall Hunt Publishing Company.

How this dances methods work →

Though having good technique is important, dancers should also be outstanding performers. Having this ability means that the dancers go beyond what is learned in technique class and bring the movements that they are performing to another level.

world dance. Additionally, studying other dance-related techniques can be helpful to a dancer's growth and development. These techniques are sometimes referred to as body therapies or somatics and include: the Alexander technique, the Feldenkrais Method, Bartenieff Fundamentals, and Rolfing.

Although all body therapies and somatic practices are different, they each help dancers to overcome bad and unsafe habits, and help them to move as efficiently as possible. The Alexander technique helps dancers to relieve tension and redirect energy. An Alexander practitioner uses gentle touch to guide dancers into positions that are less stressful and more relaxed. The Feldenkrais Method is also a gentle, hands-on approach that helps dancers overcome limitations in their bodies and improve mobility. Through this method, dancers become aware of habitual patterns and then try to change them. Bartenieff Fundamentals focuses on how the body can function better, and teaches dancers to develop appropriate alignment, coordination, sequencing, strength, flexibility, mobility, kinesthetic awareness, and expression. These elements are taught in six basic exercises that are the center of this technique. Rolfing, also known as Structural Integration, can dramatically alter a person's posture and structure, usually through a series of ten sessions with a Rolfing practitioner. These sessions include deep tissue massage, which is not a typical massage but focuses on connective tissue manipulation and retraining the body to work with gravity.

Dancers could also do Pilates training, which includes a series of mat exercises and exercises performed on specially designed equipment. Pilates conditioning focuses on increasing muscular strength in the abdominal and lower back region, as well as throughout the body. Yoga, aerobic activity, and weight training can also help to supplement more "traditional" dance training (see Figure 3.2).

Figure 3.2

Dancers can study yoga as well as traditional dance technique.
Contributed by dgarson.com. ©Kendall Hunt Publishing Company.

Though having excellent technique is important, dancers should also be outstanding performers. Having this ability means that the dancers go *beyond* what is learned in technique class and bring the movements that they are performing to another level. It is not enough for dancers to just "do steps." They must incorporate their whole being into the movements and let the audience see the passion that drives them to dance (see Figure 3.3). They must be focused and appear confident and unafraid on stage. Working this way, combined with having excellent musicality, the ability to dance through a wide

It is not enough to be able to execute movements properly. The dancer must be able to bring them to life on stage.

Figure 3.3

Dancer performs a dynamic and expressive sequence of movements.
Copyright © 2004 by Bruce Davis.

range of dynamics and qualities, and being able to perform each movement to the fullest extent, enables the dancer to go beyond technique. Unfortunately, there are many good technicians that are very well trained, but not as many outstanding performers. It is not enough to be able to execute movements properly. The dancer must be able to bring them to life on stage.

In addition to working on their technique and performance, dancers must also be concerned with having a healthy and fit body. Eating properly, maintaining the correct weight, getting enough rest and doing supplemental exercises for strength and cardiovascular fitness are a daily part of dancers' lives. Unfortunately, some dancers push things, such as dieting, too far. Since the aesthetic in the majority of the dance world is to be thin, anorexia and bulimia affect some dancers (particularly women). In these cases, the dancers must be treated by health professionals (for both physical and emotional counseling), or risk doing permanent damage to their bodies. There is no reason why dancers have to go to extremes to be thin. If dancers eat properly and do the right amount of exercise (aerobic activity is very beneficial), they will be able to reach and maintain their ideal weight. It is encouraging that many in the dance world are recognizing that different body types are acceptable for a career in dance. However, a slender body is still the desired type for many dance companies. Regardless of the desired aesthetic of some dance companies, most in the field would agree that dancers should focus on being "fit," and being healthy should be the priority for all.

In addition to physical health, dancers' psychological health is also important. Because a dancer's life is difficult (a dancer has to learn how to handle much criticism and rejection, the stress of auditioning, long working hours, little pay, etc.), it is important that he or she keep everything in perspective and keep a positive attitude. Often dancers go through periods of uncertainty, questioning whether all of the hard work is worth it. Some will remain in the profession, while others will leave it for something more secure, financially and emotionally. There is no doubt that the life of a dancer is a difficult one, whether dancing on a pre-professional or professional level.

Dancing on a pre-professional level (such as in college and university dance programs or in a professional studio school) is rigorous and time consuming. In college, an average dance major (above and beyond taking academic and dance theory courses) must also take from one to three technique classes per day. In addition to studying and doing homework, most dancers can be in rehearsals from one to four hours per day (and more on weekends), depending on when and how often they perform. Therefore, it is essential that dancers be in excellent physical, mental, and emotional health, and be prepared for any challenge. Dancers tend to be very resilient people, and even those who dance on a pre-professional level will reap the rewards of dedication and hard work (see Figures 3.4A–B).

Dancing on a professional level is also rigorous and time consuming. The average day for a dancer who is a member of a company is long, sometimes going from 9:00 A.M. to 11:00 P.M., depending on whether or not the company is performing. In order to remain financially stable, most companies have to sup-

. . . it is essential that dancers be in excellent physical, mental, and emotional health.

Figure 3.4A

Instructor directing a student dancer during a photo shoot.
Contributed by Ben Viatori. ©Kendall Hunt Publishing Company.

Figure 3.4B

The finished product.
Contributed by Ben Viatori. ©Kendall Hunt Publishing Company.

plement their incomes by doing other activities in addition to performing, such as touring, teaching master classes and dance workshops, and offering lectures and demonstrations. In relation to the average pay of a dancer, the workload is tremendous.

Annual earnings data for dancers is very difficult to track because of the wide variation in the number of hours worked and the short-term nature of many jobs—which may last from one day to one week. It is rare for many dancers to have guaranteed employment beyond three to six months per year. According to the Bureau of Labor Statistics (2016), the median hourly earnings for freelance dancers is approximately $13.47. Hourly wages can range from $8.69 to $33.34. Those dancers working for a professional dance company averaged $16.53 per hour, and those who taught in state and private schools averaged $22.41 per hour. Average pay for choreographers was $23.19 per hour.[2]

Looking at dance companies with budgets ranging from one hundred thousand to ten million dollars, average salaries can range between $15,200 for newer company members and $41,280 for veteran dancers who have significant years of experience. There are a few dancers, considered to be principal status, who can make a considerable amount, but this type of salary is only received by a few dancers who are affiliated with major dance companies and are members of the American Guild of Musical Artists (AGMA), which is a labor organization ". . . that represents the men and women who create America's operatic, choral and dance heritage."[3] Given the fact that there are many dance companies that do not have a budget of $100,000 or higher and are not affiliated with the AGMA, it should be noted that many dancers make a salary that is below the poverty line. Therefore most dancers, on top of an already busy schedule, have to supplement their incomes with additional employment. Sometimes these jobs can be dance related, such as teaching dance, but many times dancers wait tables, hold office positions, or do whatever work they can that does not interfere with their rehearsal and performance schedules.

Many dance companies cannot afford to have dancers on salary, and will instead pay per rehearsal and performance. This low wage scale, combined with the fact that most dance companies do not have health insurance, retirement plans, etc., makes being a dancer a profession that is difficult and trying, to say the least.

Summary

People are motivated to dance for many different reasons. Some began dancing during childhood, usually because a parent thought it would be a good idea for his or her child to take a dance class. Some people say dancing is relaxing and allows them to release stress and tension. Others say it is good exercise. But professional dancers and the students who aspire to be professional dancers give other reasons why they dance. Most dancers say that dance is their passion and that they are not happy or fulfilled unless they are moving and performing. This concept might be hard for the average person to understand, considering the fact that most dancers work so hard and make so little money.

Of course, there are many facets to being a dancer and every dancer is unique in his or her own way. But the common thread that runs through each and every one of them is the very strong love and passion that they have for the art form. And although the dancer's life is a hard one, most would not want to do anything else.

. . . although the dancer's life is a hard one, most would not want to do anything else.

Figure 3.5

Contributed by Candice Kaminski, clikstudiosonline.com. ©Kendall Hunt Publishing Company.

Discussion Questions

Discuss in class or provide written answers.

1. What do you think are the most important characteristics that a dancer should possess? Make a list and discuss why you chose each one. *Excellent physical, mental, and emotional health*

2. Have you ever seen anyone dance who you would consider to be an outstanding performer? What was so special about that person that led you to that conclusion?

3. If you were a choreographer and you were holding auditions, what would you look for in a dancer? Be specific and give reasons for your answers.

4. What are some other types of training a dancer could do that would be beneficial?

The Audience

Copyright ©2004 Bruce Davis.

chapter four

Dance is a performing art. Choreographers and dancers spend long hours in rehearsals with the ultimate goal of performing before an audience. Many choreographers hope that the audience will "connect" with the dance and that the viewers will find the dance aesthetically satisfying. This is not to say that a choreographer is concerned only with creating a dance that he or she thinks will please and win over an audience. Although some choreographers are motivated to create dances that will do just that, most artists put the creative emphasis on the dance as a work of art and hope that the audience will respond to it in some way.

Dance is a performing art.

One of the most important points for an audience member to remember is to keep an open mind. If a person makes the decision to be receptive to the material put before him or her, then the viewing experience has the potential to be very fulfilling.

The Audience as Participant

When viewing a dance concert, the audience must think of themselves as a participant and an equal partner in the event. In other words, the audience member must not be passive, but active and ready to receive the dances put before them. It has become difficult for many audiences to observe in this way, because in today's times many people want "instant gratification." To some, having to *think* about what they are viewing is not very appealing—they would rather be merely entertained.

Many people have gotten used to seeing dance in the flashy, quick editing style of music videos, television shows, and some movie musicals. But viewing live dances performed in a dance con-

One of the most important points for an audience member to remember is to keep an open mind.

cert setting requires more intellectual participation from viewers. Obviously, some dances will require the audience to think more than others will. But regardless of the dance genre, form, or style presented, the viewer must be an active participant; an active audience member. Of course, it is easier for the audience member to be an active participant if the choreography presented and the dancers performing the movements are interesting and exciting to watch. Therefore, from the beginning of the creative process to the final performance, the choreographers, dancers, and audiences all have roles to play:

> [Choreographers] . . . take movements, ideas and feelings from everyday and special occasions and transform them in some way. Performance is immediate, emotionally charging the performer and audience in sporadic or continuous interchange if both are receptive. Dancing often generates electricity and reflection about it that linger long after a performance in the theatre or informal setting. Dances we do, [and] see . . . sometimes haunt us. These dances can reinforce what is in society or spearhead what may be. The pulse of human affairs is action–reaction or interaction. We do not know which dances will ramify in our thoughts and behavior to shape or explain social and personal realities. Humans have the capacity for memory: the intellect often moves nimbly.[1]

The idea that a person gets out of a performance as much as he or she puts into it is an important one. If a person is receptive, viewing a performance can be a powerful, fulfilling, and enlightening experience.

Being able to clearly articulate why a dance was liked or not liked is an important part of understanding dance and an intelligent way to critique.

Understanding Dance

Some people feel confused after viewing a dance concert and that feeling is to be expected for those who have not seen a lot of dance. Over time, it is possible to become better at understanding dance. The more dance a person sees, the better equipped he or she will be to critique and analyze the works. After awhile, the audience members begin to develop their own aesthetic sense and will clearly know what they like, what they do not like and, most important, *why* they responded to the dance in the way they did. Being able to clearly articulate why a dance was liked or not liked is an important part of understanding dance and an intelligent way to critique. After viewing several dance concerts, audience members also begin to get a sense of dance as a language, thus enabling them to understand and interpret the choreography.

Understanding dance, for most, is a learned process. Since some choreographers create dances that are purely based in movement and design, it might be beneficial to look at these dances in relation to the elements of space, time, and energy (refer to *Chapter Two: The Choreographer*). For example, how does the choreographer use the space? Are there specific uses of level, direction, and floor patterns? How are dynamics and qualities used in the dance? Since all choreographers manipulate these elements, the audience could use this list to know what to look for in terms of overall dance structure. Eventually, the audience would be able to tell (through their own aesthetic sense) if the choreographer made "good" choices in the dance.

We also know that some choreographers create dances that have a definite theme, image, or storyline. In this case, it would be beneficial to try to sense the overall "feeling" of the dance by looking at the images that the choreographer evokes through manipulating the dance elements. For example, what is the choreographer trying to "say" with the specific way that he or she uses the space? Does the way the dancers use their focus portray a certain character or convey a certain emotion? Does the use of music, props, or the use of specific timing elements add to the drama of the dance (see Figures 4.1A–B)? In other words, the elements of dance can be used to analyze a dance in two different ways: as information that helps the audience look at the movements and structure of a dance (to see "how" the movements are used), or as information to help the audience see the symbols and images in the movements (to see "why" the movements are used the way they are).

Figure 4.1A

Contributed by dgarson.com. ©Kendall Hunt Publishing Company.

Figure 4.1B

In these two dances, the choreographers chose to use props. The audience must determine what these props mean or represent within the context of these dances.
Contributed by Ben Viatori. ©Kendall Hunt Publishing Company.

Other practices can enable a person to better understand dance. For example, reading the titles of the dances (some titles can give clues as to what the dance is about), reading the program notes, and even talking to the choreographer and dancers before or after the performance can give more insight into the dances. All these practices, combined with being an active participant, lead the audience member toward a better understanding of dance.

Of course, even if the above measures are taken, there may be times when a dance might not be understood. Just as there are plays, poems, and paintings that do not turn out the way that the artist intended, there are also dances that do not "succeed." The audience member should be aware that this error does happen and that all dances viewed will not always be enjoyed. People should also remember that they may view a dance that they did not care for, but that the person sitting next to them absolutely loved! Everyone comes to a performance with a different set of values, experiences, and their own aesthetic sense and therefore interprets each dance differently.

One of the most important things for audience members to remember is that their interpretation of a dance is a *correct* interpretation. Since each individual brings their own life experiences to everything that they view, not everyone will have the same interpretation. Many artists believe that this varied interpretation is one of the most exciting aspects about art and that everyone's opinion is a valid one.

The audience should also remember that the dancers are performing *for them* and that they should give the dancers their utmost attention. Believe it or not, most dancers can sense whether or not the audience is "with them." The feeling of performing in front of a disinterested or bored audience can be intimidating, or at the very least, distracting. Dance concert etiquette should be employed at all dance concerts: for example, arriving on time; reading the program for titles and notes; remaining quiet and attentive during the duration of the dances; applauding at the appropriate times; leaving your seat only at intermissions and not during the performance (unless, of course, it is an emergency); turning off cell phones and leaving them off for the duration of the performance; refraining from taking photos and videos; and showing, at the end of the concert, appreciation to the performers (which will depend on how well you like the performance). Although these seem like a lot of rules and regulations, they are actually all part of common courtesy that anyone in a performance situation would expect. Needless to say, the audience member should *enjoy* the dance concert that they are viewing. They may enjoy it so much that they will continue to attend concerts and become a member of many future dance audiences.

. . . audience members must remember that their interpretation of a dance is a correct *interpretation.*

Summary

Seeing as much dance as possible is the key to understanding and appreciating it. It must be stressed, however, that viewing dance on a television, movie, or computer screen is not the same as experiencing live dance performances. Although people may have more access to seeing dances on the internet, efforts should be made to see live dance concerts whenever possible (and preferably concerts by professional dance companies).

Viewing dance can be an experience that can enlighten, sooth, excite, infuriate, mesmerize, and thrill. It can give information about ourselves and the world around us. It can provide a view into issues and subjects that the viewer had never thought about before, or had seen in a different light. Dance is a powerful medium that can touch the deepest parts of our being.

Figure 4.2

Contributed by Candice Kaminski, clikstudiosonline.com. ©Kendall Hunt Publishing Company.

Discussion Questions

Discuss in class or provide written answers.

1. Do you think that keeping an open mind when viewing dance is important? Why or why not? Give examples to support your argument.

2. Discuss the idea of "instant gratification." How does it affect the way we view things, particularly dance? Do you think this issue is an American phenomenon, or does it occur worldwide?

3. Have you ever been in a performance situation, either as an audience member or a performer, where the audience was behaving in a less than desirable way? Describe what that experience was like and how it made you feel. Also, did it affect the performance in any way?

part three
DANCE GENRES

Most people are familiar with the styles of ballet and jazz dance, probably because these genres are readily seen on television. There are, however, many dance genres and styles, some of which had their beginnings in the twentieth century and some that have been in existence for thousands of years. The following chapters provide introductions to dance genres and styles (also referred to as "forms") that are part of the dance world.

©Shutterstock, Inc.

Ballet

Contributed by dgarson.com. ©Kendall Hunt Publishing Company.

Ballet is an art form that has a long, rich history dating back to the fifteenth century. One of the earliest records of balletic movements comes from a book of dance instruction created by a dancing master named Domenico da Piacenza.[1] Perhaps a more significant moment in ballet history—one that would pave the way for the art form from the sixteenth century to the present—was the arrival of Catherine de' Medici (1519–1589) in France. She came to France from her native Italy to marry into the ruling family of Henri, Duc d'Orleans, who would later become the King of France.

> *Ballet is an art form that has a long, rich history dating back to the fifteenth century.*

When de' Medici came to France, she brought with her several Italian dancing masters. Along with these dancing masters, she introduced a new type of entertainment to the public, later to be known as the court ballet. Balthasar de Beaujoyeulx (c. 1535–1587) was de' Medici's head dancing master. In 1573, he created the *Ballet des Polonais,* a court entertainment performed by sixteen women who each represented one of the French provinces. Beaujoyeulx went on to create the *Ballet Comique de la Reine,* which many historians point to as the first court ballet. It was produced in 1581 and was described in the following way:

> [The] ballet by [dancing master] Beaujoyeulx . . . was commissioned by Catherine de' Medici . . . The spectacle lasted from 10:00 p.m. to 3:30 a.m. The ballet was chiefly concerned with the legend of Circe and part of the set represented the Garden and Castle of Circe. The principal dancers were a group of twelve Naiads, danced by a princess and several duchesses . . . Musicians sat in a golden vault,

framed by clouds lighted from the inside . . . The cost of the spectacle was 3,600,000 gold francs. The libretto of the ballet was published in 1582 and was to become one of the first books on ballet.[2]

Early Ballet — How it went from century to century

The "ballets" presented in the sixteenth century were very different from to-day's ballets. As the above description shows, the court ballets were very much a feast for the eyes. These dazzling spectacles were a marvel to see, even though they sometimes consisted only of simple floor patterns and poses. Elaborate costumes were the rule, although they greatly restricted the performer's movements. These ballets progressed at a leisurely pace, sometimes lasting several hours.

The court ballets were performed by and for members of the nobility. The most prominent of these nobles was Louis XIV (1638–1715), commonly referred to as the Sun King. He was the King of France from 1643–1715 and during that time commissioned many ballets in which he himself performed. In 1661, he granted permission to several dancing masters to establish the Royal Academy of Dance in France and the development of the court ballet flourished. This academy later became known as the Paris Opera, which still exists today.

At the end of the sixteenth century, with the creation of the proscenium stage (that separated the audience from the performer, see Figure 5.1), ballet began to take on a more serious and theatrical quality. Dancers began to use a "turned-out" position (rotating the legs out at the hip joint) in order to move

These dazzling spectacles were a marvel to see, even though they sometimes consisted only of simple floor patterns and poses.

Figure 5.1

Example of a theatre with a proscenium stage. The stage is surrounded on the top and sides by a proscenium arch, and serves as the frame into which the audience looks.
©momente/Shutterstock.com

more efficiently. A set vocabulary of movements was developed, which included positions of the feet, arms and head, as well as locomotor (moving) and non-locomotor (in-place) movements. Thus, a rigorous technique was developed, one that required a dancer to train daily for many hours in order to become truly proficient. The new priorities set in the sixteenth century gained momentum and by the seventeenth century, ballet was recognized as a viable art form. Dance masters vigorously trained dancers to perform with technical proficiency and many ballets were created to show the dancers' abilities.

In the eighteenth century, however, the ballet aesthetic began to change. The emphasis that had been placed on technique was no longer the priority. People began to feel that the *meaning* or *message* that the movements depicted was the most important element of dance. Therefore, the priority was placed on having the audience "feel" something and receive a message from the performance.

During this time, Jean Georges Noverre (1727–1810) developed *ballet d' action*. This concept brought the importance of having a plot and using emotion in dance to the forefront of ballet choreography. He also wrote *Letters on Dancing and Ballet*, which defended ballet as a high art form—one that he felt had the power to communicate even more effectively than words.

Figure 5.2

The nineteenth century produced the Romantic ballet. "Romanticism was characterized by a passionate striving to discover meaning in human events, an effort that was uniquely reflected in all of the romantic arts, but most perfectly in its ballet."[3] Dance began to follow the path that had been developed by the Romantic artists of music, literature, painting, and sculpture. Their style of art was characterized by a number of different elements, such as love of nature, emotion, power, violence, and tranquility. The Romantic ballets, although they contained those same elements, were characterized by their use of mythical characters and places, which created atmospheres of great wonder and excitement. These ballets also featured the female dancer, and the introduction of the "romantic" style tutu (see Figure 5.2).

One of the first Romantic ballets to be performed was *La Sylphide* (1832), choreographed by Filippo Taglioni (1777–1871). Although this ballet is occasionally performed today, the ballet *Giselle* is the one that is synonymous with the Romantic era. Today many ballet companies all around the world perform *Giselle*. Choreographed in 1841 by Jean Coralli (1779–1854) and Jules Perrot (1810–1892), *Giselle* depicts

Dancer wearing romantic style tutu.
©ayakovlevcom/Shutterstock, Inc.

the story of a woman who dies of a broken heart and comes back as a "wilis" (a mythical spirit figure), not to seek revenge on her lover, but to protect him from the evil wilis.

From the fifteenth to the nineteenth century, there were great shifts in the desired aesthetics of the ballet world, and these shifts were a trend that would continue into the twentieth century. In the late 1800s, ballet took on a new look, philosophy, and aesthetic, which is referred to as "classical" ballet. Similarly, the early 1900s marked the advent of "contemporary" ballet. These two styles have remained popular and have shaped the history and ballet aesthetic of modern times.

Although there are different styles of ballet within the classical and contemporary genres (such as Cecchetti, Royal Academy of Dance [RAD] and Vaganova), certain similarities of form do exist (see Table 5.1 at the end of the chapter). There is, for example, a universal movement vocabulary that is shared by all styles of ballet. The steps (all employing the French language) remain the same from country to country. A person who only speaks one language could go to *any* country and teach ballet and would probably be perfectly understood, assuming that everyone present was familiar with the ballet terminology. As we have seen, certain differences (stylistic and historical), have separated ballet into two categories—classical and contemporary.

Several characteristics and features are always found in a classical ballet. The most obvious is the overall "look" of the ballet.

Classical Ballet

The history of classical ballet can be traced back to the late 1800s in Russia when choreographer Marius Petipa (1818–1910) began to create ballets. Several characteristics and features are always found in a classical ballet. The most obvious is the overall "look" of the ballet. Performed on a proscenium stage, spectacular scenery usually fills the upstage (farthest point away from the audience) and side areas of the stage. The dancers are always dressed in elaborate costumes typical of the characters they are portraying (see Figure 5.3). These factors enhance the storyline of the ballet, which is usually a fairytale or fable. For example, *The Sleeping Beauty*, choreographed in 1890 by Marius Petipa and first performed in Russia, tells the story of the young princess Aurora who is put under a spell by the evil fairy Carabosse. As we know from the Mother Goose version, under the spell the princess falls asleep, never to awake again. The kiss of a prince revives her, however, and they live happily ever after. Another classical ballet entitled *Swan Lake,* choreographed by Marius Petipa and Lev Ivanov in 1895 (the first *Swan Lake,* choreographed by Wenzel Reisinger in 1877 for the Bolshoi Theatre, was not successful), also first performed in Russia, tells the story of a swan, Odette, who is changed to a beautiful woman for a brief period of time by a mysterious sorcerer named Von Rotbart. She meets and falls in love with Prince Siegfried. The two can never be together, however, because Odette is under the powerful spell of Von Rotbart. In the end, both Odette and Siegfried realize that they can only be together in the afterlife and they both throw themselves into a lake. This ballet has an uncharacteristically sad ending for a classical ballet, but is one of the most popular ever created.

Figure 5.3

Dancers in the classical ballet "Swan Lake." The *corps de ballet* provide balance and symmetry to the stage, and the female dancers wear the classical tutu.
©Jack Q./Shutterstock.com

Another characteristic of classical ballet is the use of music. The choreographer brings the music to life by creating the steps to "move along" with the music. For example, if the music was in 3/4 or "waltz" time, the choreographer would follow this rhythm with the movement, paying close attention to the counts, phrasing, accents, and crescendos. Large orchestral pieces of music are the norm for a classical ballet. Although there are many composers who have created music specifically for ballets, there are two particularly prominent Russian-born composers who are known throughout the ballet world. Pyotr (Peter) Tchaikovsky (1840–1893) and Igor Stravinsky (1882–1971) both created some of today's best-loved orchestrations. Tchaikovsky's compositions for classical ballets include *Swan Lake* (1877), choreographed by Marius Petipa and Lev Ivanov; *The Sleeping Beauty* (1890), choreographed by Marius Petipa; and *The Nutcracker* (1892), choreographed by Marius Petipa and Lev Ivanov. Some of the contemporary ballets that Stravinsky created musical compositions for are *The Firebird* (1910), choreographed by Michel Fokine; *Rite of Spring* (1913), choreographed by Vaslav Nijinsky; and *Les Noces* (1923), choreographed by Bronislava Nijinska. Other popular composers such as Claude Debussy,

Large orchestral pieces of music are the norm for a classical ballet.

Figure 5.4

Margot Fonteyn in *Swan Lake*, 1959.
Bettmann/Getty Images

Pantomime and the use of literal gestures are often seen in classical ballets.

Maurice Ravel, Erik Satie, and Sergey Prokofiev have also created musical scores that were (and are) used in ballet choreography.

The use of dancers in classical repertory is similar from ballet to ballet. For classical repertory, the dancers are usually divided into three categories—the principals (who have the leading roles in the ballets), the soloists (who have solo and character roles) and the *corps de ballet* (the remaining members of the company). The principals, particularly the male and female leads, are always the main focus of the ballet and are the dancers who move the storyline from beginning to end (see Figure 5.4). The climax and most prescribed moment of classical ballet is the *grand pas de deux,* or step for two. The *grand pas de deux* follows a specific format, beginning with the entrance of the male and female dancers, who then perform an *adagio* (slow duet). This *adagio* is followed by variations (solos) for each dancer, beginning with the male, which is usually comprised of difficult and quick movements, such as leaps, turns, and jumps, also known as *grande allégro* movements. The female dancer usually performs quick footwork and turns, known as *petit allegro* movements. The two dancers then return together for a final coda (or final movements) to complete the *grand pas de deux.* The female dancer, or ballerina, is the main focus of the duet parts of the *pas de deux.* The role of the male dancer is to support her in the difficult turns and lifts that are found in most classical ballet repertoires.

The *corps de ballet* serves almost as part of the elaborate scenery, sometimes standing perfectly still in a pose for minutes at a time while the principals and/or soloists dance downstage (closest to the audience). Usually the *corps de ballet* are costumed to look exactly alike and execute the same movements at the same time. Their movements on stage are usually very linear and their floor patterns give a balanced and symmetrical look to the stage space (see Figure 5.3).

Pantomime and the use of literal gestures are often seen in classical ballets. For example, if a male dancer wanted to pantomime "I love you," he might point to himself, put his hands over his heart, and then point at the person that he loves. As classical ballets always feature a strong storyline, pantomime is often utilized to ensure that the plot remains intelligible to the audience.

In classical ballet, the female dancers wear *pointe* shoes. *Pointe* shoes are specially designed so that the ballerina can stand directly on the tips of her toes (see Figure 5.5). In professional companies, each ballerina has her shoes made specifically for her. Usually, a pair of *pointe* shoes lasts for one performance. The ballerinas would also wear the classical style tutu, which was shortened from the romantic style so the legs and footwork could be seen more clearly (see Figure 5.6).

Figure 5.5

In classical ballet, the female dancers wear *pointe* shoes specially designed so the ballerinas can stand directly on their toes.
© Andrew Williams/Shutterstock, Inc.

Figure 5.6

Dancer in classical style tutu.
©KOSTYAKOVA EKATERINA/Shutterstock, Inc.

Contemporary Ballet

Contemporary ballet evolved in Russia in the early 1900s due mainly to the work of choreographer Michel Fokine (1880–1942). Fokine was the first master choreographer of the Ballet Russes, a Russian company developed in 1909 by Serge Diaghilev (1872–1929). Diaghilev was neither a dancer nor a choreographer, but a producer who had a passion for dance and brought together many of the ballet world's most recognized figures, such as Vaslav Nijinsky, Anna Pavlova (see Figure 5.7), Leonide Massine, Enrico Cecchetti, George Balanchine, and others (see "Major Figures in Ballet"). He also wished to highlight collaborative efforts among some of the leading composers, musicians, and visual artists of the day, and therefore employed composers such as Igor Stravinsky, Maurice Ravel, Erick Satie, and Claude Debussy, and artists such as Léon Bakst, Pablo Picasso, and Henri Matisse. Fashion designer Coco Chanel was called upon to create costumes for several Ballet Russe performances.

Anna Pavlova as the Dragon Fly.
Photo by Herman Mishkin/George Eastman House/
Getty Images.

Figure 5.7

Fokine and Diaghilev shared the same aesthetic, one that pushed the boundaries and introduced a new dance to the public. Fokine had several principles that he infused in all of his choreography. One idea was that classical steps should be reshaped and modified to fit the theme of a dance. Also, the movement in a dance should give insight into what is happening on stage, therefore pantomime, as seen in classical ballets, should not be used. He felt strongly that the members of the *corps de ballet* be more than just a part of the scenery, but should be an important part of the entire dance. And finally, in keeping with the concept of collaboration developed by Diaghilev, all aspects of the ballet—movement, music, costumes, and set—should be presented with equal importance.[4] Fokine's choreography also served to heighten the status of the male dancer in a society that was used to seeing the female as the center of the ballet.

The Ballet Russes not only had Fokine to present a new type of ballet to the masses, but also employed Nijinsky (1889–1950), first as a dancer and then as a choreographer. Like Fokine, Nijinsky presented a truly contemporary form of ballet, but also used so-called taboo themes in his choreography. In his ballet, *L'Apresmidi d'un Faune* (*The Afternoon of a Faun,* 1912), audiences were shocked to see the overt sexual references, as well as the truly unorthodox choreography, which included two dimensional movements, the use of the parallel leg position, and unconventional costumes.

Contemporary ballet is similar to classical ballet in that they both use the same movement vocabulary and French terminology. The treatment of the movement in contemporary ballet, however, can appear vastly different from classical ballet (see Figure 5.8). Contemporary ballet choreographers also use more freedom of movement in the torso, upper body and arms, giving the movements a more "modern dance" flavor.

> *Contemporary ballet is similar to classical ballet in that they both use the same movement vocabulary and French terminology.*

Figure 5.8

Dancer performing a *grande jeté*. The costume and arm position gives the movement a contemporary look.
Contributed by dgarson.com.
©Kendall Hunt Publishing Company.

The dancers who perform in both classical and contemporary ballets must be highly trained (technically) and must have an outstanding performance quality. The *use* of music in both forms is also the same, with much emphasis placed on meter, counts, phrasing, etc., although the musical "styles" used might be very different. For example, contemporary ballet might use music that is abstract (atonal, having mixed-meters), whereas classical would not. The female dancers, or ballerinas, usually wear pointe shoes while performing, although some contemporary ballets might employ the use of ballet slippers or even bare feet. Choreographers of contemporary ballet reject the use of pantomime and literal gestures and abstract the movements that appear within the dances.

Although there are some similarities between classical and contemporary ballet, the differences are striking, with the most prominent being the lack of storyline or plot. Contemporary ballet is usually concerned with movement as the primary focus. Although most of Fokine's and Nijinsky's work usually had a strong narrative, many contemporary choreographers do not hold to this dance aesthetic. One major figure that is known for outstanding contemporary ballet choreography was George Balanchine (1904–1983, see Figure 5.9). He was a Russian choreographer who worked with the Ballet Russes, and in 1924 defected from Russia to the West. In 1933 Balanchine came to the United States. He was one of ballet's greatest innovators and is considered by many to be the greatest contemporary ballet choreographer of our time (his choreography is also referred to as being "neoclassical"). He eliminated the elaborate sets and costumes used in classical ballets (that he felt took the focus away from the dancer's movements) and presented the dancers as equals on stage (not as principals and corps). The typical *grand pas de deux* that was usually seen in classical ballet works was not always seen in his choreography. Instead, he sometimes presented what could more accurately be called "duets" (although they would always be referred to as *pas de deux* in the ballet genre). Balanchine is known for his "plotless" ballets that have as their focus the marriage of movement and music rather than a storyline. Two of his most famous plotless ballets are *Concerto Barocco* (1941) and *Agon* (1957). Balanchine did, however, choreograph some narrative ballets, with two of the most popular being *The Prodigal Son* (1929 and revised in 1950) and *A Midsummer Night's Dream* (1962).

Figure 5.9

George Balanchine.
Bettmann/Getty Images

The Balanchine legacy lives on in many of today's leading ballet companies, who perform one or more of his hundreds of dances and full-length ballets. New York City Ballet, which Balanchine began in 1948 with Lincoln Kirstein (1907–1995), is one company whose repertory is made up mostly of dances by Balanchine. Other companies, such as American Ballet Theatre, the Joffrey Ballet, and Dance Theatre of Harlem, perform Balanchine's works on a regular basis.

There are many contemporary ballet choreographers. Maurice Béjart (1927–2007) was one of the most recognized contemporary ballet choreographers in the world. He was the artistic director of The Béjart Ballet, and was recognized for his witty and often flamboyant dances. Operating on the premise that dance is a powerful form of communication, he was inspired to choreograph about different cultures and what he felt were the religious and social aspects of dance. He often blurred male and female identities, which was a trademark of his work. His angular yet elegant movements were also prominent features of his exciting and theatrical dances.

In 1995, London choreographer Matthew Bourne (b. 1960) created a version of *Swan Lake* in which all of the swans are male, powerful, and aggressive, though the production is also infused with comic moments. Among the many awards he has received for this production are two Tony awards for Direction and Choreography. Bourne's *Swan Lake* has been seen worldwide, and its edgy and inventive choreography has added another dimension to the dance world. Other projects of Bourne's include choreographing and co-directing Disney's *Mary Poppins* (2004) and a stage version of *Edward Scissorhands* (2005). He is the artistic director of a dance company called New Adventures.

There are also many modern dance choreographers who have created works specifically for ballet companies. In 1947, Valerie Bettis (1919–1982) was the first modern dance choreographer to set a work on a ballet company (the Ballet Russes de Monte Carlo). In 1973, Twyla Tharp (b. 1942) was invited to choreograph two dances for the Joffrey Ballet; *Deuce Coupe* (which was performed to music by the Beach Boys), and *As Time Goes By*. In 1976, Tharp choreographed *Push Comes to Shove* for the American Ballet Theatre (ABT). The dance starred Mikhail Baryshnikov, who in 1980, became the artistic director of ABT and hired Tharp as a resident choreographer for the company. In 1993, the Joffrey Ballet commissioned four modern and contemporary ballet choreographers to create an evening-length work entitled *Billboards*. *Billboards* featured the music of Prince and was a tremendous box office success. The practice of modern and contemporary choreographers who create dances for ballet companies continues today.

Summary

Both classical and contemporary ballets are performed all over the world and are as popular today as they were years ago. There are approximately sixty major nationally and internationally known professional ballet companies in the United States and abroad including American companies such as American Ballet Theatre, Atlanta Ballet, Ballet Tech, Boston Ballet, Joffrey Ballet, Lines Contemporary Ballet, Miami City Ballet, New York City Ballet, Pacific Northwest Ballet, Pittsburgh Ballet Theatre, San Francisco Ballet, The Washington Ballet, and international companies such as The Bolshoi, *Compañía Nacional de Danza*, Kirov Ballet, Lyon Opera Ballet, The National Ballet of Canada, *Nederlands Dans Theater*, Paris Opera Ballet, Royal Winnipeg Ballet, Stuttgart Ballet, and the Zurich Ballet. There are also hundreds of smaller regional and local ballet companies around the world. All of these companies perform ballets that were created years ago, as well as new ballets. An audience member would quickly be able to recognize if the ballet they were viewing were a classical or contemporary ballet, simply by looking at the costumes, scenery, staging, music, and how the dancers are used on stage. The similarities and differences between classical and contemporary ballet can be found in Table 5.1. Refer to Table 5.2 for an outline of ballet events.

Figure 5.10

For the most part, dancers in classical ballet keep their spines erect.
©Kristian Sekulic/Shutterstock, Inc.

Table 5.1 The Similarities and Differences between Classical and Contemporary Ballet

Similarities	Differences
■ Both use a vocabulary of movement that employs the French language. ■ Both emphasize a strong relationship to music. ■ Both utilize dancers who are highly trained in their technique and performance abilities. ■ Both the male and female dancers are featured on stage (in the Romantic period, the female dancer took prominence).	■ Classical ballet always has a storyline; most contemporary ballets focus on the movement. ■ Classical ballet appears very symmetrical, with both sides of the stage equally "balanced" by having the same number of dancers (*corps de ballet*) on each side executing the same movements. Contemporary ballet does not focus on symmetry, and having a stage that is "unbalanced" is a characteristic of the style. ■ Classical ballets are always danced to classical music. Contemporary ballets may also use this type of music, but can also use music that is abstract or from a specific genre, such as jazz music. ■ There is always a *pas de deux* in classical ballet; there may or may not be one in contemporary ballet. ■ Classical ballet choreography may incorporate pantomime and literal gestures; contemporary ballet never does. ■ Female dancers always wear pointe shoes in a classical ballet; they may or may not wear them in contemporary ballet. ■ For the most part, dancers in a classical ballet keep their spines erect (see Figure 5.10); dancers in a contemporary ballet curve, twist, and bend their upper bodies.

Table 5.2 Outline of Ballet Events

1400–1700	Renaissance Period
1559	Catherine de' Medici brings ballet masters from Italy to France.
1573	Balthasar de Beaujoyeulx, dé Medici's head dancing master, creates *Ballet des Polonais*.
1581	Balthasar de Beaujoyeulx creates *Ballet Comique de la Reine*, considered the first court ballet.
1661	Louis XIV, the Sun King, establishes the Royal Academy of Dance.
1661	Pierre Beauchamp creates the five positions of the feet.
1681	The first female ballet dancer appears on stage. Women are now permitted to perform in professional ballets.
1754	Jean Georges Noverre creates his first ballet and eventually brings *ballet d' action* to the forefront of ballet choreography.
1760	Jean Georges Noverre publishes *Letters on Dancing and Ballet*.
1822	Dancing *en pointe* is introduced.
1832	Filippo Taglioni choreographs *La Sylphide*, considered the first Romantic ballet.
1841	Jean Coralli and Jules Perrot choreograph *Giselle*.
1870	Arthur Saint-Léon choreographs *Coppélia*, one of the last great Romantic ballets.
1877	Wenzel Reisinger choreographs the first production of *Swan Lake* for the Bolshoi Theatre. This production was not successful.
1890	Marius Petipa, the father of classical ballet, choreographs *The Sleeping Beauty*.
1895	Marius Petipa and Lev Ivanov choreograph *Swan Lake*, and it is a great success.
1909	The first season of Diaghilev's Ballet Russes.
1909	Diaghilev hires Vaslav Nijinsky, Anna Pavlova, and Michel Fokine, the father of contemporary ballet.
1910	The first ballet company in America is established; The Chicago Opera Ballet.
1924	George Balanchine joins the Ballet Russes.
1929	Diaghilev dies.
1933	Balanchine comes to the United States.
1934	George Balanchine and Lincoln Kirstein start the School of American Ballet.

Table 5.2 Outline of Ballet Events (continued)

1937	The Mikhail Mordkin Ballet is established, later to become the American Ballet Theatre.
1947	Valerie Bettis is the first modern dancer to choreograph on a ballet company (The Ballet Russes de Monte Carlo).
1948	After having a series of ballet companies, Balanchine and Kirstein officially establish The New York City Ballet.
1950	Nijinsky dies.
1967	Arthur Mitchell establishes the Dance Theatre of Harlem, featuring African-American dancers.
1974	Mikhail Baryshnikov defects to the United States.
1976	Modern dance choreographer Twyla Tharp sets *Push Comes to Shove* on the American Ballet Theatre, with Baryshnikov as the lead dancer.
1977	*The Turning Point*, a movie about ballet starring Baryshnikov, is made.
1980	Baryshnikov becomes artistic director of the American Ballet Theatre.
1983	Balanchine dies and leaves over 460 dances and full-length ballets. Peter Martins becomes artistic director of New York City Ballet.
1985	Baryshnikov and tap dancer Gregory Hines star in the movie *White Nights*, with choreography by Twyla Tharp.
1990	Baryshnikov leaves the American Ballet Theatre and, with modern dance choreographer Mark Morris, begins the White Oak Dance Project, a modern dance repertory company.
1993	The Joffrey Ballet produces *Billboards,* which uses music by Prince and choreography by modern dance and contemporary ballet choreographers Laura Dean, Charles Moultan, Peter Pucci, and Margo Sappington. It is a box office success.
1994	American Ballet Theatre dancers form their own union, the Independent Artists of America.
1995	Choreographer Matthew Bourne creates a version of *Swan Lake,* which differs radically from all other versions. The swans in Bourne's ballet are all male, and appear powerful, aggressive, and violent. This ballet had successful runs in theatres all around the world.
1997	Ballet dancer Edward Villela receives the Kennedy Center Honor.
1999	Seven ballerinas from American Ballet Theatre perform in the Romantic ballet *Giselle*.
2000	American Ballet Theatre debuts in China with a performance of the classical ballet *La Bayadere*.
2000	Mikhail Baryshnikov receives the Kennedy Center Honor.
2001	Christopher Wheeldon is named Resident Choreographer at New York City Ballet.
2002	Mikhail Baryshnikov disbands the White Oak Dance Project.
2003	New York City Ballet holds a year-long celebration of the centennial of George Balanchine's birth. It begins on November 25 and continues through the 2004 season.
2004	The U.S. Postal Service issues stamps honoring four choreographers for their contributions. The stamps honor George Balanchine, Alvin Ailey, Agnes deMille, and Martha Graham.
2004	Dance Theatre of Harlem experiences major financial difficulties. Artistic Director Arthur Mitchell begins a massive fund-raising effort, and new Board members are elected. A new Executive Director, Laueen Naidu, is hired to help save the company and the Dance Theater of Harlem School.
2004	Ballet star and White Oak Dance Project co-founder Mikhail Baryshnikov appears in the final episodes of the HBO hit series *Sex and the City*.
2005	The Baryshnikov Arts Center opens in New York. Its purpose is to be an international center for artistic experimentation and collaboration.
2005	Ballet dancer Suzanne Farrell receives the Kennedy Center Honor.
2007	Although the company is still on hiatus, Dance Theatre of Harlem's educational program *Dancing Through Barriers* functions as a "traveling classroom" and introduces thousands of school-age students to the art of dance.
2007	Nearly 300 former members of American Ballet Theatre celebrated the sixty-seventh year of the company by appearing on stage during the final curtain call of the May 26 performance.
2007	Matthew Bourne wins a Drama Desk Award for *Edward Scissorhands*.
2007	New York City Ballet presents *Honoring Lincoln,* an evening of dance dedicated to honoring co-founder Lincoln Kirstein.
2008	New York City Ballet mounts the *Jerome Robbins Celebration,* performing thirty-three of Jerome Robbins's ballets during their 2008 season.

(continued)

Table 5.2 *Outline of Ballet Events (continued)*

Year	Event
2008	As part of the Balanchine Preservation, Suzanne Farrell, best known as Balanchine's last muse, recreates *Pithoprakta*, a lost ballet, which she danced with Arthur Mitchell in 1968.
2008	Modern dance choreographer Mark Morris creates *Romeo and Juliet; On Motifs of Shakespeare*, based on the original Sergey Prokofiev score, and creates a modern dance based on a ballet classic.
2008	The Kennedy Center awards choreographer Twyla Tharp the Kennedy Center Honor.
2009	The Joffrey Ballet opens its official school, The Joffrey Academy of Dance, in Chicago and operates as a separate entity from the Joffrey Ballet School in New York.
2009	The *Youth America Grand Prix*, an international ballet competition featuring dancers age 9–19 from around the world, celebrates its tenth year.
2009	Ballet companies around the world celebrate the *Ballet Russe Centennial* by remounting famous works from that era, paying homage to Serge Diaghilev.
2009	The New York Public Library for the Performing Arts mounts the exhibition, *40 Years of Firsts: Dance Theatre of Harlem*.
2009	The Bolshoi Ballet from Russia (220 dancers strong), perform in the United States, with their most talented stars appearing on the tour.
2011	The Joffrey Ballet cancels the beginning of its season amid negotiations between the ballet company and the dancers union, the American Guild of Musical Artists. The two sides eventually settled on a contract for the dancers.
2012	The Kennedy Center awards ballet dancer Natalia Markarova the Kennedy Center Honor.
2014	Having disbanded the company in 2004 due to budgetary constraints, the Dance Theatre of Harlem resumed performances in the 2012–2013 season, with Virginia Johnson serving as artistic director.
2014	New York City Ballet celebrates the 60th anniversary of George Balanchine's *The Nutcracker*.
2014	The Kennedy Center awards ballet dancer Patricia McBride the Kennedy Center Honor.
2014	New York City Ballet names Justin Peck resident choreographer.
2015	Sylvie Guillem, one of the world's leading ballet dancers, retires after a thirty-year performance career.
2015	Misty Copeland is the first African-American dancer to be promoted to principal dancer status with the American Ballet Theatre.
2015	The Joffrey Ballet (Chicago) celebrates its 60th anniversary season.
2015	Modern dance choreographer Mark Morris creates a new dance for American Ballet Theatre's fall season.
2015	The Center for Ballet and the Arts at New York University announced the establishing of the Virginia B. Toulmin Fellowship for Women Choreographers, which was created to address the scarcity of female choreographers in ballet.
2016	After twenty years as artistic director of the Atlanta ballet, John McFall retires. Gennadi Nedvigin becomes the new artistic director.
2016	The Grand Audition is developed in Europe and allows dancers to audition for ten ballet companies over a two-day period.
2017	Amid accusations of sexual harassment, Peter Martins steps down as artistic director of the New York City Ballet. An artistic team including Jonathan Strafford, Justin Peck, Craig Hall, and Rebecca Krohn is appointed to run the company.
2018	New York City Ballet, Joffrey Ballet, Miami City Ballet, San Francisco Ballet, and the Boston Ballet present dances choreographed by Jerome Robbins in celebration of what would have been his 100th birthday.

Discussion Questions

Discuss in class or provide written answers.

1. What are some of the similarities between classical ballet and contemporary ballet? What are some of the differences?

2. Discuss some of the important contributions to ballet by those mentioned in "Major Figures in Ballet." What is the significance of the Russian influence?

3. If you have seen examples of both classical ballet and contemporary ballet, which do you enjoy watching most? Why?

Figure 5.11

Contributed by Candice Kaminski, clikstudiosonline.com. ©Kendall Hunt Publishing Company.

MAJOR FIGURES IN BALLET

Ballet, which has its roots in the court dances of Italy and later France (sixteenth and seventeenth centuries), has in its long history many outstanding choreographers and dancers. Here is a list of some of the artists that helped shape the world of ballet.

The Beginnings: Sixteenth through the Eighteenth Century

Catherine de' Medici (1519–1589)—A member of one of Italy's royal families, de' Medici married into the French monarchy. Neither a dancer nor a choreographer, de' Medici had a love for dance and brought several dancing masters with her from Italy to France. Thus began the long reign of the court ballet.

Balthasar de Beaujoyeulx (c. 1535–1587)—Beaujoyeulx was one of de' Medici's dancing masters. He is credited with producing the *Ballet Comique de la Reine*, the first court ballet of note.

Pierre Beauchamp (1631–c. 1705)—Beauchamp was a dancing master and the first ballet master of the Academy of Dance in France. He created the five ballet positions of the feet and legs used today and developed the technique of using the turned-out leg. He also devised a system of dance notation.

Jean Baptiste Lully (1632–1687)—A dancer and composer, Lully was the director of the Royal Academy of Music and Dance, which opened in 1672. Louis XIV granted permission for this academy, which later came to be known as the Paris Opera. Lully was instrumental in elevating the status of opera and ballet in the courts from entertainment to a professional art form.

Louis XIV (1638–1715)—Also known as the Sun King, Louis XIV was the King of France from 1643–1715. He was a great lover of dance and appeared in several court ballets. He granted permission to establish the first Academy of Dance.

Louis Pecour (1653–1729)—One of Beauchamp's former students, Pecour succeeded Beauchamp as director of the Paris Opera. He also introduced the minuet to the nobility of France.

John Weaver (1673–1760)—Weaver was an English choreographer who published the first written history of ballet. He also was the first choreographer to employ the use of pantomime in his ballets.

Francoise Prevost (1680–1741)—A star of the Paris Opera, Prevost was also an outstanding teacher. She was mostly known for her dramatic ability and was gifted in her use of pantomime.

Marie Salle (1707–1756)—Salle was a student of Prevost's and was known for her dramatic ability. She performed in both Paris and London and is credited with being the first female choreographer.

Marie Camargo (1710–1770)—One of Prevost's students, Camargo was a Paris Opera dancer who was known for her great technical ability, especially in performing "beats."

Jean Georges Noverre (1727–1810)—Noverre authored *Letters on Dancing and Ballet*, which presented the concept of *ballet d' action*. In this article, choreographers were called upon to create a new type of ballet—one that had a plot and followed a logical progression, rather than being abstract.

The Romantics of the Nineteenth Century

Charles Didelot (1767–1837)—Didelot was a French dancer, choreographer, and teacher whose choreography was characteristic of the Romantic style. He also introduced several changes to the typically worn ballet costumes, including flesh-colored tights for women. He also employed "flying machines" in his ballets and the newly introduced pointe technique.

Filippo Taglioni (1777–1871)—An Italian dancer and choreographer, Taglioni choreographed *La Sylphide* in 1832. This ballet is said to have begun the Romantic Era.

Carlo Blasis (1795–1878)—Blasis opened one of the most important dance schools in Milan (Royal Academy of Dance), where his method of teaching dance shaped much of the teaching of ballet technique. He was also an author of instructional textbooks.

Marie Taglioni (1804–1884)—Daughter of Filippo Taglioni, Marie performed in many of her father's ballets. She introduced a new costume design (bare neck and shoulders, tight fitting bodice, and skirt reaching just below the knee, also known as a "romantic" tutu), and is known for her beautifully executed jumps and leaps. She also perfected dancing *en pointe,* and her dancing appeared effortless.

August Bournonville (1805–1879)—Once a student of the Paris Opera, Bournonville brought the Romantic ballet to his native Denmark and became director of ballet at the Royal Theatre. His dance aesthetic became a part of the Royal Danish Ballet and he worked to elevate ballet and the dance profession.

Fanny Elssler (1810–1884)—A dancer born in Vienna, Elssler was a rival of Marie Taglioni while they were both employed by the Paris Opera. Elssler is known for her ability to execute small, quick steps. One of Elssler's most famous roles, *Cachucha,* was a Spanish-style dance that she performed very sensuously, which led critics to call her "pagan."

Jules Perrot (1810–1892)—Co-choreographer of *Giselle* (with Jean Coralli), Perrot used movement (as opposed to pantomime) to move the storyline of the ballet along. One of his most famous ballets that was strictly movement-based was *Pas de Quatre,* choreographed in 1845 and danced by Maria Taglioni, Carlotta Grisi, Fanny Cerrito, and Lucile Grahn.

Carlotta Grisi (1819–1899)—Grisi was an Italian ballerina who created the leading role in *Giselle,* a ballet of the Romantic Era that is still performed today.

Arthur Saint-Léon (1821–1870)—One of the last great choreographers of the Romantic era, Saint-Léon was also a dancer and violinist. He became ballet master of the Imperial Theatre in St. Petersburg in 1859 and attempted to develop a system of dance notation. The last ballet he choreographed, *Coppélia* (1870), is still performed today, although there are many different versions that are based on Saint-Léon's theme.

The Russian Influence (1910–1930s)

Marius Petipa (1818–1910)—A French-born choreographer, Petipa came to St. Petersburg in 1847. Petipa formulated "classical ballet," which stressed formal values such as symmetry and order of movements, staging, etc. Much of what we know today to be "classical" ballet directly descends from the teachings and choreography of Petipa. Some of his famous ballets are *The Sleeping Beauty* and *Swan Lake* (the latter choreographed with Lev Ivanov).

Lev Ivanov (1843–1901)—Ivanov was Petipa's assistant who collaborated with him to develop two of today's most loved classical ballets: *Swan Lake* and *The Nutcracker.* Ivanov's choreography is best known for expressing emotion through pure classical dancing (without pantomime).

Enrico Cecchetti (1850–1928)—Cecchetti was an Italian whose outstanding teaching ability made him important in Russian ballet. He became the private ballet instructor for Anna Pavlova and then the ballet master for Diaghilev's Ballet Russes. The Cecchetti method of teaching is used around the world today. In 1922, the Cecchetti Society was established in England and in 1939 the Cecchetti Council of America was formed in the United States.

Alexander Gorsky (1871–1924)—Gorsky began the turn away from the formality of the established classical ballet in Russia. He did away with symmetry and used character dances to embellish the storyline. He wanted to use the ideas of drama teacher and director Konstantin Stanislavsky (working from the "inside" to the outside) in his ballets. Therefore, he gave his dancers different motivations and characters to portray on stage.

Serge Diaghilev (1872–1929)—Diaghilev was the director of the Ballet Russes, which was a company made up of dancers from the Imperial Theatre of St. Petersburg (Fokine was hired as the company's first master choreographer). He promoted the idea of collaboration between choreographers, composers, and set and costume designers, and worked with visual artists such as Jean Cocteau and Pablo Picasso, and composers Erik Satie and Igor Stravinsky. Diaghilev is also credited with giving **Vaslav Nijinsky** (1889–1950) his first opportunity as a choreographer. Nijinsky, known for his outstanding dancing ability, shocked audiences with his ballets *L'Apresmidi d'un Faune (The Afternoon of a Faun)* and *Le Sacre du Printemps (The Rite of Spring).* Audiences were shocked due to the storylines which included references to sex and death, and to the unique movement style. In these ballets, Nijinsky abandoned the well-known technique of classical ballet and replaced it with stylized movements that were asymmetrical, heavy, and employed both turned-in and parallel positions.

Agrippina Vaganova (1879–1951)—Vaganova was the founder of the Soviet system of ballet education. She created a method of teaching ballet (known as the Vaganova method) that was adopted by all Soviet dance schools. Russian dancers trained in this method for many years. Today, the Vaganova method is still taught around the world.

Michel Fokine (1880–1942)—Fokine followed the path that Gorsky had set up, although he believed strongly in technique. Fokine also believed that a fusion of dance, music, drama, scenery, and costumes was necessary and he broke many rules of ballet to fit his aesthetic. His choreography is known as contemporary ballet.

Anna Pavlova (1881–1931, see Figure 5.12)—A principal dancer with Russia's Imperial Ballet and the Ballet Russes, Pavlova was known for her beautiful and dramatic dancing. One of her most famous dances was *The Dying Swan,* choreographed for her by Fokine in 1907. After she left Russia in 1911, she went to London and formed a company of English dancers (who changed their names to sound Russian). She and her company toured all over the world for many years.

Figure 5.12

Anna Pavlova is one of the world's most recognized ballerinas.
Courtesy of Photofest.

Bronislava Nijinska (1891–1972)—Nijinska was the great Nijinsky's sister and became an outstanding choreographer in her own right. Diaghilev hired her to choreograph for the Ballet Russes, and she created ballets such as *Les Noces* in 1923, and *Les Biches* in 1924. Her choreography was as experimental and abstract as her brother's.

Leonide Massine (1895–1979)—Massine was another choreographer hired by Diaghilev for the Ballet Russes. By 1917, with the premiere of Massine's *Parade,* the Ballet Russes had established the reputation for offering modern, or contemporary, ballets.

George Balanchine (1904–1983)—A student of the Russian Imperial School of Ballet, Balanchine toured with a small troupe of dancers until he was offered a job at the Ballet Russes, where he stayed for four years. In the year of Diaghilev's death (1929), Balanchine created one of his best-loved ballets, *The Prodigal Son,* which is still performed today. After serving as a resident choreographer for the Ballet Russes de Monte Carlo (a company created by Sergei Denham), Balanchine came to the United States in 1933 at the invitation of art patron **Lincoln Kirstein** (1907–1995). In the United States, Balanchine established the School of American Ballet and had four successive companies: The American Ballet, American Ballet Caravan, Ballet Society, and the New York City Ballet (developed in 1948, it is the only one still in existence). Balanchine is best-known for his sophisticated use of music, plotless ballets, and minimal costume and set design. His artistic neoclassical style has continued to keep him, even years after his death, at the forefront of today's choreographers.

Beyond the Russian Borders: Britain, France, and the United States (1930s–1940s)

Marie Rambert (1888–1982)—Rambert developed the Ballet Rambert in England in the mid-1920s. Although not a choreographer, she was a master teacher and trained many outstanding dancers. The company still exists today and is known as the Rambert Dance Company.

Lucia Chase (1897–1986)—An American ballerina, Chase, along with dance director **Richard Pleasant** (1906–1961), organized Ballet Theatre (now American Ballet Theatre) in New York. Beginning in 1940, Chase went on to direct the company for many years.

Ninette de Valois (1898–2001)—de Valois developed the Sadler's Wells Ballet in England in the late 1920s, which eventually became the Royal Ballet. Together with Rambert, she helped sustain the Carmargo Society, an organization developed to provide financial support for Britain's ballet companies.

Frederick Ashton (1904–1988)—Ashton was a choreographer and director of the Royal Ballet, succeeding de Valois in 1963. As a student of Marie Rambert, he was encouraged to choreograph. He is best-known for the outstanding *pas de deux* sections that appear in his ballets.

Serge Lifar (1905–1986)—Lifar was a Russian dancer who, in 1929, became ballet master of the Paris Opera Ballet. He believed that dance should not follow the rhythm that music dictated, but should have its own rhythm. He is credited with elevating the position of the male dancer in ballet and provided several outstanding dance sequences for males in his choreography.

Anthony Tudor (1908–1987)—Tudor danced in both the Ballet Rambert and Sadler's Wells (Royal Ballet) dance companies. He also choreographed for Ballet Rambert, before coming to the United States in 1940, where he joined Ballet Theatre (now the American Ballet Theatre) in New York. Tudor's choreography is known for its psychological meaning depicted through movement.

Alicia Markova (1910–2004)—An English dancer, Markova danced with Diaghilev's Ballet Russes for five years, where she changed her name to sound Russian (her birth name was Marks). She also danced with Ballet Rambert in the works of Ashton and Tudor. Markova was loved by the American and European dance audiences.

Roland Petit (1924–2011)—A French choreographer who believed the Paris Opera Ballet was too restrictive, Petit developed the *Ballet de Paris* in 1948. He is known for blending jazz and ballet techniques in his highly dramatic choreography.

Rudolf Nureyev (1938–1993)—Nureyev, a Russian, was a soloist with the Kirov Ballet before he defected from the Soviet Union (while the Kirov was on tour in Paris). He remained and danced in France before being hired by the Royal Ballet. Here, he was partnered with ballerina **Margot Fonteyn** (1919–1991), who was a British dancer. Their partnership is among the best-known and loved in the ballet world. Together they danced in many famous ballets and are well-known for their work in *Romeo and Juliet*, choreographed by Kenneth MacMillan.

Into the Present

Agnes de Mille (1905–1993)—An American dancer trained in ballet, de Mille choreographed for such companies as the Ballet Russes de Monte Carlo and the American Ballet Theatre. She is also known for her choreography of musical theatre productions such as *Oklahoma!*, in 1943, and *Carousel*, in 1945.

Catherine Littlefield (1908–1951)—Littlefield was the founder of the Littlefield Ballet, later to be known as the Philadelphia Ballet. She is credited with presenting the first full-length American production of *The Sleeping Beauty*. She also choreographed for ice skaters and presented ballet on ice in a 1940s production entitled *It Happens on Ice*.

Jerome Robbins (1918–1998, see Figure 5.13)—An American dancer and choreographer, Robbins performed with the Ballet Theatre (later called American Ballet Theatre) and was affiliated with the company for eight years. He choreographed for several ballet companies, particularly New York City Ballet, of which he was associate artistic director from 1949 to 1963. He also co-directed New York City Ballet with Peter Martins in the 1980s, until the end of the 1990–1991 season. Robbins is also known for his musical theatre choreography, such as *West Side Story* (1961).

Figure 5.13

Jerome Robbins, an American choreographer.
Courtesy of Photofest.

Maurice Béjart (1927–2007)—Béjart, from France, danced with many leading European companies. His debut as a choreographer was in 1954. In 1959, he was appointed director of the *Theatre Royal de la Monnaie* in Brussels, Belgium, where he stayed until 1988. He then established *Béjart Ballet Lausanne* in Switzerland. Béjart's choreography is referred to as contemporary, sexy, and dramatic.

Yuri Grigorovich (b. 1927)—A Russian, Grigorovich danced with the Kirov and eventually became a prolific choreographer. In 1964, he became chief choreographer of the Bolshoi Ballet, where he is credited with the creation of characterization through dance.

Kenneth Macmillan (1929–1992)—Macmillan was a Scottish dancer and choreographer who succeeded Frederik Ashton as artistic director of the Royal Ballet. He was known for creating ballets that employed large casts and lavish costumes.

Robert Joffrey (1930–1988)—An American ballet dancer and choreographer, Joffrey established the Joffrey Ballet in 1954. This company is primarily known for dancing contemporary works by leading choreographers such as Joffrey and Alvin Ailey. Previously housed in New York, the company is now located in Chicago and opened its own academy. The original Joffrey Ballet School is still located in New York. **Gerald Arpino** (1928–2008) also choreographed for the company and served as assistant director. After Joffrey's death, Arpino took over artistic directorship of the company.

Arthur Mitchell (b. 1934)—Previously a dancer with New York City Ballet, Mitchell wanted to develop a company where African-American dancers could perform in classical ballets. In 1972, he established Dance Theatre of Harlem. Today, the company is under the artistic direction of Virginia Johnson.

Natalia Makarova (b. 1940)—A Russian dancer who defected to the United States, Makarova is one of the most well-known and admired ballerinas.

Eliot Feld (b. 1942)—Previously a dancer with American Ballet Theatre, Feld established the Feld Ballet in 1974, later called Ballet Tech, which performed contemporary ballets that were described as fast-paced and sexy. Although Ballet Tech disbanded in 2003, Feld still choreographs and presents concerts.

Helgi Tomasson (b. 1942)—Tomasson has been the artistic director of the San Francisco Ballet since 1985. Originally from Iceland, Tomasson studied at the School of American Ballet in New York in the early 1960s, and joined the Joffrey Ballet in 1962. Today, the San Francisco Ballet is an internationally known company, whose dancers are recognized for their powerful technique and dramatic performance ability.

Peter Martins (b. 1946)—A Danish dancer and choreographer who performed with New York City Ballet for many years, Martins was the artistic director of New York City Ballet from 1983 to 2017, when he was forced to resign amid sexual harassment allegations.

Jiri Kylian (b. 1947)—Originally from Czechoslovakia, Kylian trained as a ballet dancer before going to the Royal Ballet School in London. The Stuttgart Ballet soon hired him as a dancer, where he also began to choreograph. Kylian is the artistic director of the *Nederlands Dans Theater*, whose works are a combination of modern dance, contemporary dance, and ballet. Kylian's works are dramatic and usually fast-paced and powerful, and push the limits of the body, space, drama, and humor.

Mikhail Baryshnikov (b. 1948)—A Russian dancer with the Kirov Ballet, Baryshnikov defected while on a tour in Canada in 1974. After several guest appearances with different companies, Baryshnikov came to American Ballet Theatre where he danced for several years. He also served as artistic director of the company. Baryshnikov has been involved in several projects, including dancing with the White Oak Dance Project, which he cofounded in 1990 with choreographer Mark Morris. (The company disbanded in 2002.) He has since opened the Baryshnikov Arts Center in New York, an organization dedicated to artistic experimentation and collaboration. He is still an active performer in dance, television, and theatre.

William Forsythe (b. 1949)—Born in New York, Forsythe has spent much of his dance career in Europe. After dancing with the Joffrey Ballet, he was hired by the Stuttgart Ballet where he was encouraged to choreograph. In 1984, he became artistic director of the Frankfurt Ballet. His work, influenced by Pina Bausch and Jiri Kylian, is considered provocative and elegant. He has choreographed on major ballet companies all around the world, including New York City Ballet, *Nederlands Dans Theater*, the Joffrey Ballet, and the Australian National Ballet. He also collaborated with dance educators and media specialists to create new approaches to dance documentation and research. His computer program, *Improvisation Technologies: A Tool for the Analytical Dance Eye*, is used in universities and by professional dance companies worldwide.

Alexander Godunov (1950–1995)—A principal dancer with the Bolshoi Ballet, Godunov defected from the Soviet Union to the West in 1979. He became a principal dancer with American Ballet Theatre, and performed with them until 1982. He left his dance career for a career in movies, with one of his most popular roles as an Amish farmer in the movie *Witness*.

Karole Armitage (b. 1954)—Although trained in ballet, Armitage joined the modern Cunningham Dance Company in 1975. After she left the Cunningham Company, she began, in the late 1970s, to create ballets that have been referred to as "punk-rock" ballets, because of their use of punkrock music, costumes, hairstyles, and make-up. She is still an active choreographer today.

Nacho Duato (b. 1957)—A native of Spain, Duato studied in both Europe and New York before taking his first professional position as a dancer with the Cullberg Ballet in Stockholm. He soon began choreographing and had major successes, which led to the appointment of resident choreographer for the *Nederlands Dans Theater* in 1988. In 1990, he was invited to become the artistic director of Compania Nacional de Danza. He is currently the artistic director of the Berlin National Ballet, a position he will hold until 2019. His ballets are performed by the leading ballet companies in the world, including American Ballet Theatre, Royal Danish Ballet, San Francisco Ballet, and the Australian Ballet.

Lourdes Lopez (b. 1958)—A former principal dancer with New York City Ballet, Lopez took over as artistic director of the Miami City Ballet in 2012. She is one of the few female artistic directors of a major ballet company in the country.

Matthew Bourne (b. 1960)—Bourne, from London, is the former artistic director of Adventures in Motion Pictures, and the current artistic director of New Adventures. In 1995, he choreographed a critically acclaimed version of *Swan Lake* in which all of the swans are men. This production has been called groundbreaking and has won a record number of awards, including two Tony awards for Choreography and Direction. In 2004, Bourne choreographed and co-directed Disney's *Mary Poppins,* and later worked on a stage version of *Edward Scissorhands* (2005).

Sylvie Guillem (b. 1965)—A native of France, Guillem trained at the Paris Opera Ballet School and then became a dancer with the Paris Opera. She is known for her extreme flexibility and the ability to extend her legs and hold them in difficult lines, shapes, and positions. Some critics say that this use of the legs distorts the classical ballet line, but audiences worldwide are mesmerized by her abilities. She was a principal guest artist with the Royal Ballet, as well as other ballet companies around the world, and has since retired from performances after a thirty-year career.

Richard Siegel (b. 1968)—Siegel is the artistic director of the Richard Siegal/Ballet of Difference dance company, which is based in Germany. Siegel created this company in order to present "ballet of the 21st century." The company fosters a contemporary view of ballet that includes different aesthetics, including Eurocentric and Afrocentric movement vocabularies.

Trey McIntyre (b. 1970)—For years, McIntyre worked as a freelance artist, creating dances for such companies as American Ballet Theatre, Stuttgart Ballet, and The Washington Ballet. In 2004, he founded the Trey McIntyre Project, which was based in Boise, Idaho until it was disbanded in 2014. McIntyre frequently uses pop music in his dances, and creates works that are full of details within a contemporary ballet vocabulary.

Christopher Wheeldon (b. 1973)—Wheeldon was born in England and began his ballet training when he was 8 years old. In 1991 he danced with the Royal Ballet, and in 1993 he was invited to join New York City Ballet. In 2001, Wheeldon was named Resident Choreographer of New York City Ballet, where he stayed for seven years. In 2008, Wheeldon created his own dance company, Morphoses/The Wheeldon Company, which included dancers from New York City Ballet, The Royal Ballet, the Bolshoi Ballet, and other prominent companies. He was affiliated with that company until 2010. Today, Wheeldon has expanded into television, film, and theatre, and received a Tony Award for choreography for the Broadway show *An American in Paris*.

Annabelle Lopez Ochoa (b. 1973)—Once a prolific ballet dancer, Ochoa made the decision in 2003 to focus on working solely as a choreographer. She has created ballets for over 50 dance companies around the world and has won several awards for her work in ballet, musical theatre, and opera.

Aszure Barton (b. 1975)—A Canadian whose movement vocabulary ranges from the graceful to the bizarre, Barton has choreographed for ballet companies as well as modern companies and Broadway. She is the artistic director for Aszure Barton and Artists, creating work both traditional and unexpected.

Benjamin Millepied (b. 1977)—This French dancer and choreographer, who performed with the New York City Ballet for sixteen years, is now the Director of Dance for the Paris Opera Ballet. He is also widely known as the choreographer and one of the stars of the movie *Black Swans*.

Yabin Wang (b. 1984)—Wang is one of China's renowned contemporary ballet choreographers. She combines Western and Chinese aesthetics in her powerful and moving dances. She created Yabin and Her Friends in Beijing, with the goal of commissioning dances by choreographers from all over the world.

Liam Scarlett (b. 1987)—Scarlett is a British choreographer and the artist in residence for the Royal Ballet. He is the youngest choreographer to ever assume this position. He wants people to respond emotionally to his work and show that "everyone on stage has a story."

Troy Schumacher (c. 1987)—Schumacher has been a dancer with New York City Ballet since 2005, and is also being recognized as an innovative choreographer. In 2010, he established BalletCollective, which performs contemporary ballet in intimate settings, focusing on artistic collaboration between the choreographer, dancers, musicians, and artists.

Justin Peck (c. 1988)—Peck is a soloist and resident choreographer for the New York City Ballet. He received this position after participating in the New York Choreographic Institute. Peck was the focus of a documentary entitled *Ballet 422*, which provides a backstage look at Peck's process in creating a dance for New York City Ballet.

Modern and Contemporary Dance

Contributed by dgarson.com.
©Kendall Hunt Publishing Company.

This chapter explores the genres of modern and contemporary dance, post-modern dance, and dance-theatre from the beginning to the present day. Although these genres are closely related in aesthetic and artistic principles, they also have unique and distinct characteristics. Today, these genres are widely recognized, and are studied and performed throughout the world.

Defining and categorizing modern dance, however, is difficult. While at one time, the newness of the form allowed for a specific definition and categorization, today it is not that simple, since each of these terms is now used to describe work that may vary widely in style, approach, and methodology. For example, currently in modern dance it is not uncommon for a choreographer or an instructor to approach choreography and teaching from a "post-modern" aesthetic or a "traditional" modern aesthetic that may be different from the founders of the original techniques. Similarly, the term "contemporary dance" may be used to describe a certain modern form, although this term means different things to different people, depending on the context in which it is used. For some, contemporary dance denotes a technique that focuses on a fusion of techniques and styles, while for others it defines a technique that is based in emotion and story-telling. A third definition of contemporary dance has to do with the "newness" or "modernness" of the form, as in the "Martha Graham School of Contemporary Dance." Many would agree, however, that contemporary dance draws on influences from modern dance, ballet, jazz, as well as other genres, such as world dance, hip-hop, release technique and even technology. There are no limits as to the influences and dance aesthetic of today's contemporary choreographers, and using the term contemporary to define a specific style or aesthetic is one way this next generation of dance artists can distinguish themselves from the predecessors of modern and post-modern dance.

Today, what is often taught and choreographed is an "eclectic" type of technique, meaning that instructors and choreographers have drawn from the many traditional, post-modern, and contemporary techniques that fall under the broad heading of "modern dance" to develop their own personal styles. This practice grows increasingly common as the newest generation(s) of teachers and choreographers move further away in time from the work of modern dance's founding mothers and fathers. For this discussion, the terms modern dance, post-modern dance, dance-theatre, and contemporary dance will be used as historical terms.

In comparison to ballet, modern dance is a dance form . . ., evolving as a direct revolt against what was perceived as the "restrictions" of ballet.

Figure 6.1

Isadora Duncan helped pave the way for modern dancers and choreographers.
Bettmann/Getty Images

Modern Dance: The Beginning

In comparison to ballet, modern dance is a dance form that came about much later (beginning in the late 1800s and early 1900s), evolving as a direct revolt against what was perceived as the "restrictions" of ballet. Many dance historians credit Isadora Duncan (1877–1927, see Figure 6.1), with being the first dancer to present "modern dancing" to the public, although performers such as Loïe Fuller (1862–1928, see Figure 6.2) and Maud Allan (1883–1956, see *Major Figures in Modern Dance*) certainly did present to audiences dancing that was new and different.

Duncan's reasons for moving and creating, however, were different from those of Fuller's and Allan's. After years of ballet training, Duncan began to feel that the pointe shoes and costumes that ballerinas wore were too confining, as was the ballet vocabulary. She decided to leave her technical training and began to dance in a way that seemed to her to be more natural. She was inspired by the movements of the trees, the ocean, and by all of nature. Duncan developed a technique that used movements such as hopping, running, swaying, and skipping; movements that seemed natural and expressive to her. The solar plexus, in the center of the body, was the area from which all movement was generated. She was inspired by the history of the Greeks and she danced barefoot and in sheer tunics similar to the Greek style. She felt that these tunics did not restrict her movements and that they also showed the beauty of the female body. Duncan, known to many in America as a rebel, found fame (and an enthusiastic audience) in several parts of Europe and Russia. She traveled and performed there between 1904–1927, initially coming at the invitation of Loie Fuller, who admired Duncan's great potential and artistry. While she was in Russia, many believe that Duncan's "new" dance form inspired many of the contemporary ballet choreographers, such as Michel Fokine. Eventually, the American audiences accepted her and she paved the way for all of the modern dancers and choreographers who were to follow.

Duncan danced to music composed by Beethoven, Schubert, and Wagner, among others, but had a particular love for music by Chopin. Many of her dances clearly portrayed her love and passion for moving. However, in 1913, Duncan's two children were killed in a tragic car accident. This event led her to create a dance, entitled *Mother*, which depicted a sorrowful and broken figure. Eventually, Duncan opened a school of dance. Six of her students, referred to by dance critics as the "Isadorables," were all adopted by Isadora and took the Duncan last name. Three of these students, Irma, Ana, and Maria Theresa, were the people responsible for teaching the Duncan technique after Isadora's death. Today, there are individuals and dance companies who are dedicated to keeping the Duncan legacy alive.

Many modern dance choreographers emerged after Isadora Duncan, each contributing their own aesthetic and philosophical opinions to the dance world, as well as their own "technique" or "style" of dance. For example, Ruth St. Denis (1878–1968, see Figure 6.3) and Ted Shawn (1891–1972) were two dancers who married and formed a school in 1915 that they called Denishawn. St. Denis and Shawn were greatly influenced by different cultures, particularly of the Asian countries. Though the dances they performed were not authentic, Denishawn brought a view of the dance of other countries to the American audience. The main educational purpose of the Denishawn school, however, was to educate the "total" dancer—meaning the body, mind, and spirit.

St. Denis and Shawn developed a company using pupils from the school. They performed on the vaudeville circuit (See *Chapter Nine: Jazz Dance, Musical Theatre, and Tap Dance*), as well as in other theatres across the country. They eventually toured several Asian countries, where they not only performed but also studied the dances of the countries that they were so fond of depicting. In the early 1930s, Denishawn (as well as St. Denis and Shawn's marriage), came to an end, and both branched out on their own with other endeavors. St. Denis opened a school in California, while Shawn created an all-male dance company, Ted Shawn and His Men Dancers. This company was established in

Figure 6.2

Loie Fuller used special lighting techniques that she developed, along with costumes that had many yards of fabric, to create unique effects on stage.
Courtesy of Library of Congress Prints and Photographs, LC-USZ62-86015.

Figure 6.3

One of the founders of
Denishawn, Ruth St. Denis.
Photofest.

Figure 6.4

Martha Graham, dancer and choreographer,
developed a technique based on "contracting"
and "releasing" through the center of the body.
Courtesy of Photofest.

order to bring the importance of the male dancer to the forefront, and performed all over the United States. With this company of men, he also created Jacob's Pillow in Massachusetts, which to this day is one of the country's most prestigious dance schools and presenting organizations.

Three major dance figures to come out of the Denishawn School were Martha Graham, Doris Humphrey, and Charles Weidman. These three artists, sometimes referred to as the "pioneers" of modern dance, had a major impact on the dance world. Although most ballets can be easily divided into the categories of classical or contemporary, many different "techniques" or "styles" can be categorized under the heading of modern dance (refer to *Major Figures in Modern Dance* for an overview of different dancers who created specific techniques).

Dancer and choreographer Martha Graham (see Figure 6.4) developed a technique that was based on the idea of "contracting" and "releasing" through the center of the body. These specific movements are connected to the breath and allows for body parts to move in opposition from each other. The principle of contraction and release can be seen throughout her dances and also in the exercises of a modern dance class taught by a "Graham" teacher. Many other dancers and choreographers were and are recognized for creating a specific technique or style of dance.

Erick Hawkins (1909–1994), a dancer in Graham's company for many years and her former husband, developed a technique that stressed the ease and free flow of movement. Dancers studying his technique learn to perform movements using the minimum amount of muscular energy necessary, instead focusing more on the movements of the bones and skeleton.

On the other hand, Doris Humphrey (1895–1958) and Charles Weidman (1901–1975), developed a technique that was built around the premise of "fall and recovery." Dancers studying this technique learned to be proficient in balancing and ceding to the pull of gravity. José Limon (1908–1972), a student of Doris Humphrey, further developed (using many of the principles of his teacher) a technique that develops balance, speed, and control.

Thousands of dancers have trained in the modern dance genre since the days of Isadora Duncan. Today, a dancer can choose to study one specific technique, or several. Many teachers today choose to teach an eclectic type of dance technique, drawing concepts from the more formalized and traditional styles. Unfortunately, several teachers teach a "watered-down" version of a particular technique and their students do not learn the appropriate methods of the original style. Since the years are passing and we are getting further away from the original pioneers and their first students, it is now up to those people who are schooled in the specific techniques to keep them alive and pure. Although many great artists have died, their dances live on in their still-active companies such as the Martha Graham Dance Company, Erick Hawkins Dance Company, and the José Limon Dance Company.

Modern dancers and choreographers were concerned not only with developing different styles of moving, but also with creating different themes and ideas to depict in dance. In comparison to the fairy-tales of classical ballets, modern dance choreographers were (and are) more concerned with, among other things, the human condition and real-life situations and emotions. For example, Martha Graham created dances that dealt with psychological issues. She used themes relating to American life, Native Americans, and Greek mythology to initiate her choreography. One famous dance she choreographed, entitled *Appalachian Spring* (1944), celebrates traditional domestic values of the American pioneers by depicting the life of a young married couple. In contrast, Graham also created *Cave of the Heart* (1946), where she portrayed the jealous and bitter Medea from Greek mythology. Nevertheless, all Graham dances utilize her strong technique, which demonstrates intense muscular energy and control, sharp angles, and contraction and release of the center of the body.

Doris Humphrey and Charles Weidman (see Figure 6.5), although both part of the same company (the Humphrey-Weidman Dance Company), had different interests when it came to creating dances. Humphrey was interested in group dynamics and choreographed many dances that highlighted the group instead of soloists. She also had a strong connection to the music and worked with a technique called "music visualization," which Ruth St. Denis had introduced to her. Music visualization is a way to "see" the music through the dance, sometimes having the dancers follow specific instruments or rhythmic

In comparison to . . . classical ballets, modern dance choreographers were (and are) more concerned with, . . . the human condition and real-life situations and emotions.

Figure 6.5

Creators of the Humphrey/Weidman technique, Charles Weidman and Doris Humphrey.

Charles Weidman photo Bettmann/Getty Images

Barbara and Willard Morgan Photographs and Papers, UCLA Department of Special Collections. Reprinted by permission.

patterns. Humphrey also choreographed dances that were performed in silence. In this way, she greatly influenced how the dancers performed the movement, stressing specific rhythms, dynamics, and the use of breath phrasing. Her dance entitled *Water Study* (1928) is a perfect example of a dance that is not bound to music, but is truly musical, simply because of the unique way in which the dance is choreographed. All sixteen dancers who originally performed the dance had to be very much in tune with each other in order to perform the ocean-like movements in correct sequence and at the right time. Weidman, although he held the same values and beliefs as his partner, was also interested in comedy in dance. Whereas Humphrey's dances were dramatic and emotional, such as *The Shakers* (1931), a dance about members of a religious sect, Weidman's dances were often comic in nature. He used a technique he called "kinetic pantomime," in which music, and movement performed in silence, would alternate. He did, however, choreograph many serious and dramatic dances. *Lynchtown* (1935), was a dance that depicted the evil and sadistic behavior of a crowd present at a lynching.

Anna Sokolow (1910–2000, see Figure 6.6), a former Graham dancer, created dances that reflected the reality of her time. In 1955, Sokolow created *Rooms*, which depicted life in the inner-city, showing people in their most vulnerable and depressed states. This depiction was a realistic and profound one in the 1950s and remains pertinent today. Not all modern dance choreography, however, has a theme, storyline, or conveys an emotion, as evidenced in the following discussion of post-modern choreographers.

Since the term "modern dance" has meant so many things to so many people, can it be clearly defined? Dance critic Selma Jeanne Cohen wrote:

> *The modern dance is a point of view, an attitude toward the function of art in the contemporary world. As the world changes, the modern dance will change, for the symbols will again—as they become acceptable—lose their power to evoke the hidden realities. They will again have to be recharged, revitalized; even demolished and recreated anew in order to serve their function. Unless this happens, the modern dance is not modern—it is dead.*[1]

This quote provides a powerful message for all dancers and dance audiences, but particularly for choreographers; the dance is modern if it is "recreated anew." Regardless of the themes or issues that modern dance choreographers choose to deal with, one role of the modern dance artist is to provide for the audience a view into life's realities, complexities, and experiences.

Post-Modern Dance

In the 1950s, dancers and choreographers began to feel restricted by the teachings of their predecessors. Until this time, most dance techniques were rigorous, requiring dancers to study and train for many years in order to become proficient at their art. As Isadora Duncan had revolted against ballet, this generation of dancers wanted to take their choreography in a different direction than their teachers. These new choreographers were not concerned with the dramatic and the realistic, as many of their predecessors had been, but believed that other factors were more important to include in their choreography. One of these factors, for example, was to reflect *movement*, rather than the storyline, as the primary focus of the dance. Because of this philosophy, the works of these choreographers, for the most part, came to be known as "abstract." These people were also commonly referred to as being part of the "avant garde," meaning that they were leaders in a new and unconventional movement—specifically, the post-modern movement.

Merce Cunningham (1919–2009, see Figure 6.7) was one of the first choreographer to emerge from using traditional modern dance choreographic meth-

Not all modern dance choreography has a theme, storyline, or conveys an emotion . . .

Figure 6.6

Anna Sokolow created dances that reflected reality.
Photofest.

Figure 6.7

Merce Cunningham was one of the first post-modern choreographers to develop a new style of choreography.

Jack Mitchell/Archive Photos/Getty Images

Indeterminacy . . . is a method in which the elements of the dance can change from performance to performance. . . . Therefore, . . . a dance that is performed a certain way one night might not be performed the same way the next.

ods and developed a new style of choreography. Unlike his predecessors, Cunningham did not believe that a dance had to possess a theme or storyline. His concept of dance revolved around the idea of "movement for movement's sake." In other words, *movement* should be the primary focus in the dance and should not be executed in order to depict a story to the audience. According to writer Sally Banes, Cunningham's philosophy holds the following beliefs:

> . . . *any movement can be material for a dance; any procedure can be followed and used as a compositional method; any part of the body can be used; music, costumes, set design, lighting and the movements all have their own identity and simply occur in the same place at the same time; any dancer in the company can be a soloist; a dance can be performed in any space; and a dance can be about anything, but it is primarily about the human body moving.*[2]

Cunningham, who referred to his concerts as "events," often used "chance" and "indeterminacy" methods in his choreography. These methods are tools that Cunningham believed helped him to break old habits and to create new and exciting moments in his dances. For example, chance methods were used to determine specific movement order, phrase order, dancer's directions and floor patterns on stage, or in what order the sections of a dance will be. In 1953, Cunningham created a dance called *Suite by Chance*, in which a toss of a coin determined different aspects of spatial designs, timing, and order of movement sequences. Indeterminacy, an entirely different concept, is a method in which the elements of the dance can change from performance to performance. In *Field Dances,* created in 1963, the dancers were permitted to take the movements that they were previously given and perform them in different ways, such as repeating a section, reversing a section, etc. Therefore, using indeterminacy methods, a dance that is performed a certain way one night might not be performed the same way the next.

Cunningham also collaborated with several post-modern musicians, including David Tudor, Toshi Ichiyanagi, and Gordon Mumma. His most noted collaborations were with the composer John Cage (1912–1992), who held the same philosophical beliefs as Cunningham and also used chance and indeterminacy methods in his compositions. Contemporary visual artists such as Andy Warhol, Jasper Johns, and Robert Rauschenberg created set and costume designs for several of Cunningham's works.

Alwin Nikolais (1912–1993), another choreographer who rebelled against the traditional methods of choreographing, did not feel that the "self" always had to be the main focus on stage. Dancers appearing in his works were often presented in costumes that made them appear more as objects than humans, and his dances often utilized props (see Figure 6.8). For example, Nikolais choreo-

Figure 6.8

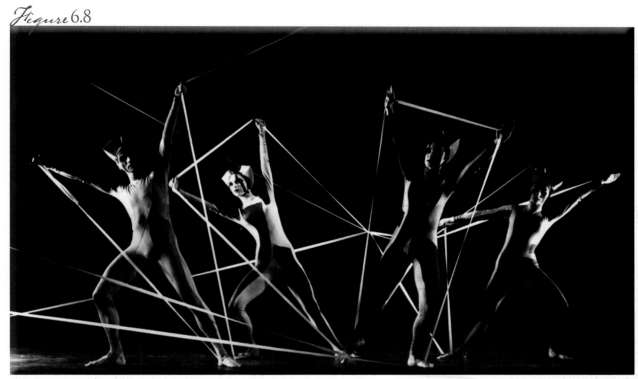

Alwin Nikolais Dance Company in "Tensile Involvement."
Photofest.

graphed a dance entitled *Noumenon* (1953), in which the dancers appear totally encased in bags made of material. The dancers inside manipulate the bags. The visual effect was unlike anything many dance audiences had ever seen. Nikolais is also known for integrating dance, music, and design. He often created his own sound scores, costumes, props, and lighting designs for his dances.

Nikolais' works were primarily abstract, and it was the *motion*, not the *emotion* that he was concerned with. In his early days as a choreographer, many dance critics accused him of dehumanizing the dancers in his works, but Nikolais did not perceive his work in this way. He believed that he was presenting to the audience a view of another experience, one that was not concerned with human feelings and emotions, but with the beauty and power of movement.

Paul Taylor (b. 1930, see Figure 6.9) is another choreographer who is credited with influencing the post-modern movement. Taylor danced with both Graham and Cunningham, but went on to

Figure 6.9

Paul Taylor in "Aureole."
© Artistic License.

develop his own personal aesthetic. His earlier works utilized untraditional music, often referred to as sound scores, as well as pedestrian movements. In 1957, Taylor presented *Duet*, where he stood and his partner sat motionless for four minutes, while composer John Cage sat quietly at the piano. In the newspaper review of the dance, the critic Louis Horst (1884–1964), responded by leaving a blank space in the review column. Taylor, however, did go on to develop a very athletic and dynamic dance vocabulary. His dances sometimes have a strong narrative, such as *Big Bertha* (1971), which depicts a seemingly innocent family whose world is turned upside-down during an outing to an amusement park. He also created such works as *Aureole* (1962), which is a pure movement piece.

Throughout the 1950s and 1960s, the works of Cunningham, Nikolais, and Taylor inspired another group of choreographers to create in a different vein. During the 1960s and 1970s, this new group of post-modern dancers extended the limits, just as Cunningham, Nikolais, and Taylor had done, but went even further away from traditional technique. Choreographers such as these new postmoderners wanted to reduce dance to its simplest form and to examine what they thought dance really was. Similar to Cunningham and Nikolais, they eliminated the idea of theme and storyline. They also, however, eliminated the use of formal technique, instead examining the basic movements of dance, such as walking, running, skipping, and hopping. They began to create dances based on these premises. In order to remain true to these ideas, some of these choreographers refused to work with trained dancers, so many used untrained performers in their works.

During the 1960s and 1970s, many of these choreographers and dancers performed at the Judson Memorial Church in New York (an actual church with a performance space in it), and they came to be known as the Judson Dance Theatre. The dancers were determined to reject the conventional teachings of their predecessors. Dance critic Deborah Jowitt recalled that ". . . it was a reaction against an existing art and also perhaps a comment on the times. Modern dance had become super-charged and the Judson people wanted to express a different kind of rhythm."[3] Visual artists, writers, musicians, as well as dancers came together and presented different types of material that they called dance. They performed in places other than theatres, such as gymnasiums, city streets, and even rooftops. They used improvisation, theatre games, and other experimental tools in their performances, many of which had the look and feel of the "Happenings" of the 1960s. Happenings were events that were popular with avant garde artists, musicians, writers, and dancers and usually involved participation from audience members. Many of the Judson Dance Theatre members had participated in the Happenings and therefore had experiences in spontaneous and collaborative work and taking risks in dance making.

The beginnings of the Judson Dance Theatre can be traced back to 1960, when Robert Ellis Dunn (1928–1996), began to give dance composition classes at the Cunningham School. These classes were experimental in nature and had a strong basis in improvisation and analysis of compositions. In 1962, he organized the first concert at the Judson Memorial Church. For a long time, the Judson Dance Theatre was ignored by the press and the dance critics, but had a strong and consistent following. Eventually, it was accepted that "The experiments and adventures of the Judson Dance Theatre . . . laid the groundwork for a post-modern aesthetic in dance that expanded and often challenged the range of purpose, materials, motivations, structures and styles in dance."[4]

After the Judson Dance Theatre disbanded (in 1968), several of its initial members regrouped and, along with new members, formed the Grand Union. The Grand Union was a collaborative effort—there was no specific director and all members had equality. Everyone contributed to the artistic processes of the group. Improvisations containing both dance and theatre were the focus of the company, with some of the material being political, some comical, some abstract, and some literal. Sally Banes stated that the Grand Union ". . . [stretched] the material and formal limits of their art by incorporating objects (and gestures) from everyday life, using imagery (including sounds) from popular culture and making long, rambling works in a flexible format with a consistently changing stream of images and meanings."[5]

Many important dances were created during the time of the Judson Dance Theatre and the Grand Union. A popular dance from this time was choreographed by Judson Dance Theatre member Yvonne Rainer (b. 1934). This dance, entitled *Trio A* (1966), showed movement that was reduced to its bare essentials. There were no dynamic changes of the movements throughout the dance. Even though some of the movements were fairly difficult to execute, the dancers did not have to be technically trained to perform them. It was acceptable for the audience members to witness dancers struggling with particular movements. Rainer also used this dance as a protest against the Vietnam War. In 1967, she renamed the dance *Convalescent Dance* and performed it on a concert with other protesting choreographers.

It was Rainer, who in 1965 created her *NO Manifesto*, which became the creed of the post-modern movement:

> *No to spectacle no to virtuosity no to transformations and magic and make believe no to glamour and transcendency of the star image no to the heroic no to the anti-heroic no to trash imagery no to involvement of performer or spectator no to style no to camp no to seduction of spectator by the wiles of the performer no to eccentricity no to moving or being moved.[6]*

Trisha Brown (1940–2017), also a Judson Dance Theatre member, gave us *Man Walking Down Side of Building* (1970), which is self-explanatory and was performed in New York City as people on the street looked on. Brown also went on to create many complex choreographic works by using the act of repetition. Simple movement patterns were developed and repeated in several different ways (such as changing the direction, level, or timing of the movement), turning the simple, fundamental motor patterns into visually complicated dances. In addition to these choreographers, several others presented dances that had a tremendous impact on the way we now look at dance (see *Major Figures in Modern Dance*).

Throughtout the 1960s and the 1970s, the post-modern choreographers created works that were a radical departure from the work of their predecessors.

Figure 6.10

Alvin Ailey created dances that were accessible to audiences.

Bettmann/Getty Images

Throughout the 1960s and the 1970s, the post-modern choreographers created works that were a radical departure from the work of their predecessors. During that time, however, some choreographers would not negate technique, theme, or storyline and were not considered to be "post-modern." That is to say that their work was not considered to be abstract or avant garde. Alvin Ailey (1931–1990, see Figure 6.10) was one such choreographer and was concerned with making dances that were accessible to the general public. He wanted his audiences to feel totally fulfilled and entertained while they were watching his dances. He was concerned primarily with creating works that had a definite form, unlike the improvised dances of the Judson Dance Theatre and Grand Union. One of Ailey's most popular dances is entitled *Revelations* (1960) and is performed to African-American spirituals. It is a highly technical dance that contains dramatic as well as comical moments. *Revelations*, seen by many as a celebration, depicts the religious heritage of African-Americans. It is still performed today by the Alvin Ailey American Dance Theatre and is considered to be their signature dance.

Dance-Theatre

In the dance world, a great many works fall under the heading of dance-theatre. This genre blends dance and theatre, so that both forms are an integral part of the performance. These performances may include spoken words, text, singing, and choreography (see Figure 6.11), which is propelled by theme, dramatics, and "theatrics." In the United States, the term *dance-theatre* covers a broad spectrum of creations, but mostly applies to dance companies or choreographers who infuse into their performances dramatic action that is similar to what we see in the theatre. Sometimes, these creations can also come under the heading of "modern dance," because the choreography used is typically from the modern dance genre. For example, some works of the Judson Dance Theatre members, such as Meredith Monk, Lucinda Childs, and Yvonne Rainer, can be referred to as dance-theatre, as well as falling under the "post-modern" heading.

Dance-theatre was developed in Europe, specifically in West Germany, and came directly out of the modern dance genre:

> In Europe . . . the development of modern dance was brutally interrupted by World War II. The movement was centered in Germany. Under the Nazis, some modern dance choreographers fled; others collaborated and discredited the movement. By the end of the war, European modern dance was all but wiped out and it did not revive until the sixties, when a new form, the German *Tanztheatre*, or dance-theatre, rose from the ashes of German expressionist dance of the twenties and thirties.[7]

It is important to note that in the United States, the *movement*, or the dancing, usually takes priority in dance-theatre work; in Europe, the focus of dance-

Figure 6.11

Movement and spoken word are two aspects of dance-theatre.
Contributed by Ben Viatori. ©Kendall Hunt Publishing Company.

theatre is usually much more *theatre* than dance. Therefore, there is a great difference between the two continents and what the valued aesthetic is in reference to dance-theatre. In the past, some European dance critics viewed the American version of dance-theatre as "outdated," while some American critics viewed the Europeans as negators of dance vocabulary.

One of the major figures in the dance-theatre (or *tanztheatre*) genre in Germany was Pina Bausch (1940–2009), who created works since the late 1960s. Her company, the *Wuppertaler Tanztheatre*, combined dance and theatre to create disturbing pictures of real-life situations. These situations were almost always based on the male/female relationship, which Bausch showed in a bleak and disturbing way. "Especially unresolved are the images of gender and sexual relations. Bausch shows men and women locked into power plays and obsessive patterns of physical and emotional violence."[8] Some American critics thought that what Bausch created was not dance at all and have called her work "indulgent" and "superficial." On the other hand, other American dance critics felt that Bausch's work was (and is) riveting and important, and that she presented issues to audiences that must be addressed.

Germany is not the only country where dance-theatre is prominent. France also has a widespread following for dance-theatre, and French choreographers, such as Maguy Marin (b. 1951), are popular not only in Europe, but in the

United States as well. The Japanese dance form *Butoh*, developed in the 1960s by Kazuo Ohno (1906–2010), also falls under the category of dance-theatre. *Butoh* (which is referred to as "dark soul dance" or "dance of utter darkness") is characterized by its use of slow, sustained movements. Sometimes, the performers move at such a slow pace that it is difficult to see them move from one shape to another. One famous company that performs *Butoh* is *Sankai Juku* (founded in 1975 by Ushio Amagatsu), whose members have shaved heads and cover their bodies with white makeup for each performance. This company, like many dance-theatre companies, presents painful images of devastation that they perceive to be in the world around them.

In today's world of modern and contemporary dance, there are no rules and regulations, just an underlying freedom to create in whatever way one wishes.

Modern and Contemporary Dance Today

Today, there are many choreographers who maintain a connection to a traditional modern dance aesthetic, as well as those whose work reflects the philosophy of the post-modern dancers. Still others are forging new ground and carving their own niche in the world of contemporary dance. It is virtually impossible to categorize or label today's choreographers, because the category of modern dance has become so broad. In today's world of modern and contemporary dance, there are no rules and regulations, just an underlying freedom to create in whatever way one wishes. To say that in dance "anything goes" would be an understatement, since today's choreographers have gone well beyond any traditional definition of modern dance.

For example, in recent years aerial, or vertical dance, has become popular. There are many different companies around the world that call themselves aerial dance companies, but every company has a different aesthetic. There are some companies, for example, that do all of their aerial work outside—on mountain cliffs, in canyons and on rock formations—while other companies utilize indoor spaces and theatres. All of these companies use harnessing and mountain climbing equipment and other special apparatus to perform their dances.

One popular aerial dance company is Project Bandaloop, based in San Francisco. In one event in Houston, the company performed *Romeo and Juliet* on the twenty-third story of a skyscraper. The dancers were 350 feet in the air, while the Houston Symphony played below. It is estimated that there were 40,000 people who viewed that performance. Project Bandaloop also presents outdoor work (on the cliffs of Yosemite, for example), as well as performances in theatres.

There are other dance companies that have extended the limitations of the body by adding props, set pieces, and what some would consider death-defying movements to their performances. Elizabeth Streb's (b. 1950) company, Streb Extreme Action, combines virtuosity and technical skill to produce some of today's most exciting, if not heart-stopping, performances. Often performed on large set pieces, the dances have been described as a combination of dance, athletics, gymnastics, and the circus. Dancers are tossed from one place on stage to another, seeming to fly through the air. They run up and climb over walls, jump through set pieces, and perform work that has earned them the title of "action hero" in Streb's company. A company with a similar aesthetic, Diavolo: Architecture in Motion, also uses large and complex set pieces that are usually in constant motion as the dancers perform on top of, in, and around the apparatus. Diavolo, created by artistic director Jacques Heim (b. 1964), shows work that depicts the relationship between the human body and its surroundings, specifically between the body and architecture.

Another popular aesthetic that has been seen in the modern and contemporary dance field is the idea of dance fusion, which is the combining of different dance genres, as well as aspects from theatre, music, and visual art. There are many choreographers who blend genres in their work, such as Doug Elkins, Jennifer Muller, and Ron Brown (see *Major Figures in Modern Dance*). In these dances, it is not uncommon to see modern, ballet, jazz, hip hop, African (or another world dance form) all blended together into one dance. There are also choreographers who use text, singing, and other theatrical elements in a dance. These dances not only display a fusion of genres, but sometimes call attention to the multicultural aspects of the art form.

Technology is also having an influence on the way people create, including the use of video, live feed, motion capture, and other advancements that allows dance to go beyond what is happening live on stage (see *Chapter Eleven: Dance Production: Behind the Scenes of a Dance Concert*). Dance for the camera (or screen dance), where dances appear only in film form, is another area of dance in which many artists are working. Many feel that technology has opened up a new area for creativity, and screen dances are made that depict every dance genre, can be based in narrative or be abstract, and can show actual dancers, a manipulated version of the dancers, or even animation. There are festivals, conferences, and competitions dedicated specifically to this genre, and even colleges and universities are including dance for the camera (and dance and technology in general) in their curricula.

A trend in the dance world is the migration of established, professional dancers who are accepting teaching positions in colleges and universities. These choreographers, such as David Dorfman and Bebe Miller, still maintain a connection to the professional dance world (many still are the artistic directors of a company), but have the security of a full-time position. This situation is a positive one for all parties involved—the universities get to have outstanding artists and educators on their faculty, while the artists have a stable base from which to work.

Of course, there are choreographers who only focus on their companies and choreographing for other professional companies. One contemporary choreographer of note is Mark Morris (b. 1956, see Figure 6.12). Morris has created some of today's most critically acclaimed dances and has established himself as an outstanding choreographer. One aspect of Morris's choreography that critics and audiences alike note is his use of music. *Dido and Aeneas* (1989), in which Morris portrayed dual rolls of Dido and the witch, is a clear example of Morris's ability to use music in an extremely sophisticated way. Before Morris

Mark Morris and company members performing Morris' dance *A Spell*.

Robbie Jack/Corbis Entertainment/Getty Images

Figure 6.12

choreographs a dance, he studies the musical score and learns every phrase, note, and nuance of the piece. Only then will he begin to choreograph. He is also committed to only using live music during his dance concerts. In the end, the audience views a beautiful marriage of dance and music. His dances range from the wildly comic to the dark and dramatic. He is one of today's most famous choreographers, and his company is known worldwide.

Bill T. Jones (b. 1952) is also one of today's most popular modern dance choreographers. He, along with his partner Arnie Zane (1948–1988), created the Bill T. Jones/Arnie Zane Company. Jones's choreography follows a strong narrative and dramatic line. Though it is often controversial (see *Major Figures in Modern Dance*), there is never an absence of passion and feeling in his work. In *D-Man in the Waters* (1989), which Jones created as a tribute to a friend who had died of the AIDS virus, swimming motifs are combined with subtle gestures in a piece that is at once witty and poignant. In this dance, the dancers explode onto the stage with power, strength, and commitment, which are signature qualities of this company. Jones also includes theatrical elements in his work, such as singing, text, and dialogue, as seen in his 2017 work *Analogy: A Trilogy*.

Regardless of the style, technique or method, modern dance has and always will be about the world in which we live, reflecting all that the world encompasses in the form of movement.

Summary

All the aforementioned choreographers continued to create dances for many years, and many are still active choreographers today (see *Major Figures in Modern Dance*). Students of modern and contemporary dance still study the formalized techniques created by many of these artists, while others choose to

Figure 6.13

study with people who teach a more eclectic form. Regardless of the style, technique, or method, modern dance has and always will be about the world in which we live, reflecting all that the world encompasses in the form of movement (see Figure 6.13).

The contributions that the post-moderners made to the dance world have had a profound effect on the way that people choreograph and view dance. In providing their audiences with a view of the abstract, they created a rich language of symbolic expression. Writer Selma Jeanne Cohen stated:

> *Unquestionably the members of the avant garde have made a significant contribution to the art of dance. They have tremendously broadened the range of the dance vocabulary and revealed its wealth of connotative power. They have explored new relationships between movement and sound, movement and light and color. They have stimulated a fresh awareness of the uniqueness of the medium of dance. If they have not demonstrated that dance must do away with content and narrative or emotional continuity, they have shown that dances can be formed without them.*[9]

Today, the term *post-modern* is used mostly to describe those people active from the 1950s to the 1970s who held to the post-modern aesthetic. The next generation of modern dance choreographers, such as Mark Morris and Bill T. Jones, are referred to in this book as "the next wave" (see *Major Figures in Modern Dance*). Although Morris, Jones, and other

Contemporary dancer.
©Volodymyr Leshchenko/Shutterstock, Inc.

current choreographers have forged their own paths, many also maintain a connection to both the modern and post-modern dance aesthetics. Like choreographers past, these artists provide a contemporary view on issues that range from the mild to the controversial, from the comic to the thought-provoking, and from the beautiful to the horrific. The work created by these different artists are based both in reality and in the abstract, and provide for the viewers a glimpse into different facets of life.

Dance-theatre is an exciting art form, but one that is defined in different ways, depending on what country is being referenced. In the United States, the movement is usually the primary focus, while in other countries, the theatre aspect takes preference. Although most dance-theatre that is seen worldwide has its roots in modern and post-modern dance, only in the United States is this fact still obvious. Table 6.1 outlines the similarities and differences between traditional modern dance and post-modern dance. Events in modern dance history can be found in Table 6.2.

Table 6.1 *Similarities and Differences between Traditional Modern Dance and Post-Modern Dance*

Similarities	Differences
■ Both presented dances that displayed innovative movement. ■ Both utilized themes that were social, political, and global. ■ Both utilized the elements of space, time, and energy in a way that was different from ballet.	■ Many traditional modern dances had strong narrative lines; most post-modern dances were plotless and devoid of narrative. ■ Traditional modern dances employed trained dancers; some post-modern choreographers used untrained dancers. ■ Traditional modern dances often utilized costumes; post-modern dances were often presented in everyday street clothes. ■ Traditional modern dance was often presented in theatres. Post-modern dance was presented in a number of different places.

Table 6.2 *Outline of Modern, Post-Modern, and Contemporary Dance Events*

1900	Isadora Duncan has her first solo performances in the United States, which were not well received. She then travels to Europe.
1902	Duncan's first successful performance, which occurs in Budapest.
1903	Duncan travels to Greece to study Greek culture and perform.
1904–1909	Duncan performs several times in Russia; she is said to have had a major impact on the choreography of Michel Fokine.
1914	Ruth St. Denis and Ted Shawn begin Denishawn.
1915	Doris Humphrey becomes a student at Denishawn.
1916	Martha Graham becomes a student at Denishawn.
1920	Charles Weidman becomes a student at Denishawn.
1926	Martha Graham presents her own concert as an independent artist. She then begins to develop her dance company as well as the Graham technique.
1928	Doris Humphrey and Charles Weidman begin the Humphrey-Weidman Dance Company and develop the Humphrey-Weidman technique.
1931	Final Denishawn performance.
1931	The premier of Doris Humphrey's *The Shakers*.
1933	Ted Shawn develops an all-male dance company, Ted Shawn and His Men Dancers.
1941	Ted Shawn begins Jacob's Pillow.
1944	Martha Graham choreographs *Appalachian Spring*.
1944	After performing with the Martha Graham Dance Company, Merce Cunningham creates his first works as an independent artist.
1948	Alwin Nikolais becomes director of the Henry Street Playhouse and develops his own company.
1955	Anna Sokolow creates *Rooms*.
1957	Paul Taylor creates the Paul Taylor Dance Company.
1958	Alvin Ailey establishes the Alvin Ailey American Dance Theatre.
1960	Alvin Ailey choreographs *Revelations*.
1960	Robert Ellis Dunn begins to teach dance composition classes at the Judson Memorial Church.
1962	The Judson Dance Theatre is formed.
1966	Yvonne Rainer choreographs *Trio A*.
1968	The Grand Union is formed.
1970	Trisha Brown creates *Man Walking Down Side of Building*.
1980	Mark Morris develops the Mark Morris Dance Group.
1982	The Bill T. Jones/Arnie Zane Dance Company is formed.
1988–1991	Mark Morris is the artistic director of the Brussel *Theatre Royal de la Monnaie*.

Table 6.2 Outline of Modern, Post-Modern, and Contemporary Dance Events (continued)

1989	Mark Morris choreographs *Dido and Aeneas*.
1989	Bill T. Jones choreographs *D-Man in the Waters*.
1994	Bill T. Jones choreographs *Still/Here*, which dance critic Arlene Croce labels "victim art."
2001	The Mark Morris Dance Center is opened in Brooklyn, N.Y.
2001	The Dance Camera West Film Festival is established to provide a forum for the genre of Dance Art Film.
2002	Dance Theatre Workshop, a New York City performing institution dedicated to nurturing artistic talent, constructs a new facility. It is called the Bessie in honor of master teacher Bessie Schonberg, and is a state-of-the-art performance space.
2003	Bill T. Jones receives the prestigious Dorothy and Lillian Gish Prize, which recognizes outstanding talents in the arts.
2003	Mark Morris creates a dance, *Non Troppo*, for the leading men of American Ballet Theatre. The work is for a PBS special, *Born to be Wild: The Leading Men of American Ballet Theatre*.
2003	The American Dance Festival celebrates its seventieth anniversary with performances by artists from France, India, Russia, Japan, China, Taiwan, and the United States.
2004	Since the early part of the new century, aerial, or vertical dance has become popular worldwide. Aerial dance has been around since the 1970s but has become a part of mainstream dance in recent years. Some companies performing aerial dance are: Project Bandaloop (San Francisco, CA), Frequent Flyers Productions (Boulder, CO), Stage Fright (London), Legs on the Wall (Australia), and High Strung Aerial Dance (Toronto).
2006	The Limon Dance Company celebrates its sixtieth anniversary. Carla Maxwell has been with the company for over forty years, first as a principal dancer, then as the artistic director.
2007	Jacob's Pillow, founded by Ted Shawn, celebrates its 75th anniversary.
2007	Bill T. Jones wins the Tony Award for Best Choreography for the Broadway hit *Spring Awakening*.
2007	The Dance Camera West Film Festival enters its sixth year, having presented over 600 dance films from around the world.
2008	The Alvin Ailey American Dance Theatre celebrates its 50th season.
2008	The Lar Lubovitch Dance Company celebrates its 40th season.
2008	Twyla Tharp receives the Kennedy Center Honor.
2009	The Bill T. Jones/Arnie Zane Dance Company celebrates its 25th season, creating two dances about the legacy of Abraham Lincoln, marking the 200th anniversary of Lincoln's birth.
2009	The Alwin Nikolais Centennial features a two-year celebration of the works of this iconic choreographer.
2010	The Kennedy Center awards choreographer Bill T. Jones the Kennedy Center Honor.
2011	Jacob's Pillow launches Jacob's Pillow Dance Interactive, an online resource of video clips featuring performances that have taken place at the festival from 1937 to 2010, including footage rarely seen.
2012	After Merce Cunningham's death in 2009, the Cunningham Trust (founded in 2000), established headquarters at New York's City Center, where it offers daily classes in Cunningham technique. The Trust serves as the custodian of the work of Merce Cunningham. Its mission is to preserve, enhance, and maintain the integrity of Cunningham's work.
2012	Choreographer Wayne McGregor creates a TEDGlobal presentation, demonstrating how a choreographer communicates ideas to an audience. For the presentation, he worked with two dancers to build phrases of dance, who improvised live on the TEDGlobal stage.
2013	Health issues cause Trisha Brown to step down as the head and choreographer of the Trisha Brown Dance Company. The dancers embark on a three-year farewell tour.
2014	The Julliard School gives an honorary doctorate to choreographer Lar Lubovitch.
2015	Web sites such as YouTube and Vimeo continue to provide access to thousands of dance clips and videos to millions of viewers.
2017	Rennie Harris wins the Dance Magazine Award.
2017	Online Dance Company, directed by Cifrão and based in Portugal, exists only online, posting one video per month and featuring dances from hip-hop to ballet to ballroom. With videos such as *There's No Age for Dancing*, and *We are (A)live*, the company has received well over one million views.
2018	Dances created with themes of social justice are more prominent than ever, with one example being Robert Battle's *Mass*, performed by the Alvin Ailey American Dance Theatre.

Discussion Questions

Discuss in class or provide written answers.

1. What are the major similarities between modern dance and post-modern dance? What are the differences? What are the characteristics of contemporary dance?

2. Who do you think were (or are) some of the most influential artists of the modern dance world? Why? What about post-modern and contemporary artists?

3. Discuss the quote by Deborah Jowitt that states that the Judson Dance Theatre members were making a "comment on the times." What do you think this quote means? What were "the times" all about when the Judson Dance Theatre was active and how do you think the artists were reacting to it?

4. Why do you think Americans place an emphasis on movement in dance-theatre performances and people from other countries put the emphasis on theatre?

5. Do you think that the different audiences that view dance-theatre have an impact on how it is performed? For example, do you think that there is a difference between an American audience and a European audience and how they perceive and receive dance?

Figure 6.14

MAJOR FIGURES IN MODERN, POST-MODERN, AND CONTEMPORARY DANCE

To give readers a perspective on the wide range of dancers and choreographers who were and are involved in the world of modern dance, post-modern dance, contemporary dance, and dance-theatre, here is a list of some of the artists that have helped shape dance history.

Figure 6.15

Loie Fuller, in her trademark costume, which was used to highlight her special lighting effects.
Courtesy of Library of Congress Prints and Photographs, LC-USZ62-90930.

The Forerunners

Loie Fuller (1862–1928, see Figure 6.15)—Fuller was an American dancer who was popular in Europe, particularly in Paris during the late 1800s, where she was known as "La Loie." She developed many lighting techniques and lighting instruments and created visual spectacles by dancing with costumes made from yards of fabrics that would pick up the different colors of the lights. She also encouraged Isadora Duncan to come to Europe, where Duncan was embraced by the public.

Isadora Duncan (1877–1927, see Figure 6.16)—Credited with being the "mother of modern dance," Duncan believed that movements should be drawn from nature. Developing the Duncan technique, comprised of basic movements such as swinging, hopping, running, skipping, and leaping, Duncan sought to "free" the body from the confines of ballet and created a truly modern form of dance.

Figure 6.16

Many dance historians credit Isadora Duncan with being the first dancer to present "modern dancing" to the public.
Courtesy of Photofest.

Ruth St. Denis (1878–1968)—At first a dancer on the theatrical stage, "Miss Ruth" began to choreograph after seeing a cigarette poster that used the Egyptian goddess Isis in its advertisement. She then became fascinated with Asia and performed for years in Europe and New York. She met and married **Ted Shawn** (1891–1972) and together they formed Denishawn, a school that also had a company that toured throughout the United States. Shawn shared St. Denis's passion for ethnicity, as well as religious expression. In the early 1930s their marriage ended, as did the Denishawn school. Shawn established Ted Shawn and His Men Dancers, an all-male dance company that toured throughout the United States for many years. He also established Jacob's Pillow, a school in Massachusetts. Jacob's Pillow is still in existence today and provides dance instruction and performances in the summers.

Rudolf Von Laban (1879–1958)—Sometimes referred to as the "father of German modern dance," Laban developed movement choirs, which consisted of large groups of people moving together at the same time. His choreography was expressionistic, and he believed that dance should be accessible to everyone. Laban is best-known for developing a system of notating dance called Labanotation, as well as a system of notating space, efforts, and shapes called Laban Movement Analysis. These two systems are still used today to record and reconstruct dances.

Maud Allan (1883–1956, see Figure 6.17)—Influenced by the work of Isadora Duncan, Allan was a dramatic dancer who also had a great knowledge of music. Like Fuller and Duncan, Allan, an American, became popular in Europe. She was not without controversy, as much in her private life went against societal norms of the time.

Figure 6.17

Maud Allan performed dancing that was dramatic and musical.

Hulton Deutsch/Corbis Historical/Getty Images

Louis Horst (1884–1964)—Horst was the musical director, composer, and accompanist for Denishawn and later Martha Graham's company and school. He was one of the first artists to develop principles on teaching dance composition, and taught composition and choreography classes that included working with musical structures. He was the founder and editor of the magazine *Dance Observer*, and authored two important books on dance, *Preclassic Dance Forms* and *Modern Dance Forms*.

The Pioneers

Mary Wigman (1886–1973)—A German choreographer and dancer whose works are considered to be "expressionistic," Wigman presented dances whose movements were full of meaning and emotion. She is also one of the first modern choreographers to use musical scores consisting mostly of percussion instruments, as well as danced in silence. A student of Laban, she introduced different concepts of spatial designs to her students.

Martha Graham (1894–1990)—A Denishawn student, Graham gave her first independent concert in 1926. In 1927, she established the Martha Graham School of Contemporary Dance (still in existence today), and a company comprised of all women. She later expanded her company to include male dancers. Graham's dances, most of them psychological dramas, were primarily based on themes drawn from Greek mythology, American pioneers, and Native Americans. Graham developed a dance technique based on a system of contraction and release of the center of the body.

Doris Humphrey (1895–1958)—A Denishawn student, Humphrey eventually became a teacher at the school and developed, along with Ruth St. Denis, a technique known as "music visualization," in which movement phrases, patterns and rhythms correspond with musical phrases, patterns and rhythms (and enables one to "visualize" the music). In 1928, she left Denishawn and together with **Charles Weidman** (1901–1975), another Denishawn student, developed the Humphrey-Weidman School and Dance Company. They developed a dance technique that revolved around fall and recovery, with a major emphasis on balance. Their company disbanded in 1945 and Humphrey became artistic director of the José Limon Dance Company (Limon was one of her students). Weidman went out on his own and choreographed dances, many of a comic nature. Weidman was truly gifted in the art of pantomime and had a wonderful sense of comic timing.

Hanya Holm (1898–1992)—A student of Mary Wigman, Holm came to the United States in 1931 to establish a Wigman school. For a short time she had a company, and became a master teacher using the theories of Wigman as well as her own. Holm is also known as one of the first modern dance choreographers to choreograph for musicals on Broadway such as *Kiss Me Kate, Out of This World,* and *My Fair Lady*.

Kurt Jooss (1901–1979)—Jooss was also a student of Laban and he carried much of Laban's principles into his own work. He is famous for choreographing *The Green Table*, in 1932, which was a protest against war. This powerful anti-war statement was created one year before Adolf Hitler came into power. In 1933, Jooss was ordered to fire all of the Jews in his company, which he refused to do. The company fled Germany and eventually settled in England.

The Second Generation

Martha Hill (1900–1995)—One of the best-known dance educators, Hill established the first bachelor of arts degree in dance at Bennington College in 1932. She is also credited with providing teaching and performing opportunities for Martha Graham, Doris Humphrey, Charles Weidman, and Hanya Holm, first at Bennington College, and then at the newly established American Dance Festival. In 1951, she created the dance division of the Julliard School, where dancers from all over the world still train.

Helen Tamiris (1905–1966)—Tamiris came to modern dance through the ballet world. In 1927, she began to choreograph solo dances for herself. She also choreographed several musical theatre productions such as *Show Boat* and *Annie Get Your Gun*. She is best-known for creating a dance called *Negro Spirituals*. Although she was white, she was the first choreographer to use these spirituals for concert dance. She often collaborated with **Daniel Nagrin** (1917–2008), who is known for his choreography and master teaching, particularly in the areas of improvisation and composition.

Lester Horton (1906–1953)—A West Coast choreographer, Horton developed his company in 1932 and was focused on presenting works depicting Native American culture. He developed the Horton technique, which requires a strong torso and symmetrical and asymmetrical movements of the arms and legs.

José Limon (1908–1972)—A student of Humphrey and Weidman, Limon was a Mexican-American whose heritage influenced his work. After World War II, he formed the José Limon Dance Company and, using the principles of weight, and fall and recovery, developed a technique that was closely linked to the technique of Humphrey and Weidman.

Katherine Dunham (1909–2006, see Figure 6.18)—In 1931, Dunham had her first concert in Chicago entitled *Negro Rhapsody*. This concert was to be the beginnings of black concert dance. Dunham is known for combining native Caribbean and modern dance and is also known as a researcher and a scholar. She appeared in several musical theatre productions as well as movie musicals, and her work also had an influence on jazz dance.

Bonnie Bird (1914–1995)—Bird's career included both academic and professional performing experiences. She was one of the first dancers in Martha Graham's dance company and also served as her teaching assistant. She was a

Figure 6.18

Katherine Dunham helped lead the way in opening stage doors and overcoming racial prejudices for entertainers of color.
Courtesy of Photofest.

prolific writer and wrote for many leading dance periodicals and magazines. She also served as the Head of International Development at the Laban Centre of Movement and Dance in London.

Anna Sokolow (1910–2000)—One of the first members of the Martha Graham Company, Sokolow also worked during that time as an independent choreographer. Over the years, Sokolow developed professional and personal relationships with dancers in Mexico and Israel and traveled to these places to teach and choreograph. Sokolow's dances were both political and social comments on societal issues.

Bella Lewitzky (1916–2004)—Lewitzky was a student of Lester Horton. Her choreography is most noted for its intricate movement patterns and strong technique. She is recognized as a champion for freedom of expression and anti-censorship. The Lewitzky Dance Company was housed for many years in Los Angeles, but has since disbanded.

Erick Hawkins (1909–1994)—Hawkins was originally a ballet dancer and became the first male dancer to join Martha Graham's dance company. He later became her husband. After their breakup, he left her company and in 1951 began to establish himself as an independent choreographer. He created a new technique that put emphasis on ease and free flow of movements. Today, the Erick Hawkins Dance Company is still a viable part of the dance community.

Valerie Bettis (1919–1982)—Bettis, a student of Hanya Holm, was known as a master teacher as well as a choreographer. She is also credited with being one of the first modern dancers to choreograph for a ballet company (the Ballet Russes de Monte Carlo).

Pearl Primus (1919–1994)—A student of Graham, Humphrey, Weidman, and Holm, Primus is also credited with bringing black concert dance to the forefront. In her choreography, her focus was mainly on African dance and African subject matter. In contrast to Dunham, whose movements were flowing and smooth, Primus' movements were athletic and dynamic (see Figure 6.19).

Talley Beatty (c. 1923–1996)—Beatty performed in the first company that Katherine Dunham established. He eventually established his own company, which performed for about five years. His choreography combined modern and jazz techniques and often revealed the racial injustice suffered by African-Americans. One of his most popular dances is *The Road of the Phoebe Snow*, created in 1959, which portrayed life along the famous railroad line.

Figure 6.19

Pearl Primus was a powerful and dynamic performer.

Donald McKayle (b. 1930)—McKayle studied with Graham and Cunningham, among others. His choreography calls attention to the black experience and is currently performed by such companies as the Dayton Contemporary Dance Company and the Alvin Ailey American Dance Theatre.

Alvin Ailey (1931–1990)—A student of Lester Horton, Ailey developed his own company in the mid-1950s. Called the Alvin Ailey American Dance Theatre, the company is located in New York. Ailey was always concerned with making his dances accessible to the audience. He combined modern, jazz, and world dance to create a unique style. The Ailey company and school, still in existence today, is world-renowned.

Carmen de Lavallade (b. 1931)—A student of Horton, de Lavallade danced with many dance companies, but is widely known for her dancing with the Alvin Ailey American Dance Theatre. She is a recipient of the Kennedy Center Honor.

Eleo Pomare (1937–2008)—Like Beatty's works, Pomare's choreography often represented the struggles of blacks in America. His powerful *Blues for the Jungle*, created in 1972, was a realistic look at life in Harlem. He studied with Kurt Jooss in Germany and eventually established his own company that made their New York City debut in 1966.

The Post-Moderners

Alwin Nikolais (1912–1993)—A student of Hanya Holm, "Nik" is best remembered for his choreography that explored the use of lighting, costumes, and props in a purely theatrical way. Nik was not concerned with showing emotion on stage, but rather motion, and is known as one of the forerunners of the post-modern movement. In 1970, along with fellow choreographer **Murray Louis** (1926–2016), he established the Nikolais-Louis Dance Lab in New York, as well as the Nikolais-Louis Dance Company established in later years. Louis, once a student of Nikolais, continued the artistic directorship of the Nikolais-Louis Dance Company after Nikolais' death. Today, the Nikolais/Louis Foundation for Dance, in collaboration with the Rire/Woodbury Dance Company, tours and performs repertory by Nikolais and Louis.

Merce Cunningham (1919–2009)—Cunningham came to dance because of tap dance lessons he received at a young age. He was a dancer with the Martha Graham Dance Company for five years before establishing the Merce Cunningham Dance Company in 1953. He developed the Cunningham technique, in which the spine acts as a spring and can coil, twist, and turn. His technique also employs intricate direction changes and many shifts of weight throughout a given phrase of movement. He created dances that were devoid of meaning and were "movement for movement's sake." He is credited with being "the father of post-modern dance."

Anna Halprin (b. 1920)—One of the leading figures in the Judson Dance Theatre, Halprin had, as a student, studied the more formalized techniques of her predecessors. Today, she is best-known for her work in improvisation.

Paul Taylor (b. 1930)—In a career spanning both the modern and post-modern movements, Taylor was both a student of Martha Graham and a dancer with the Merce Cunningham Dance Company. He is considered to be one of the forerunners of the post-modern movement. In 1955, Taylor began to create his own dances and in 1961 formed his own company. Taylor's choreography is a combination of athletic dynamics and beauty. Today, the Paul Taylor Dance Company is world-renowned.

The Post-Moderners: Second Generation

Robert Ellis Dunn (1928–1996)—Dunn, a musician, taught dance composition and improvisation classes at the Cunningham School in the 1960s. In 1962, he organized the first dance concert at the Judson Memorial Church in New York and thus began the activities of the Judson Dance Theatre.

Viola Farber (1931–1998)—As a choreographer, Farber was very much influenced by her former teacher, Merce Cunningham, although some of her works were on the comical side. Farber began her own company in 1953. She is also known for succeeding Alwin Nikolais as artistic director of the *Centre National de Dance Contemporaine* in France.

Dan Wagoner (b. 1932)—Wagoner came to New York in the late 1950s and danced with the Martha Graham, Merce Cunningham, and Paul Taylor companies before he established his own company in 1969. Dan Wagoner and Dancers performed for almost twenty-five years, but had to disband because of financial reasons.

Yvonne Rainer (b. 1934)—A student of Cunningham, Rainer was one of the founding members of the Judson Dance Theatre. Rainer was concerned with reducing dance movement to a minimum, without the inclusion of emotion, theatricality, or spectacle. Today, Rainer is still an active choreographer and filmmaker.

Simone Forti (b. 1935)—A student of Anna Halprin, Forti's works took on an improvisational feel, much like those of

her teacher. Today, a master teacher herself, Forti continues to create works from an improvisational base.

Rod Rodgers (1938–2002)—For several years, Rodgers was a member of the Erick Hawkins Dance Company. In the mid-1960s he formed the Rod Rodgers Dance Company, which performed choreography that was a mix of modern and jazz. He was also a founding member of the Association of Black Choreographers.

Steve Paxton (b. 1939)—Paxton is best-known for developing "contact improvisation" (see *Chapter Seven: Improvisation and Creative Movement*). Paxton was also a founding member of the Judson Dance Theatre and was a student of Cunningham.

Trisha Brown (1940–2017, see Figure 6.20)—Another founding member of the Judson Dance Theatre, Brown's choreography employed the use of repetition. She created intricate movement patterns that seemed to logically build from one movement to the next. She established the Trisha Brown Dance Company in 1970.

Figure 6.20

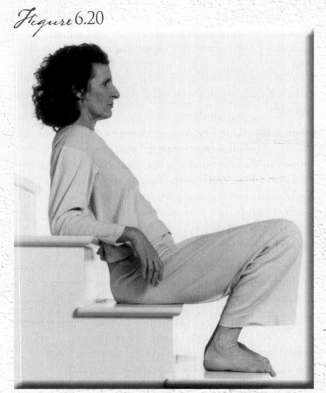

Trisha Brown was one of the founding members of the Judson Dance Theatre and the Grand Union before establishing her own dance company.
© by Lois Greenfield, 1988.

Lucinda Childs (b. 1940)—Another student of Cunningham and founding member of the Judson Dance Theatre, Childs' use of repetition of movement and phrases was a trademark of her choreography. Childs has provided choreography for mixed-media performances such as Robert Wilson's *Einstein on the Beach*.

Gus Solomons, Jr. (b. 1940)—Solomons danced with the Martha Graham and Merce Cunningham dance companies, among others. In addition to choreographing, Solomons has written for many dance publications, including *Dance Magazine*.

Twyla Tharp (b. 1942)—Tharp worked with both Cunningham and Taylor, and later developed her own company and created a movement style that was a blend of several dance forms, including ballet, modern, tap, and jazz. Although seemingly "loose," Tharp's choreography is technically difficult, with its use of a relaxed torso but dynamically charged arm and leg movements. Tharp has also choreographed for several ballet companies and for a short while was a resident choreographer for American Ballet Theatre in New York. In 2002, she created the Broadway musical *Movin' Out*, with music by Billy Joel. She is an active choreographer, creating work for dance companies, movies, and Broadway productions.

David Gordon (b. 1943)—Once a student of Cunningham and founding member of the Judson Dance Theatre (as well as its offspring, the Grand Union), Gordon has been choreographing since the early 1960s. His dances, many filled with comical moments, combined movement and text. The David Gordon Performance Company is comprised of dancers who are also skilled actors, including Gordon's wife, **Valda Setterfield** (b. 1934).

Meredith Monk (b. 1943)—Another student of Cunningham, Monk combined her talents as a musician and writer within her works. Her dance aesthetic differed from most of the Judson Dance Theatre members in that her dances were full of symbolism and emotion. Today, Monk presents mixed-media events that include her original choreography, music, and text.

Margaret Jenkins (b. 1944)—Jenkins is the artistic director of the Margaret Jenkins Dance Company, which is based in San Francisco. She creates narrative works in which the dancers, through the use of improvisation and the development of movement phrases, are often collaborators.

Lar Lubovitch (b. 1944)—A student of Martha Graham, Anna Sokolow, and José Limon, Lubovitch danced with a number of modern dance companies before creating his own. His choreography, which combines highly charged movement phrases with intricate floor patterns, has made the Lar Lubovitch Dance Company one of the best-loved in America.

Laura Dean (b. 1945)—The use of repetition, particularly spinning and spins that move in intricate patterns around the stage, are among the tools that Dean uses in her choreography. She was a Cunningham student and a founding member of the Judson Dance Theatre. Today, her company, Laura Dean Musicians and Dancers, still employs the techniques she developed in the 1960s.

Kei Takei (b. 1946)—A choreographer whose dances appear to be as sacred as primitive rituals, Takei came to the United States from Japan in 1966. Her use of repetition is essential in her work, which has a mesmerizing effect on the audience. Her company, Moving Earth Orient Sphere, has been performing a series of dances for many years, all with the word "light" in the title.

Ulysses Dove (1947–1996)—Dove performed with many leading dance companies, such as the Merce Cunningham Dance Company and the Alvin Ailey American Dance Theatre. His choreography received critical acclaim, and has been seen on such companies as the American Ballet Theatre, New York City Ballet, and Alvin Ailey American Dance Theatre.

The Next Wave

Pina Bausch (1940–2009)—Bausch was a German choreographer whose company *Wuppertaler Tanztheatre* (dance-theatre), combined dance and theatre to create disturbing and haunting pictures of real-life situations. Many of her dances dealt with gender issues, specifically focusing on fear and brutality. Today, her company is called *Tanztheater Wuppertal Pina Bausch*, and continues to perform world-wide.

Garth Fagan (b. 1940)—Jamaican-born Fagan was a student of Martha Graham, Pearl Primus, and Alvin Ailey, among others. His company, Garth Fagan Dance, uniquely blends modern, jazz, and world dance. Based in Rochester, New York, his company is internationally known. He also created the choreography for the Broadway production of *The Lion King*.

Judith Jamison (b. 1944)—Jamison was one of Alvin Ailey's principal dancers for many years. He created several roles and dances specifically for her, including the beautiful solo *Cry*. After Ailey's death in 1990, Jamison assumed the position of artistic director of the Alvin Ailey American Dance Theatre, remaining in this position until 2011, and becoming Director Emerita after her retirement.

Jennifer Muller (b. 1944)—Jennifer Muller/The Works is a company that often blends several genres into one dance. It is not uncommon to see a Muller work that includes modern, ballet, jazz, text, and singing. Her work is sometimes referred to as dance theatre and is often inspired by Eastern philosophy. Another signature of her choreography is the inventive partnering sequences that her dancers perform.

Liz Lerman (b. 1947)—One of our country's most political choreographers, Lerman's dances are always a commentary on societal and political issues. The use of dance and text is a trademark of her work, as was her intergenerational dance company, The Dance Exchange. Lerman also directed Dancers of the Third Age, a company with members over age sixty.

Bebe Miller (b. 1949)—Miller's works are among today's most highly acclaimed in the modern dance world. Using a variety of music, such as classical pieces and the music of Jimi Hendrix, Miller's works are thought-provoking and dramatic.

Elizabeth Streb (b. 1950)—Streb's company, Streb Extreme Action, is known for its fierce athleticism that has sometimes been called "violent," although she does not see it as such. Streb has expanded the definition of dance to include movements that seem to defy gravity and use space unlike any other dance company. Her dances often include props or large set pieces, that the movements center around, in, under, over, etc., and provide the viewer with images unlike any they have ever seen before in a dance concert.

Eiko (b. 1951) and **Koma** (b. 1947)—These dancers from Japan present what seems to be *Butoh*-inspired choreography, although they refer to their technique as "Delicious Movement." Their movements are performed so slowly that at times the audience does not see their transition from one movement to the next. Their dances usually have dark and dramatic themes.

Joe Goode (b. 1951)—Goode resides on the West Coast where he is a choreographer, theatre director, and teacher. After dancing with the Margaret Jenkins Dance Company, he formed the Joe Goode Performance Group (in 1985). Mostly all of his dances incorporate movement, music, text, and singing. Much of the work he creates has been influenced by the HIV/AIDS epidemic.

Maguy Marin (b. 1951)—Born and raised in France, Marin trained in classical ballet as a young child and was eventually introduced to modern dance. She danced in Maurice Béjart's company for three years, and then eventually established the *Compagnie Maguy Marin*. Her choreography has been categorized as dance-theatre, and she is known as one of France's most innovative choreographers. Some of her most popular works, such as *Cinderella* and *Coppelia*, were created for the Lyons Opera Ballet.

Bill T. Jones (b. 1952, see Figure 6.21)—Artistic director of the Bill T. Jones/Arnie Zane Company (Zane is now deceased, a victim of the AIDS virus), Jones's choreography follows a strong narrative and dramatic line and are both poignant and controversial. One of his dances, *Still/Here* (1994), created a major controversy. Because of Jones's

Figure 6.21

Bill T. Jones creates dances with strong narratives and dramatic themes.

Robbie Jack/Corbis Entertainment/Getty Images

use of people with terminal illnesses in the dance, critic Arlene Croce refused to review the dance, which she said was "victim art." Because of this disagreement, the dance world, as well as the popular media, began a long and heated debate on "victim art" and Jones's *Still/Here*.

Ralph Lemon (b. 1952)—Lemon's emotion-filled dances were the driving force of his popular company (which has disbanded). He is concerned with showing real ideas and real people in his works. His unique movement style combines physical strength and strong technique with pedestrian gestures and free-flowing movements.

Ohad Naharin (b. 1952)—Naharin began dancing with the Batsheva Dance Company in Israel. He was then invited by Martha Graham to join her company in New York. While there, he was also a scholarship student at the School of American Ballet. In 1980, he made his debut as a choreographer, and to date has choreographed on major dance companies, including *Nederlands Dans Theatre*, Frankfurt Ballet, Hubbard Street Dance, and Rambert Dance Company. From 1990–2018, he was the artistic director of the Batsheva Dance Company, which is based in Israel. He will continue to be associated with the company as a resident choreographer. He will also continue teaching Gaga technique, which emphasizes sensation and efficiency of movement.

Peggy Baker (b. 1952)—Baker, a Canadian, has won international acclaim for her choreography and performances. From 1981–1988, she was a dancer and rehearsal director with the Lar Lubovitch Dance Company. In 1990, she toured with Mikhail Baryshnikov's White Oak Dance Project. Today, she is the artistic director of Peggy Baker Dance Projects.

Margie Gillis (b. 1953)—Gillis is a Canadian artist mostly known for her solo work. Her ability as a solo artist is outstanding and she is known worldwide as a spectacular performer. She has said that she uses dance as a catharsis to express joy, sorrow, and uncertainty.

Molissa Fenley (b. 1954)—Once the artistic director of a small company, Fenley began performing almost exclusively as a solo artist. Her works are primarily abstract and her movements are a display of pure, clean lines. Today, she still performs as a soloist, as well as with her company, Molissa Fenley and Company.

Homer Avila (1955–2004)—A dancer with Momix and the Bill T. Jones/Arnie Zane Company, Avila was an outstanding performer. In 2001, he lost a leg and hip to a rare form of cancer, but continued to perform even after his surgery. A dedicated and inspiring performer, Avila performed up until the time he died.

Art Bridgman and **Myrna Packer**—This modern dance duet company has been collaborating since 1978. In their latest work, they have been exploring integrating live performance with video technology and have developed the concept of "video partnering." Their theatrical choreography has strong emotional and visceral appeal, and their partnering sequences are daring and exciting.

David Dorfman (b. 1956)—Dorfman came to dance late in life, having been an athlete throughout much of his youth. He began dancing in college, and though he had originally set out to be in the business world, he ended up receiving an M.F.A. degree in dance. He now has a company, David Dorfman Dance, which is based in New York and performs dynamically and emotionally charged dances, often blending movement, music, and text. He has also been known to do community projects, working with people of all levels of dance experience.

Mark Morris (b. 1956)—One of today's leading choreographers, Morris is well-known for his sophisticated use of music in his dances. Now residing in the United States, his company also had a three-year residency in Brussels, where he was the artistic director of the *Theatre Royal de la Monnaie*. In 2001, the Mark Morris Dance Center was opened in Brooklyn, NY.

Doug Varone (b. 1957)—Varone's company, Doug Varone and Dancers, is one of the most dynamic and exciting companies performing today. Varone is extremely versatile, creating dances that range from being abstract to those that have strong emotional content. In 1997, he choreographed and staged the Broadway musical, *Triumph of Love*.

Susan Marshall (b. 1958)—Marshall formed her dance company, Susan Marshall and Company, in 1982. She is known for taking gestures and pedestrian movements and utilizing them in her highly dynamic and athletic choreography. She is concerned with showing emotion and human interaction in her choreography.

Stephen Petronio (b. 1958)—Petronio danced with Trisha Brown from 1979–1986. In 1984, he founded the Stephen Petronio Dance Company. Petronio has been known to create very emotional and intellectual dances, and often uses costumes that blur and confuse sexual identity.

Sarah Skaggs (b. 1958)—Interested in blending social and concert dance, Skaggs has created a unique dance vocabulary for her choreography that she has set on numerous dance companies. In 1991, she developed her company, Sarah Skaggs Dance, which performs in both traditional dance settings as well as in site specific works.

David Parsons (b. 1959)—Parsons was a dancer with the Paul Taylor Dance Company for nine years. He left Taylor's company in 1987 to begin his own, the Parsons Dance Company, which is internationally known today. Parsons' choreography is dynamically charged and he encompasses a broad range of emotions in his dance repertory.

Anne Teresa De Keersmaeker (b. 1960)—De Keersmaeker's company, Rosas, is based in Brussels, Belgium. In 1995, she established the Performing Arts Research and Training Center that provides interdisciplinary education in music, theatre, and dance. In 2011, she made international news due to Beyoncé's use of De Keersmaeker's movements in the pop icon's music video *Countdown*, igniting a discussion regarding movement plagiarism.

Doug Elkins (b. 1960)—A self-proclaimed "style thief," Elkins combines ballet and modern dance with break dancing and hip-hop to create his unusual choreography. In his dances, Elkins presents the audience with humorous contradictions, such as men in women's clothing and break dancing done in Catholic school uniforms.

Sean Curran (b. 1961)—Formerly a dancer with Bill T. Jones/Arnie Zane Company, Curran is now an exceptional choreographer in his own right. After performing in the Broadway show *Stomp* for four years, Curran began making and presenting dances with the Sean Curran Dance Company, that are personal expressions shown through a wide range of themes and dynamics.

Michael Clark (b. 1962)—Formerly a ballet dancer, Clark came to modern dance after arriving in the United States from Britain and studying at the Cunningham School. He is one of Britain's most controversial choreographers. His dances, many of which use rock music and stylized clothing, are some of the most innovative dances seen today.

John Jasperse (b. 1963)—Jasperse began to choreograph and perform professionally in 1985. In 1989, he established the John Jasperse Company, now called John Jasperse Projects. He is known for doing experimental work influenced by a post-modern aesthetic.

Rennie Harris (b. 1964)—Harris created Rennie Harris Puremovement, based in Philadelphia, which is dedicated to preserving and bringing hip-hop culture to the public.

One of his most famous works is *Rome and Jewels*, a hip-hop version of Shakespeare's *Romeo and Juliet*.

Andrea Woods (b. 1964)—Woods is the artistic director of Souloworks/Andrea E. Woods and Dancers based in Brooklyn, NY. She performed with Bill T. Jones/Arnie Zane Company from 1989–1995. She is a dynamic performer with powerful stage presence. Her work is created with inspiration from the African American experience and presented as African American folklore.

Jacques Heim (b. 1964)—Heim is the artistic director of Diavolo: Architecture in Motion, which utilizes large scale set pieces that the performers dance on, under, through, and around, mostly while the apparatus is in motion. Diavolo was featured on the television show *America's Got Talent*, which brought a new audience to this company. Heim has also created choreography for the *Cirque du Soleil* performance of KÀ, which featured apparatus inspired by Diavolo's structures and architecture.

Ron Brown (b. 1966)—Brown is the founder and artistic director of the Ronald K. Brown/Evidence Dance Company. In his choreography, he fuses modern dance with West African dance, a combination that is exciting and inspiring to observe. His highly physical choreography has been described as storytelling through the body. Today, he is one of the most sought-after choreographers, creating dances for professional companies, such as the Alvin Ailey American Dance Theatre.

Shen Wei (b. 1968)—Shen Wei is a Chinese-born American choreographer, visual artist, and director. He creates original works that include dance, painting, sound, sculpture, theater, and video, demonstrating a blend of Asian and Western aesthetics. In 2000, he founded the contemporary dance company Shen Wei Dance Arts. This company is known for innovative concerts and site specific works. Wei was the lead choreographer for the 2008 Beijing Olympics.

Wayne McGregor (b. 1970)—McGregor has been recognized as one of the most innovative choreographers of today. In 1992, Wayne McGregor Random Dance Company was formed and became the first resident company at the new Sadler's Wells in England. Since 2006, he has been resident choreographer of the Royal Ballet. He has also created dances for the Australian Ballet, Stuttgart Ballet, and San Francisco Ballet. His 2010 piece *Far*, which features a pin board of 3,200 LED lights, has been seen worldwide.

Crystal Pite (b. 1970)—Pite is a Canadian choreographer and dancer who performed with Ballet Frankfurt, where she worked with William Forsythe. In 2002 she created Kidd Pivot, which integrates movement, music, text, and visual design. The company tours their innovative performances around the world.

Miguel Gutierrez (b. 1971)—This dance and music artist is the artistic director of Miguel Gutierrez and the Powerful People, a company whose work questions the nature of existence, and presents a collaborative mix of dance, music, and media. He prefers to be called a "dance artist" and not a choreographer. Gutierrez is the recipient of numerous grants and awards and a 2002 "Bessie" Award for his work as a dancer in John Jasperse Company.

Robert Battle (b. 1973)—This choreographer creates fast-paced, frenetic movement that requires the dancers to dance with abandon. A former dancer with the Parsons Dance Company, he developed his own company, Battleworks Dance Company, in 2001. In 2010, he was named the artistic director of the Alvin Ailey American Dance Theatre, succeeding Judith Jamison.

Tania Isaac (b. 1975)—A native of St. Lucia, West Indies, Isaac is interested in giving voice to social concerns and creating community through art. A former dancer with Rennie Harris Puremovement and Urban Bush Woman, Isaac is now the artistic director of Tania Isaac Dance. Her work is at the same time witty, political, and sensual.

Kyle Abraham (b. 1977)—Abraham's company, Abraham.In.Motion, is concerned with presenting dances about identity as it relates to personal history. Abraham danced with several companies before creating his own, but it is his work as a choreographer where he has garnered critical acclaim.

Camille A. Brown (b. 1979)—A voice for her generation, Brown is a dancer, choreographer, and activist. She is the artistic director of Camille A. Brown and Dancers, and has choreographed for major dance companies such as the Alvin Ailey American Dance Theatre and Philadanco!, as well as for Broadway musicals. She is the recipient of numerous awards, and strives to empower communities through dance.

Travis Wall (b. 1987)—Wall is a contemporary and jazz dance choreographer. He is best known for his 2006 appearance as a competitor on the second season of the television show *So You Think You Can Dance*. In 2012, he was hired to choreograph for the contestants on the show, receiving an Emmy nomination for his work on the show's seventh season.

Improvisation and Creative Movement

Improvisation and creative movement are two dance genres that do not necessarily require the participants to have a background in traditional dance techniques. These two genres are focused on self-expression and self-exploration.

Improvisation in dance is the act of creating movement spontaneously.

Improvisation

Improvisation in dance is the act of creating movement spontaneously. For some, creating movement on the spur of the moment can be easy and natural, while for others it may seem impossible. It is interesting to note that it may be easier for a person who has little or no training in dance to improvise than it is for an advanced dancer. Most people might think that the opposite would be true. The scenario, however, is played over time and time again in dance classes across the country—while improvising, the advanced dancer with a lot of technical training will fall back on what they know, whereas the beginning dancer, who does not have any preconceived notions of what they think they "should" do, or what the steps "should" be,

111

moves freely and organically. What does moving "organically" mean? Since improvisation is not about doing actual dance steps that a person would learn in a class, the participants are encouraged to move in a way that is unique and original to *themselves*. Many times, this type of movement is referred to as organic movement, or movement that comes naturally from within.

Regardless of technical level and ability, all dancers and people who wish to dance can benefit greatly from improvisation. For example, when a person does free-style dancing at a social gathering, such as a party, he or she is basically improvising. This type of dancing usually feels good to people. It is during these times that people are able to "cut loose" and enjoy moving with friends to good music. Therefore, one benefit of improvising is that it helps to develop the ability to move freely, without inhibitions or self-consciousness.

In a more structured setting, such as an improvisation class, participants can still experience this kind of freedom, but in a different way. Improvisation sessions or classes can be taught using several different methods. For example, an "improv" class can be structured, with the instructor setting ground rules for the participants. Directions such as "move only at high and low levels," or "move very fast for thirty seconds and then very slow for a minute," can be used to elicit movement while providing a framework in which the participants move. Actually, having some "rules" to follow during improvisation sessions can make it less difficult. In a loosely structured improv session, the only direction a dancer may get is "begin moving." In this instance, the participant must be someone who is highly skilled in improvisation, either because they are an advanced dancer with a knack for improv, or because they are a natural mover.

The use of improvisation is not only limited to dance, but can be found in other art forms. For example, a director of a theatre production could utilize improvisation to help the actors discover more about their characters. A painter may improvise brush strokes on a canvas to see what different textures he or she can create. A musician could improvise on an instrument to develop a new melody. In dance, improvisation can have several functions. For the dancer, it is an important tool that can be used as a way to break old movement patterns. For example, if a dancer is very good at performing slow and sustained movements, but not so skilled in performing fast and sharp movements, then improvising movements using these different dynamics would be a good exercise for them.

Improvisation is also a good way for dancers to learn more about themselves as movers, not only on a physical level but also on cognitive and emotional levels. Because improvisation requires a tremendous amount of spontaneity and exploration on the part of the participant, a great deal can be learned relative to likes and dislikes, as well as strengths and weaknesses.

Many choreographers use improvisation as a means of creating new movement for their dances. In a rehearsal session, a choreographer might ask the dancers to improvise in certain sections of the dance and then make the improvised movement a permanent part of the dance (often, this process is referred to as setting the movement). Some choreographers may ask the dancers to always improvise certain parts of a dance on stage, although improvising during

Figure 7.1

a live performance usually requires the talents of highly skilled dancers in order for it to be effective each time. There are even dance companies that are purely based on improvisation and these companies improvise during all or most of their performances.

Members of the Judson Dance Theatre and the Grand Union (during the late 1960s and early 1970s) used a great deal of improvisation in their work, sometimes holding improvisation sessions similar to ones that jazz musicians hold. They often invited people from the audience to improvise with them during a performance (this act was a frequent practice of the Grand Union). An off-shoot of improvisation, called contact improvisation, was developed by Judson Dance Theatre member Steve Paxton (b. 1939, see Figure 7.1). It is an extension of "traditional" improvisation in that the people performing it remain in almost constant contact with each other. This constant contact is attained by equally giving and receiving the weight of each person's body. A great amount of trust is necessary for the dancers to successfully work together. In contact improv sessions, very difficult movements, such as lifting someone, can be achieved with minimal amount of effort because of the momentum that is built up.

Steve Paxton created contact improvisation.
© Johan Elbers.

Improvisation is a wonderful tool that all dancers and choreographers can use in order to find out more about themselves, create new movements, and experience the freedom of moving spontaneously.

Creative Movement

Creative movement is similar to improvisation in that both genres require the participant to create movements spontaneously. The difference between the two dance forms is that improvisation is usually focused on the movement, whereas creative movement is usually focused on moving for self-discovery. Creative movement specialist Mary Joyce explains: "In creative dance there is no 'right' or 'wrong.' There are no set routines the dancer has to learn. What is important in creative dance is that the dancer draw upon inner resources to make a direct and clear statement."[1] It is important to note that the main focus of creative movement is not the *product*, but the *process*.

Dance teachers will often use this dance form with children, and many feel that children (particularly pre-kindergarten through third grade) benefit more from practicing creative movement than some of the more formal techniques, such as ballet. With creative movement, the children's individual personalities influence how they are going to move (see Figure 7.2). The teacher usually

Creative movement is similar to improvisation in that both genres require the participant to create movements spontaneously.

It is important to note that the main focus of creative movement is not the product, *but the* process.

Figure 7.2

Child dancing in a creative movement class.
Copyright © 2004 by Bruce Davis.

leads and guides (instead of dictating or demonstrating) the students through different exercises, so that participants make most of the creative decisions. Many wonderful creative movement exercises allow children to learn about different life skills, such as self-awareness, socialization, cooperation, and discipline, in addition to experiencing the joy of moving. For example, if a teacher wanted the children to learn about spatial awareness, she or he might instruct the children to move as close together as possible without touching or bumping into each other. This exercise would allow the children to concentrate on one another and also work together to achieve their goal.

Creative movement has also been used to teach dance to older adults. Since some older adults are limited in their range of motion, creative movement is a perfect form of dance for them. Individuals can choose how they want to move and with how much speed and force. Creative movement can also be done with individuals who are seated in chairs. This option is beneficial to senior groups, or people who are physically challenged.

Summary

Both improvisation and creative movement are dance genres that have significant benefits for the participants. Not only do they provide opportunities for experiencing the pleasures of movement, but they also provide opportunities for focusing on the "self."

When doing improvisation or creative movement, it is important for the participants not to feel intimidated or shy about what they are doing (this statement is easier said than done!). But if participants realize that there isn't a "right way" or "wrong way" when participating in these movement experiences, they can feel secure in knowing that what they create is appropriate.

Figure 7.3

Discussion Questions

Discuss in class or provide written answers.

1. What are the similarities between improvisation and creative movement? What are the differences?

2. What are some of the benefits that a person can gain from participating in improvisation and creative movement classes? Give specific examples.

3. In improvisation, why might it be easier to work within a set of rules than to work without them?

Dance in World Cultures

This chapter focuses on two world dance genres: world concert/ritual dance and folk dance. As discussed, these genres are complex and have deep and historic traditions that today remain significant to the dances. Before beginning an actual discussion of the genres, however, several items have to be clarified in relation to the terms that are used to describe them. In the past (and still today in some cases), these genres were referred to as "ethnic" dance, but this label is no longer accurate or appropriate. Therefore, the beginning of this chapter serves as an explanation of certain terms and the concerns surrounding their usage.

Contributed by dgarson.com.
©Kendall Hunt Publishing Company.

Defining World Concert/Ritual Dance and Folk Dance

There have been many scholarly discussions and writings on dances that are found in different world cultures. Specifically, the focus has been on world concert, ritual dance, and folk dance (also sometimes referred to as "ethnic" dance). Two major concerns have been identified when referring to these dance genres. The first is the common use of the word "ethnic" to define world dance forms. Ethnochoreologists, such as Joann Keali'inohomoku (who studies different cultures through their dances), argue that "In the generally accepted anthropological view, ethnic means a group which holds in common genetic, linguistic, and cultural ties, with special emphasis on

117

cultural tradition. By definition, therefore, every dance form must be an ethnic form."[1] Keali'inohomoku presents an excellent argument against the use of the word *ethnic* to define only dances that are from non-Western countries. In other words, she believes that the term *ethnic* should also encompass dance genres such as ballet, which she argues is a ". . . product of the Western world and it is a dance form developed by Caucasians who speak Indo-European languages and who share a common European tradition."[2]

Over the years, other labels used to describe this dance genre have been *primitive* and *non-Western,* each also presenting its own problems in relation to interpretation and meaning. In recent years, the term *world dance* has become the most accepted term to describe dances that are specific to a certain country. Some of these dances are based in ritual, meaning that they pertain to certain rites—religious or otherwise—that are ceremonial and formal and follow a certain prescribed procedure. Also, some dances are meant for presentation on the concert stage and some are used both for ritualistic purposes and for public performance. Therefore, for purposes of discussion, this dance genre is referred to as *world concert/ritual dance.* The reader should be aware, however, that there are some ritual dances that would never be performed before an audience (due to the sacredness of the ritual).

The second concern in regard to this genre is the difficulty in defining world concert/ritual dance and folk dance as separate forms. Some feel that these two forms are the same thing or, at the very least, share common denominators. For this discussion, we shall examine world concert/ritual dance and folk dance as two separate forms, acknowledging that these two forms do indeed share common denominators and overlap in historical, present-day, and practical information.

One of the basic differences between world concert/ritual dance and folk dance is that while world concert/ritual dances are in most cases performed for an audience, folk dances are usually a participatory activity.

World Concert and Ritual Dance

One of the basic differences between world concert/ritual dance and folk dance is that while world concert/ritual dances are in most cases performed for an audience, folk dances are usually a participatory activity. For this discussion, the world dances being referred to are those dances that are specifically *performed for an audience,* such as the dances in *noh* and *kabuki,* which will be discussed later. Although folk dances can also be viewed by an audience (there are many folk dance companies), their main function is to provide a social activity that gives people a sense of community and culture. Although certain folk dances might have begun as a dance purely performed for ritualistic purposes, gradually these dances were modified, and thus took on a different function. These dances were no longer based in ritual but more in recreation and social involvement.

What exactly are world concert/ritual dances? These dances usually portray something that is important to a specific culture, such as religion, moral values, work ethic, or historical information relating to the culture. Some were and are used as a form of communication. Ritual dances are passed down from generation to generation and are often performed as part of traditional gatherings, such as weddings, births, and funerals. Many of these dances are now presented for public viewing on the concert stage (hence the term "world concert/ritual dance"). Many countries have specific dances that are a major part of their culture (we have already seen one example in the discussion of the Yanomami of South America in *Chapter One: Dance as an Art Form*). Other examples can be found in African countries such as Senegal, Guinea, Ghana, Nigeria, Zaire, Tanzania, Kenya, and the Congo. There are also Asian countries where dance and dance rituals form a major part of the culture, such as India, Burma, Thailand, Cambodia, Laos, Malaya, Indonesia, the Philippines, China, Vietnam, Hong Kong, and Japan. Other countries known for their strong connection to dance are Haiti, the Caribbean, Cuba, Greece, and Spain, to name a few. Although examples of specific dances and dance styles can be cited for any of these countries, it might be beneficial to take an in-depth look at the dances of two countries: Japan and Nigeria.

Japan

Similar to many countries, Japan has a fascinating history of cultural dances that are considered concert dance and that are also based on rituals. The following explanation of some of the dances of Japan provide an example of dances in a world culture.

The dances and dance dramas of Japan (which, when created, were influenced greatly by the cultures of China and India) are hundreds and even thousands of years old and have been passed down from generation to generation. When they are performed today, they employ much of the same music, movements, and costumes that were used by the original creators, although some changes have occurred throughout the ages. A Japanese audience would refer to this type of dance as "classical," as opposed to the more modern forms that were created in Japan during the twentieth century (such as the fascinating form of *Butoh,* discussed in the "Dance-Theatre" section in *Chapter Six*). Three classical forms of Japanese dance are *bugaku,* which began in the seventh century; *noh,* developed during the fourteenth and fifteenth centuries; and *kabuki,* which began in the seventeenth century.

Bugaku, when first developed, was a dance reserved for viewing by nobility and important guests. Since the seventh century, it has been accompanied by a type of music known as *gagaku.* In his writings on Asian dance and drama, Faubion Bowers stated that *bugaku* and *gagaku* are the oldest regularly performed dance and music in the world today. He describes a *bugaku* performance in the following way:

> *Gagaku (pronounced nga-nga-koo and meaning literally "graceful, authorized music") begins with a series of reverberating thuds on the orchestra's giant drum. . . . As the windows and skylights shudder with the drum's sound, the musicians and dancers, dressed in costumes whose styles of long silk sleeves, baggy pants that tie at the ankle and soft felt-soled shoes have been traditionally repeated for the last thousand years, take their places at the far end of the hall. . . . Then the*

. . . Japan has a fascinating history of cultural dances that are considered concert dance and that are also based on rituals.

Three classical forms of Japanese dance are bugaku, noh, *and* kabuki.

dances begin. As the dancers move they extend their arms stiffly and symmetrically with the fingers held taut. They bend their legs in deep plies. Sometimes they wear huge frightening masks with gaping maws. . . . Somehow the antiquity of the dance and music is immediately evident.[3]

Today, *bugaku* is characterized by its unison dancing, usually by two or four dancers. The dramatic aspects, specific characters, and storylines utilized long ago are still elements of *bugaku*.

The second oldest form of dance drama in Japan is *noh*. There were several hundred plays written for the *noh* theatre, about two hundred and forty of which are still performed today. All *noh* plays combine dance, music, and acting. The most distinguishable trait of *noh* that separates it from other theatrical forms is the uniquely slow way in which the play unfolds. For most of the play, the performers move, speak, sing, and dance very slowly, and audiences who are unfamiliar with *noh* sometimes find it difficult to sit through a performance. If people are willing to experience a *noh* production, however, they will see an art form that is full of symbolism and meaning. Bowers states that "Once the spectator becomes geared to *No's* [sic] rhythms, each lift of the hand, each movement of the tightly stockinged foot, the opening and closing of the fan, the twirling of a long, rustling sleeve, assume immense meanings."[4] These plays are spiritual and place a great emphasis on the ideas of life and death.

These plays are spiritual and place a great emphasis on the ideas of life and death.

Although thought of as a theatre form in the West, the Japanese culture sees *noh* as a blend of many art forms, with dance playing a prominent role. *Noh* cannot exist without dance. The main performer, or the *shite* (the "doer"), must train in all aspects of the *noh*. For a *noh* performer, training begins as a child, and professional status is not achieved until much later in life.

In order to be a professional *noh* performer, a person must belong to one of the five schools of *noh* (Kanze, Hosho, Kongo, Komparu, or Kita), which are usually only open to people who are born into a *noh* performer's family. All professional *noh* performers are male, and they play all of the roles and characters, including gods, warriors, beautiful women (usually portrayed as ghosts), mad women, and demons. The *noh* performer wears special masks to portray most of these characters. Elaborate costumes are always worn, and beautiful fans and other props are used to symbolize specific aspects of the play. In addition to the *shite*, there is always a chorus on stage, musicians, a *waki* (who explains the story), stage assistants, and a *kyogen* actor (usually a "commoner"). The *kyogen* actor also performs in comic interludes that occur between *noh* plays. From theatre to theatre, the *noh* stage always looks the same and must be built to certain specifications. Simply stated, it is a raised wooden stage with four pillars and a bridgeway that the main characters use to enter and exit. There is a pine tree displayed on the back wall, which many believe symbolizes divinity and the idea of the stage as a divine space. When props or set pieces are used, they are usually very simple, and not at all realistic.

Kabuki is a form that was essentially derived from *noh,* and is similar in that it combines dance, drama, and music, and employs movements that are

Figure 8.1

very stylized. *Kabuki* is much more of a spectacle than *noh*, however, boasting elaborate scenery, costumes, makeup (see Figure 8.1) and movement that is quicker and more acrobatic. Therefore, a *kabuki* performer is required to be multi-talented. Like *noh* performers, many of these performers begin their careers at an early age and remain in this profession well into their senior years. The older performers are held in high regard, and many are said to reach their "peak" during their final years as performers. Although *kabuki* was started by a woman named *Okuni* (around 1600), only males perform *kabuki* professionally. Women were actually banned from performing *kabuki*. Therefore, the role of the *onnagata*, or actor of female roles, was created. *Kabuki*, much more than *bugaku* and *noh*, has allowed contemporary ideas to seep into the current performances. The *kabuki* dances, however, still retain a strong sense of tradition, and are performed today very closely to the way they were performed when they were first created.

Nigeria

The many dances of Africa vary in style, movements, music, costumes, and meaning, from country to country and region to region. There are some common denominators, however, that are found in most African dances, regardless of the region that they are from:

Kabuki, a classical form of Japanese dance, includes dramatic makeup and costumes.
DAJ/Getty Images

> First, because it is danced on the naked earth with bare feet, . . . the African style is often flat-footed and favors gliding, dragging, or shuffling steps. Second, African dance is frequently performed from a crouch, knees flexed and body bent at the waist. . . . Third, African dance generally imitates animals in realistic detail. . . . Fourth, African dance also places great importance upon improvisation, satirical or otherwise, allowing freedom for individual expression; this characteristic makes for flexibility and aids the evolution and diffusion of other African characteristics. Fifth, African dance is centrifugal, exploding outward from the hips. . . . Sixth and most significantly, African dance is performed to a propulsive rhythm, which gives it a swinging quality. . . .[5]

Though the previous description certainly does not address all the many facets of African dance, it does provide a perspective of the form on a basic level. It would be a tremendous undertaking to give the details of dances from the many cultures found in Africa, such as those of the Zulu, Nalu, Bini, Senufo, Bamessi, Sembla, Ashanti, Ibo, or Ogoni peoples. A look at one culture, however, would be beneficial in understanding African dance.

The Yoruba are situated in western Nigeria (as well as portions of Benin, a small Republic in West Africa). "Yoruba civilization was founded on a firm sense of historical destiny and cultural superiority. . ."[6] Therefore, the current Yoruba culture places a great emphasis on art, as did their ancestors. For the Yoruba people, "Art and motion further the attainment of truth and meaning through spirit possession and/or initiation."[7] In this culture, dance is used as a way to communicate to gods and ancestors. The dancing is deeply based in past ritual and religious experiences of the culture, and is rich in symbols and deities (gods) from the spirit world. These deities induce possession over certain members of the community, who dance the movements and the message of the deity. Yoruba movements are usually directed downward, toward the earth, which is a typical characteristic of many African movements. The Yoruba are a complex people, engulfed in tradition and religion:

> *Yoruba cosmology recognizes two closely related realms of existence: the tangible world of the living and the invisible realm of gods, ancestors and other spirit-beings. Despite their differences, these two realms are closely linked because both partake of the life force that runs through the universe. The ultimate source of life is the divine creator, an indefinable figure neither male nor female, who mostly stands aloof from the created universe. Human interaction is with the potent . . . gods and ancestors; the dancing body is the place where the two realms meet.[8]*

Contemporary Influences on World Dance

To most societies, it is difficult to understand the power and important function that dance has in the Yoruban culture as well as other cultures. It is also difficult to know exactly how much contemporary influences have had an impact on these cultures and their dances. Because of outside influences, some of the dances of Africa have undergone changes. It has been noted that ". . . the external forms, rhythms and syncopations [have] been torn apart from their spiritual and sacred contexts and made popular to the point of distortion."[9] The fact that some of these dances have undergone major transformations and are performed very differently than originally intended is a major cause for concern among many of the native people.

The influence of contemporary society upon world concert/ritual dances is a hotly emotional topic in all *countries that have a strong dance tradition.*

The influence of contemporary society upon world concert/ritual dances is a hotly emotional topic in *all* countries that have a strong dance tradition. In past centuries, even if dances were performed for an audience (as opposed to being performed purely for ritualistic purposes), they still retained their sense of tradition and were performed as closely to the originally created ritual as possible. Today, however, many world concert/ritual dances are being commercialized and presented in ways that are unrecognizable in comparison to the ways they were once performed. People of many different cultures, especially the elders, are upset and frustrated with what they see as the trivialization of their dance forms.

One example of this shift into the mainstream is found in the Hula of Hawaii. For years, Hula was known mostly as a dance that was performed for tourists as they arrived at the hotels on their Hawaiian vacation. But in its original form, Hula was a hand dance that was "a celebration of man's communion with the elements and nature," and those performing it had to be knowledgeable about the "social context, language and melody [of Hula]"[10] in order for it to be performed properly (see Figures 8.2 and 8.3). As Keali'inohomoku noted, the "Hula has adapted to a new social order. It was once a ritual; today it is taught as an art that's accessible to non-Hawaiians."[11] The fact that Hula is now recognized as an art form (and not only as a tourist attraction), is an important step in the preservation of Hula. There are many people, however, who are still trying to preserve the sacredness of Hula. Many Kumu Hula (or master teachers) instill the traditional values related to Hula in their students, and ensure that Hula is presented and performed in a traditional manner.

> *Hula is a moving encyclopedia inscribed into the sinews and postures of dancers' bodies. It carries forward the social and natural history, the religious beliefs, the philosophy, the literature, and the scientific knowledge of the Hawaiian people. It is, therefore, more than the dance form of a particular Polynesian people, more than swaying hips and talking hands, more than competitions, vacation entertainment, or a weekly workout routine. Because the story of native Hawaiians is an ongoing one, hula is important in the living present, and . . . it is important to understand hula as a vital, creative art form and a lived experience that preserves a culture's values, continually forming and reforming identity in and through movement.[12]*

Today, many world concert/ritual dances are being commercialized and presented in ways that are unrecognizable in comparison to the ways they were once performed. People of many different cultures, especially the elders, are upset and frustrated with what they see as the trivialization of their dance forms.

Figure 8.2

Hula in its original form was a hand dance that was a "celebration of man's communion with the elements and nature."
©Steve Adamson/Shutterstock, Inc.

Figure 8.3

Woman in traditional dress performs Hula on the island of Kauai.
©Boykov/Shutterstock, Inc.

As stated earlier, some members of the specific cultures discussed are not pleased with what is happening to the tradition of their dances. One reason why these dances are becoming so commercial is, of course, a financial one. On many concert stages, such as in the United States, there is a great demand for performances by companies from other countries. For these performances, sometimes the movements are changed to ones that are perceived to be more pleasing to an audience. For example, most dances in world cultures have a lot of repetitive movements. To the culture where the dance originated, this use of repetition is important and may symbolize many things, such as ensuring that the gods receive a certain message, emphasizing a certain important rhythm in the music, or for the participants to achieve a feeling of ecstasy and fulfillment. But an audience that is not used to such a use of repetition, or does not understand the symbolic meaning behind the movements, might get bored. Therefore, some of the movements are changed to ones that might seem to be more entertaining to the viewers.

From the few examples cited, it is easy to understand why members of certain cultures are concerned with the future of their dances. The argument that these dances are used for ritualistic purposes and should possess the traditional movements and meaning developed by their ancestors is a powerful one and should be respected. Yet, since many feel that having the opportunity to present their dances to other cultures is necessary and important, they are willing to accept this mainstreaming.

One example of a classical dance form brought into the mainstream of contemporary society (and deemed as a success by many), can be seen in the dance and cinematic genre known as Bollywood. The term Bollywood was coined in India by combining "Bombay" (now called Mumbai) and "Hollywood." Although the term was created in the 1970s, the 1990s brought the current Bollywood style to the forefront. Today, these movies include full-scale musical numbers that feature a dance style that is a combination of classical Indian dances and folk dances, combined with jazz, hip-hop, and other contemporary genres (refer to the discussion of classical Indian dance in *Chapter One: Dance as an Art Form*).

> . . . *Bollywood dancing has been heavily influenced by Western dance styles, and incorporates elements from the West. In many cases, the musical numbers are released as separate music videos, and the soundtracks are released prior to the film, in order to further advertise the upcoming feature films. . . . Currently Bollywood Dance is still influenced by Western culture, perhaps even more so today than when it began. Elements include the use of frequent costume and location changes during dances, as well as the use of larger dance troupes. And the movements have become more bold and extroverted to capture the audience's attention. The evolution of Bollywood Dance is a process that is entirely Indian and yet cross-cultural at the same time.*[13]

Bollywood dance (and film) has been immensely popular in India for years, and the United States has been introduced to this genre through mainstream movies, musicals, and television shows. The Oscar winning movie *Slumdog Millionaire* (2008) featured a Bollywood-style dance scene at the end of the movie, and for many, it was the first time that this type of dancing had been seen. Musical theatre writer and composer Andrew Lloyd Webber created the Broadway show *Bombay Dreams* (2009), which tells the story of a young, poor man who hopes to become a popular film star, only to meet and fall in love with a powerful filmmaker's daughter. The dance show, *So You Think You Can Dance*, often features a Bollywood dance category that participants learn and perform. Today, Bollywood is no longer only known on one continent, but known worldwide. Of course, it is not without controversy; scholars continue to debate the artistic significance of the form. However, the popularity of Bollywood cannot be denied. The fusion of an ancient dance form and current contemporary genres has resulted in a cinematic and cultural phenomenon.

Folk Dance

The beginnings of folk dance can be traced back to Upper Paleolithic and Neolithic times, as can the beginnings of many dances in world cultures. Folk dance and world concert/ritual dance were not distinguished from each other until the emergence of a civilized culture in Ancient times. With regard to European culture, folk dance expert Betty Casey stated:

> As civilization developed in Europe and became more sophisticated, simple folk dances changed accordingly, becoming more social in character. . . . Some folk dances are overlaid with foreign influences, reflecting cultures introduced by invaders and conquerors. The resulting choreography portrays the unique life-styles of different peoples—their religions, customs, geography, history and feelings. Folk dancing is more than just a cultural profile of a given people. Their music, costumes and background combine with rhythms, moods and patterns to form a total picture.[14]

Folk dances are also recognized as being a major part of dancing in sixteenth-century Europe, the same time that court ballets were becoming popular. Some believe that many folk dances were, in fact, created in direct response to the court ballets. Since the working class were not allowed to attend the court ballets (that were intended only for the rich), they created folk dances for their own enjoyment. In addition to being a source of entertainment, folk dances provided opportunities for socialization and gave people a sense of community.

It was not long before the dancing masters of the courts began to borrow movements from folk dances for their court ballets. "The minuet for instance, originated as a romantic, folkloric peasant dance and attained a splendid stylized dignity in the courts of France during the reign of Louis XIV"[15] (refer back

Almost every country has its own folk dances that have been passed down from generation to generation.

to Figure 1.8). In turn, the court ballets had an influence over some folk dances, and today steps from ballet vocabulary can be found in many different folk dances.

Almost every country has its own folk dances that have been passed down from generation to generation. Over the years, some of the movements have changed from what they were originally and sometimes there can be more than one version of the same dance (see Figure 8.4). This fact illustrates the major difference between folk dance and world concert/ritual dance. Ideally, world concert and ritual dances are performed today in a manner that remains true to the dance's origins. Perhaps even more important is that the dances are performed with the same *intent*—in this way, the meaning may be preserved even when specific movements are lost. The authenticity of the world concert and ritual dances is important because they hold a great deal of religious and symbolic meaning for the people who perform them.

Figure 8.4

Some folk dances have been passed down through the generations. Observing folk dancing is a way for people to learn about different cultures.
©Carlos E. Santa Maria/Shutterstock, Inc.

Many countries are known for the richness of their folk dances, including Israel, Greece, France, Germany, Mexico, Scotland, England, Italy, Colombia, and Russia. Some of these countries can trace their folk dance heritage back many centuries, while other folk dance histories are more difficult to trace. For example, the history of Greek folk dance can be traced back to Ancient times, mainly because of artifacts and drawings that depicted dance, but also because these dances have been handed down from generation to generation. Are these dances the same exact dances that were done centuries ago? Probably not, but many hold the same ritualistic, social, and celebratory elements. They are also

Figure 8.5

Greek Syrtaki Folk Dance
Ensemble
©John Blanton/Shutterstock.com

still performed in the same way, usually either in a line or a circle, and utilize a shoulder hold, a chain hold, or a handhold typically seen in Greek dances (see Figure 8.5). Today, there are still Greek dances performed for ritualistic purposes, such as a procession done by the priest, bride, and groom during a Greek Orthodox wedding service. Dancing is also an important part of the everyday lives of Greek people, who dance on many formal occasions (weddings, births), but also dance spontaneously at casual parties and get-togethers. Although Greek folk dances are performed in a similar manner each time, participants are encouraged to improvise and demonstrate their own particular style. Greek folk dances are some of the oldest in folk dance history.

Israel's folk dance history, on the other hand, is much more difficult to trace. The Bible has many dancing references, therefore we know that dancing was a part of Jewish people's heritage. There is no evidence of specific dances, however, such as in the Greek culture. We do know that many other cultures influenced the dancing of the Jewish people. For example, the *Hora* came from Romania, and is today considered the national dance of Israel. In 1944, there was a renewed interest in folk dancing in Israel, due to a major dance festival held at a *kibbutz* (a farm or settlement operated by all the members). This revival has lasted until today, and folk dance in Israel is popular and important to the culture.

In the United States, ". . . square dancing has undergone so much Americanization and modernization that it has become known worldwide as an American folk dance."[16] The movements that make up traditional square dances, however, are bits and pieces borrowed from dances of other countries, such as the Irish jig, English reels, and French quadrilles, that were brought to the United States by

Greek folk dances are some of the oldest in folk dance history.

immigrants.[17] Today, many people in America and around the world enjoy international folk dancing. It is a way for people to not only learn about other cultures, but also have the pleasure of socializing, communicating, and participating in a physical activity.

Summary

Viewing and participating in dances from world cultures can be a wonderful way to learn about countries, cultures and aesthetics (see Figure 8.6). In our diverse and multi-ethnic world, we can look to dance and all of the arts to provide us with a view of other's lives. In this way, we can explore what our similarities and differences are. Most important, we can learn how to appreciate and celebrate these similarities and differences. Table 8.1 details the Characteristics of World Concert/Ritual Dance and Folk Dance.

Figure 8.6

Dancers performing *Cumbia*, a dance from Colombia.
Contributed by dgarson.com. ©Kendall Hunt Publishing Company.

Table 8.1 The Characteristics of World Concert/Ritual Dance and Folk Dance

World Concert/Ritual Dance	Folk Dance
■ Can be performed for an audience or for ritualistic purposes. ■ The dancing portrays what is essential and important to a specific culture. ■ The dancing was and is used as a form of communication. ■ There is a strong use of repetition in many world dance forms. ■ These dances are passed down from generation to generation. New ones are also developed. ■ Dancing rituals were and are a part of many aspects of daily life (hunting, gathering) and for traditional ceremonies (births, weddings, deaths). ■ Contemporary influences can be seen in many traditional world dance forms.	■ Folk dances can be performed for an audience and can also be participatory. ■ Social involvement and recreation are major components of folk dance. ■ Each dance portrays and represents a specific culture. ■ Music and costumes are important elements in the dance presentation. ■ Folk dances were and are passed down from generation to generation, with revisions along the way. ■ Folk dances are still developed today.

Discussion Questions

Discuss in class or provide written answers.

1. Discuss the similarities between world concert/ritual dance and folk dance. Also discuss the differences.

2. What do you think about the controversy surrounding the different world concert and ritual dances that are becoming too commercialized? Do you think that it is appropriate for dances to change in order to please an audience?

3. Have you ever participated in any folk dances? If so, what countries were they from? What were they called? Were the movements repetitive? When you danced them, did you stand in a circle or straight line? Did you hold hands with a partner or with a group of people? Discuss your experience.

Figure 8.6

Contributed by Candice Kaminski, clikstudiosonline.com. ©Kendall Hunt Publishing Company.

The world of jazz dance, musical theatre, and tap dance is an exciting and thrilling one. This chapter explores these American dance forms that all have their roots in African movements and rhythms.

Jazz Dance, Musical Theatre, and Tap Dance

Similar to the term "modern dance," "jazz dance" is also used as an umbrella term, encompassing several diverse styles. "Traditional" jazz dance, "musical theatre jazz," "lyrical jazz," "funk," "swing," and sometimes even "hip-hop" are categorized as jazz dance or as a close relation of the genre. For this discussion, the term jazz dance will be used to define a broad category of styles.

Jazz Dance

Jazz dance is an exciting dance genre that today has a place in the popular theatre and the concert stage, in small dance studios and large universities, and in movies and television programs. The history of jazz dance is a fascinating one, beginning with the origins that can be traced back to Africa.

In the seventeenth century, when slaves were brought to America from Africa, they brought with them their music and dance. The slaves on the plantations continued the dancing and drumming

The history of jazz dance is a fascinating one, beginning with the origins that can be traced back to Africa.

that was so much a part of African life. Eventually, the slave masters prohibited drumming, but the African rhythms did not diminish. They were kept alive by the slaves who clapped their hands, stomped their feet, and sang the songs of their motherland.[1] On the plantations, dances were performed for enjoyment and also for entertainment and competitions. Slave masters would often have the best dancers entertain their guests or compete against slaves from other plantations. "The presence of these dance traditions in plantation settings is evidence that dance was a communal expression that became the basis of popular black dances in the U.S. post-enslavement. The diverse cultural groups [from Africa created] a rich collection of African-derived movements that were later adopted, borrowed, and/or appropriated . . ."[2]

Eventually, the songs and dances of these people were brought into the theatres, but not by the people who had created them. The Minstrel shows, beginning in the 1830s, showcased black songs and dances. But since black people were not allowed to perform on a public stage (with the exception of those such as "Master Juba"—see *Major Figures in Jazz Dance, Musical Theatre, and Tap Dance*), white performers in blackface appeared before the audiences, performing parodies of the songs and dances of the black culture. It wasn't until the 1860s that black performers began to appear in their own minstrel shows,[3] where they performed for black audiences as well as Irish immigrants. As a way to make money and break into show business, black performers also appeared in blackface in the minstrel shows, engaging in a parody of the white performers who were doing a parody of them. Eventually, the black minstrel shows became as popular as the white minstrels, in part because of the wildly popular performances, but also due to a section of the shows (usually the close of the first act) called the "cakewalk." The cakewalk, which came directly from plantation entertainments, ". . . was a contest among dancing couples who attempted to outdo each other in the mock imitation of the white man's manners and behavior."[4] During the cakewalk, the dancers displayed their best struts, high kicks, and show-stopping footwork. Today, the entire concept of the minstrel show, and specifically white performers who appeared in blackface and appropriated songs and dances from black culture, has been examined for its racial implications and its place in early American history.

The minstrels remained popular until the early 1900s and paved the way for the vaudeville, revue, and burlesque shows that were to dominate the American stage for the next twenty years. Although all three theatrical entertainments were popular, none was as popular or as significant to jazz dance history as the vaudeville show. Writer Richard Kislan provided an explanation of the importance of the Vaudeville era:

> *More than any other entertainment alternative in its time, Vaudeville encouraged, if not precipitated, the quantitative and varietal expansion of dance acts before the public. Most vaudeville circuits included at least one song-and-dance act or minimusical revue on the bill. The system valued uniqueness and encouraged diversity. Some dancers traded on talent or technique; others developed unusual material.*

There were Dutch dancers, Russian dancers, Irish dancers, blackface minstrel dancers, whiteface minstrel dancers, flash acts, class acts, toe dancers, knockabouts, acrobatic dancers, competition acts and legomania. Even the celebrated originators of modern dance—Martha Graham, Doris Humphrey and Charles Weidman—did their stints in vaudeville. . . . It served as a professional school, a training ground and an experimental station for the dancers destined for Broadway, nightclubs and film. . . .[5]

The Vaudeville era showcased a wealth of song and dance performers. It is important to remember the contributions that African-American performers gave to this era. Though the lives of these performers were difficult, black dancers continued to create and perform new movements, keeping the African connection to the earth (hence the repeated use of the *plié* in jazz dance) and to the African rhythms. The Vaudeville era also marked the emergence of jazz music (around 1919), which was a combination of ragtime and the blues.[6] Eventually, dancers began to connect to the syncopated rhythms of jazz music. Today, the use of syncopated rhythms is what, for many, characterizes jazz dance.[7]

The advent of Latin jazz music also had an influence on the dance form. In the 19th century, a fusion of African rhythms and traditional music from the Caribbean and the United States came to be known as Latin Jazz. Evident in this music is the use of the *clave,* an instrument comprised of two wooden sticks that are hit together to produce a high pitched sound. *Clave* also refers to the specific rhythmic pattern found in Latin jazz, and that dances such as the Salsa utilize. In Latin jazz, it is not uncommon for the body to have ". . . several axes of motion. [The body] can move forward and back, up and down, and the hips create possibilities for lateral movement. Latin American dance . . . is grounded in African rhythms, which are polyrhythmic . . . there are several layers of rhythm going on at the same time."[8]

The Harlem Renaissance (1921–1933) was another significant time period in the history of jazz dance. Harlem, in New York City, was the place for all high-society people to come and be seen. At this time, many exclusive clubs opened, probably the most famous being the Cotton Club. These clubs, which catered to a white clientele, had elaborate floor shows where black singers and dancers performed. Because of the popularity of these clubs and their shows, employment for black dancers was plentiful during the Harlem Renaissance. This decade, known as the Roaring Twenties, saw many dances that were performed at these clubs, such as the Charleston and the Black Bottom, become part of a dance craze. The Charleston became immensely popular in the United States and eventually in Europe—everyone wanted to learn how to dance the Charleston. "Flappers," or women who wore their hair in a short bob and wore short, fringed dresses, are usually equated with the Charleston. There are movements in the Charleston, however, that can be traced back to African dances and also to dances in certain parts of Haiti.

During the 1930s and 1940s, jazz dance was a part of the theatre, nightclubs, movie musicals, dance concerts, and dance studios. During the 1950s

Today, the use of syncopated rhythms is what, for many, characterizes jazz dance.

During the 1930s and 1940s, jazz dance was a part of the theatre, nightclubs, movie musicals, dance concerts, and dance studios.

and the 1960s, television provided the public with many images of jazz dance, mostly through variety shows such as "The Lawrence Welk Show" and "The Ed Sullivan Show." Although much of the "television dance" that was seen at that time would probably appear very dated to a contemporary audience, many great artists regularly danced on television—Fred Astaire, Gene Kelly, Ann Miller, and Ray Bolger, to name a few. There were also outstanding musical theatre productions created during this time for both stage and screen (see *Musical Theatre*).

Today, jazz dance encompasses several different styles of movement and has come to represent a number of different attributes and characteristics.

Today, jazz dance encompasses several different styles of movement and has come to represent a number of different attributes and characteristics. While "jazz dance" has been defined in several ways, descriptive terms such as *sensual, visceral, improvisational, syncopated, hot,* and *cool* are often used in reference to jazz dance. Dancers/writers Mike Moore and Liz Williamson provide an excellent description of jazz dance by stating:

> *Basically, jazz is an approach. It is everchanging, but vitality is a constant. A continual refinement is also constant. Changes in jazz happen in very subtle ways. Jazz dancers seek the fine edge of perfection in their performance. No movement is dull, there is an unabated theatricality about jazz. No movement is perfunctory. Improvisation is the core. Jazz dance moves through delicate changes of color and shading. In jazz dance, one works toward an individual style that builds from traditional jazz origins and strikes out boldly in the contemporary. Jazz was born in America, of African parents.[9]*

As stated earlier, the term *jazz dance* has come to mean a lot of different things to different people. Certain characteristics of jazz dance, however, are essential and cannot be ignored. At times, so much of what is called jazz dance is concerned only with superficial movements. Many choreographers (particularly those who work in commercial dance) appear to believe that performing certain "dance tricks," such as high kicks and multiple turns, will please and win over audiences. This idea might be true to a certain extent, but choreographers and audiences alike must realize that there is more to a dance than staying in one place and dancing at one set speed and rhythm, which seems to be prevalent in some jazz dance choreography. Changing levels, directions, shapes, and floor patterns are an essential part of *all* choreography and should also be included in jazz dance choreography. In addition, focal changes and movements incorporating space should be considered. Also, the use of diagonal, curved, or asymmetrical groupings might be more interesting than presenting a group of dancers who face the audience in a symmetrical formation for an entire dance.

The use of music and movement in relation to phrasing is an important aspect of jazz dance.

The use of music and movement in relation to phrasing is an important aspect of jazz dance. Some jazz dances are very "square," with all of the movements happening on the "one" count. Although this use of rhythm might be appropriate for part of a dance, the use of the syncopated rhythm is a specific characteristic of jazz dance and should be used in jazz choreography. The use of varying rhythms and dynamics will enhance a jazz dance tremendously.

There is much more appeal in viewing jazz choreography that brings the audience through a range of energy than in watching a dance that stays at the same energy level throughout.

Of course, style is also an important aspect of jazz dance. Richard Kislan describes style as ". . . the specific manner of expression peculiar to a work, a period, or a personality. It implies the purposeful and consistent choice of expressive ingredients to achieve a characteristic manner"[10] Can style be taught? Maybe. Should it be encouraged? Definitely. Dancers should be encouraged to develop their own personal style. This personal style is developed when a dancer totally commits every aspect of himself or herself to the movement, including energy, focus, facial expression, and intent, while remaining true to the character or situation that the choreographer has created (see Figure 9.1). Additionally, many different categories fall under the rubric of jazz dance styles—musical theatre dance, tap, lyrical, funk, swing, and Latin jazz (to name a few)—in which dancers and choreographers can study and work.

Musical Theatre

Early examples of musical theatre productions can be found in eighteenth-century England, France, and Germany, although some historians argue that the musical performances the Ancient Greeks and Romans produced were the actual predecessors to what we today call musical theatre. Whenever the beginnings of musical theatre, the advent of the American musical theatre production is an integral part of the history of dance (as well as theatre). American musical theatre dance has its roots in jazz dance. One of the first musical theatre productions of note was *The Black Crook*. In 1866, *The Black Crook* was directed by David Costa and was the first theatre piece to use dance to move the storyline along. This work is significant because after this production, dance was seen as a positive and useful "tool," and thus was included in many theatrical productions.

There were many significant happenings in the history of musical theatre dance. One such happening was the creation of the first African-American musical in 1921, called *Shuffle Along*, created by a team of talented writers, actors, and song-makers, including jazz great Eubie Blake (1883–1983). *Shuffle Along* paved the way for the African-American performer:

> Shuffle Along *is one of the most important shows in Broadway Black history. As one of the first all-Black Broadway musical hits that was also written by Blacks,* Shuffle Along *significantly altered the face of the Broadway musical, as well as that of New York City.* Shuffle Along *opened the door for Black performers and writers on the stage during the period in the 1920s known as the Harlem Renaissance. It legitimized the Black musical, proving to producers and managers that audiences would pay to see a wealth of Black talent on Broadway, as opposed to one Black act per bill, which had been the norm. The show also contributed to the desegregation of theaters in the 1920s, giving*

Figure 9.1

Dancers displaying different jazz styles as determined by the choreographers.

many black actors their first chance to appear on Broadway.[11]

One such performer was a chorus girl and protégée of Eubie Blake named Josephine Baker (1906–1975), who became a popular international star (Figure 9.2). She popularized several dances of the 1920s, including the Charleston and the Black Bottom. Due to racism and lack of acceptance as a performer in the United States, Baker moved to Paris, where she quickly became a star. During World War II, she volunteered for the French Red Cross. Due to her celebrity status, Baker found herself among German officers who attended her performances, and she began relaying information to the French Resistance that she had overheard. She wrote notes in invisible ink on her sheet music and smuggled them to the French authorities. For her actions, she was awarded the *Croix de Guerre* and the Medal of Resistance by the French government.[12]

Another significant happening in the history of musical theatre dance was in 1926, when dance director Seymour Felix (1892–1961) introduced the marriage of book (script), music, lyrics, and dance as an important aspect of musical theatre. While working on the Rodgers and Hart musical *Peggy Ann,* Felix was determined to

Figure 9.2

Josephine Baker was an international star that popularized several dances.
Courtesy of Photofest.

> . . . devise "atmospheric" numbers, dances that unfold gradually and consist of development and climax as if they were dramatic units themselves instead of "a mere pounding of feet and kicking to music." Colorful dances could be and spectacle they could embrace, but harmonize with the story they must—and did. Then as now, the secret to successful integration of show dances lay in the discovery of valid motives for the movement. . . . Once he recognized the dependence of the dance ensemble on book, music and lyrics, Felix sought to ensure a more unified effect onstage by coordinating his efforts with that of the show's creators.[13]

From that time on, theatre productions highlighting dance sequences were the norm and were also enthusiastically received by the audiences. In 1943, Agnes de Mille (1905–1993), another pioneer of musical theatre choreography, choreographed *Oklahoma!* and presented dance in a way that had never been seen before. Until this time, dances in musicals were inserted to move the storyline, or for sheer entertainment purposes. De Mille's choreography superseded this method, creating on the stage and screen a truly artistic representation of dance. In *Oklahoma!,* one of the most popular dance sections is

The validity and artistry of de Mille's work gave musical theatre choreographers the respect they deserved, putting them on equal status with the director, composer, and playwright.

commonly known as the "dream sequence." Here, the dancers perform a surrealistic dance number whose duration is almost fifteen minutes. While adding to the storyline, this sequence is also a dramatic work unto itself, depicting frantic emotion in a nightmarish setting. The validity and artistry of de Mille's work gave musical theatre choreographers the respect they deserved, putting them on equal status with the director, composer, and playwright.

Many choreographers, who were primarily known as ballet or modern dance choreographers, created outstanding dances and dance sequences for musical theatre productions. For example, ballet greats George Balanchine, Agnes de Mille, and Jerome Robbins all choreographed for musical theatre productions. Modern dance choreographers such as Katherine Dunham, Helen Tamiris, Hanya Holm, Valerie Bettis, Twyla Tharp, and Bill T. Jones also produced musical theatre works. There were, however, a number of people who were considered choreographers and dance directors who worked exclusively in the jazz dance and musical theatre genres. One such choreographer was Jack Cole (1913–1974, see Figure 9.3).

Figure 9.3

Jack Cole.
Printed with permission from Ronald Seymour.

It is interesting to note that Cole began his career in dance by studying with modern dance greats such as Ruth St. Denis and Ted Shawn, and Doris Humphrey and Charles Weidman. He was very much influenced by the teachings of the Denishawn school, particularly the emphasis on Eastern dance styles. Therefore, he ". . . developed an entirely personal mode of jazz-ethnic (sic)-ballet that prevails as the dominant look of and technique for dancing in today's musicals, films, nightclub revues, television commercials and videos."[14] Many other choreographers who worked in the jazz dance and musical theatre idiom, such as Jerome Robbins, Bob Fosse, and Gower Champion, were greatly influenced by Cole's style.

One of Cole's most popular productions was *Kismet* (1955), where his Eastern dance influence is clearly seen in the choreography depicting the story of the Arabian Nights. Many consider Cole to be the "father of jazz dance," and the style that he developed in the 1940s is still prevalent in today's jazz dance choreography.

The realm of musical theatre belongs to both the theatrical stage and the movie musical. Many musical theatre productions are seen first as live theatre and are then recreated for the movie screen. In recent years, we have also seen many successful Broadway musicals be made into movie musicals (see Table 9.2, Outline of Jazz Dance, Musical Theatre, and Tap Dance Events). The making of a Broadway musical is quite an undertaking, mostly because of the astronomical expense required for such productions. Some popular musical theatre productions were and are *West Side Story* (1961), *The King and I* (1951), *Chicago* (1975, and revived in 1996), *A Chorus Line* (1974), *Cats* (1981), *Kiss of the Spider Woman* (1992), *The Who's Tommy* (1993), *Beauty and the Beast*

(1994), *Rent* (1996), *The Lion King* (1997), *Aida* (2000), *The Producers* (2001), *Mama Mia* (2001), *Hairspray* (2002), *Movin' Out* (2002), *Wicked* (2003), *Bombay Dreams* (2004), *Brooklyn* (2004), *Sweet Charity* (revived 2005), *Jersey Boys* (2005), *The Drowsy Chaperone* (2006), *The Wedding Singer* (2006), *Spring Awakening* (2007), *Legally Blonde* (2007), *Billy Elliot* (2008, Broadway premiere), *In the Heights* (2008), *Burn the Floor* (2009, Broadway premiere), *Rock of Ages* (2009), *American Idiot* (2010), *The Book of Mormon* (2011), *Matilda* (2012), *Newsies* (2012), *Nice Work If You Can Get It* (2012), *Kinky Boots* (2013), *Motown* (2013), *Aladdin* (2014), *An American in Paris* (2015), *Finding Neverland* (2015), *Hamilton* (2015), *Dear Evan Hanson* (2016), *Waitress* (2016), *Anastasia* (2017), *The Band's Visit* (2017), *SpongeBob SquarePants* (2017), *Come From Away* (2017), *Once on This Island* (2017), *Escape to Margaritaville* (2018), *Frozen* (2018), *Mean Girls* (2018), *Pretty Woman* (2018), *Carousel* (2018 revival), and *My Fair Lady* (2018 revival).

Tap Dance

Tap dancing is believed to have been created by the blending of ". . . the Irish jig and the English clog with the Negro Shuffle."[15] Tap dancing, introduced in the minstrel shows, dominated the vaudeville shows of the late 1800s and remained popular well into the nineteenth century. Tap dance is a style of dance in which rhythmic sounds are produced by moving the feet. Shoes are worn with metal taps on the bottom, which produce the distinctive tap sound against the floor (see Figure 9.4).

Figure 9.4

Tap shoes have metal taps on the bottom to produce the distinctive tap sound against the floor.
©Eileen Meyer/Shutterstock, Inc.

Although there are many prescribed tap dance steps, such as the "buck-and-wing," "shuffle," "flap step," and "cramp roll" (to name a few), tap dance is very improvisational. There are also many different styles of tap and tap dance performers. For example, "rhythm tappers," such as Gregory Hines and Savion Glover, call attention to intricate and percussive footwork; "class acts," such as Fred Astaire and Ginger Rogers, execute steps in a refined manner, with elegant body movements; "flash acts," such as the Nicholas Brothers, combine tap dance with acrobatic movements; and a dancer executing "soft shoe," such as vaudevillian George Primrose, would skim the floor and produce soft, muted steps.[16] Recent tap artists have developed other styles of tap, and older styles of past tap artists are being learned and practiced all the time.

Bill "Bojangles" Robinson (1878–1947) was one of the first of *many* African-American artists who popularized tap dance. Many remember Robinson as the person who tap danced with the child star Shirley Temple. Robinson, however, was a vaudeville tapper who first performed in 1891 at the age of twelve. He was also one of the first African-American performers to have regular employment in the mostly white theatre, and one of the first rhythm tap dancers.

Sammy Davis, Jr. (1925–1990) was another African-American artist who popularized tap dance and was also first seen as a child on the vaudeville stage. Davis combined his dancing talents with his wonderful ability to sing and act

Tap dance is a style of dance in which rhythmic sounds are produced by moving the feet. Shoes are worn with metal taps on the bottom, which produce the distinctive tap sound against the floor.

and became one of America's most popular entertainers. Before his death, Davis starred in a movie entitled *Tap* (1989), which brought about a new-found interest in tap dance by the general public.

Fred Astaire (1899–1987) and Ginger Rogers (1911–1995) made tap especially popular in musical theatre productions (see Figure 9.5). In addition to performing tap routines, they included ballroom dancing in their movies, bringing this unique combination of dance styles to the public. One famous movie musical in which they performed was *Top Hat* (1935), which contains many wonderful tap sequences. Gene Kelly (1912–1996), was another dancer who popularized tap dance. Known for his athletic ability, he presented tap dance in a very different manner from Astaire and Rogers, who were known for their gracefulness. His most famous tap dance can be seen in the movie *Singin' in the Rain* (1952), in which he actually does sing and tap dance in the rain.

Today, popular dancers like Savion Glover (b. 1973) use tap dance in many endeavors, thus allowing audiences to view and appreciate this dance form. Tap dance legend and Glover's mentor Gregory Hines (1946–2003), starred in movies where tap sequences were highlighted. A movie entitled *White Nights* (1985, which also starred ballet great Mikhail Baryshnikov) features Hines in one of the most exciting tap dances ever to be captured on film. Hines also starred in the movie *Tap*, which featured some of the best known-tappers, such as Sammy Davis, Jr., Sandman Sims, and the Nicholas Brothers.

Singer and dancer Paula Abdul (b. 1962) also utilized tap dancing in her work, specifically in her music videos. These videos provided opportunities for audiences to view tap dance on televisions (and computers), thus increasing the popularity and visibility of this exciting dance form. Savion Glover developed choreography for the Broadway show *Bring in 'da Noise, Bring in 'da Funk* (1995), which mixed tap with hip-hop, break dancing, and Glover's unique style. Shows like *Stomp* (1994) and *Tap Dogs* (1996) are still performed worldwide and demonstrate a wide variety of tap styles.

Summary

Jazz dance is an American art form whose roots can be traced back to Africa. Within the realm of jazz dance, we find a number of different styles, each one adding to the history of this popular dance form. Jazz dance, probably more than any other dance form, has reached across many cultural and socioeconomic boundaries and has thrilled the lives of viewers and participants.

Musical theatre and tap dance have been an important part of the American theatre and dance worlds. Seen on both the live stage and in movie musicals, these two dance forms have a historical and artistic link to jazz dance. Many artists from the jazz, ballet, and modern dance worlds have contributed to the growth and development of these forms. These popular dance forms will continue to excite and entertain audiences for years to come. Table 9.1 details the characteristics of jazz dance, musical theatre dance, and tap dance. Table 9.2 details some major events in jazz dance, musical theatre dance, and tap dance.

Figure 9.5

Fred Astaire and Ginger Rogers in "Follow the Feet."
John Springer Collection/Corbis Historical/Getty Images

Table 9.1 Characteristics of Jazz Dance, Musical Theatre, and Tap Dance

Jazz Dance	Musical Theatre	Tap Dance
■ Strong use of syncopated rhythms. ■ A repeated use of the *plié*. ■ The dancing has an improvisational feel. ■ Individual style is developed and demonstrated. ■ The dancing is presentational, visceral, and sensual. ■ There is a strong use of varying dynamics. ■ Jazz dance can be seen on the theatrical stage, concert stage, and in movie musicals and popular music videos.	■ Dance in musical theatre productions can be used to enhance the storyline and to move the storyline along. ■ Dance sequences can also stand alone as artistic works. ■ The script, music, lyrics, and dance have a strong relationship. ■ Musical theatre dance can be seen on the theatrical stage and in movie musicals.	■ Shoes are worn with metal taps on the bottom. ■ Rhythmic sounds are produced by moving the feet. ■ Tap dance has a strong use of syncopated rhythms. ■ Tap dance has a vocabulary with prescribed steps, but mostly, tap dance is improvisational. ■ There are different styles of tap and tap dancers: class acts, flash acts, soft shoe, rhythm tappers, etc. ■ Tap dance can be seen on the theatrical stage, concert stage, and in movies, movie musicals, and popular dance videos.

Table 9.2 Outline of Jazz Dance, Musical Theatre, and Tap Dance Events

17th Century	Slaves brought to America. Dancing and drumming is eventually seen on plantations.
1830s	Development of Minstrel shows. White performers perform in blackface.
1860	Black performers appear in Minstrel shows.
1866	One of the first musical theatre productions, *The Black Crook,* is presented.
1900s	Vaudeville, revue, and burlesque shows begin. The Vaudeville era is a significant part of jazz dance history. Tap dance also becomes immensely popular during this time.
c. 1919	Emergence of jazz music.
1921	Beginning of the Harlem Renaissance.
1921	First African-American musical performed, *Shuffle Along.*
1920s	Dance crazes such as the Charleston and the Black Bottom become popular.
1926	The musical *Peggy Ann* introduces the concept of connecting the script, music, lyrics, and dance.
1935	Fred Astaire and Ginger Rogers appear in *Top Hat.*
1936	The Lindy Hop becomes popular across America, and paves the way for the Jitterbug of the 1940s.
1943	Agnes de Mille choreographs *Oklahoma!,* and presents dance numbers that not only help move along the storyline but also can stand alone as dramatic works. Agnes de Mille's work elevates the status of the musical theatre choreographer.
1955	Jack Cole, the father of jazz dance, choreographs *Kismet.*
1961	Jerome Robbins choreographs *West Side Story.*
1974	*A Chorus Line* opens on Broadway, with choreography by one of America's most popular musical theatre choreographers, Michael Bennett.
1981	*Cats* opens on Broadway.
1989	The movie *Tap* is made, starring tap dance "royalty," Gregory Hines, Sammy Davis, Jr., the Nicholas Brothers, Arthur Duncan, Bunny Briggs, Steve Condos, Jimmy Slide, and Sandman Sims.
1991	The First American Jazz Dance World Congress, established by Gus Giordano, is held.
1995	*Bring in 'da Noise, Bring in 'da Funk* starring Savion Glover opens on Broadway.
1997	*The Lion King,* with choreography by modern dance choreographer Garth Fagan, opens on Broadway.
2000	*Aida,* with music by Elton John and Tim Rice, opens on Broadway.

Table 9.2 *Outline of Jazz Dance, Musical Theatre, and Tap Dance Events (continued)*

2001	Mel Brooks's *The Producers* opens on Broadway.
2002	Twyla Tharp choreographs the award winning *Movin' Out* for Broadway, which features music by Billy Joel.
2002	*Hairspray* opens on Broadway, which is based on a movie that was not a musical, created in 1988.
2005	A movie musical of *Chicago* choreographed and directed by Rob Marshall is created, which is based on the original Broadway musical of 1975 and the revival of 1996. The movie features an all-star cast and wins many major awards, including the Academy Award for Best Picture.
2005	After the success of the Broadway musical *The Producers,* a movie musical was made starring actors from the original Broadway cast. The original movie, which was not a musical, was created in 1968.
2005	A revival of *Sweet Charity* opens on Broadway.
2006	A revival of *A Chorus Line* opens on Broadway.
2006	*The Drowsy Chaperone* opens on Broadway.
2006	*The Times They Are A-Changin',* choreographed by Twyla Tharp and featuring the music of Bob Dylan, closes on Broadway after only 35 previews and 28 performances.
2006	Billy Siegenfeld, artistic director of the Jump Rhythm Jazz Project receives the Ruth Page Award, given to individuals who have made significant contributions to the field of dance.
2006	*The Wedding Singer* opens on Broadway as a musical, based on the movie of the same name.
2007	The movie musical *Dreamgirls* opens nationwide. With an all-star cast, it is based on the Broadway production, created in 1981.
2007	The Jazz Dance World Congress holds its sixteenth jazz dance festival.
2007	*Spring Awakening* opens on Broadway and features choreography by modern dance choreographer Bill T. Jones, who wins the Tony Award for Best Choreography.
2007	*Legally Blonde* opens on Broadway as a musical, based on the movie of the same name.
2007	A movie musical is made of *Hairspray,* starring John Travolta.
2008	*Billy Elliot* opens on Broadway.
2008	*In the Heights* wins the Tony Award for Best Musical.
2009	The three young boys who share the role of Billy in *Billy Elliot* are awarded the Tony Award for Best Actor.
2009	The revival of *West Side Story* opens on Broadway.
2009	*The Sixth Annual New York Musical Theatre Festival* features outstanding musical-theater talent, and this year included 27 musicals, featuring subjects ranging from vampires to Jesus.
2009	*Fela!* opens on Broadway featuring choreography by modern dance icon Bill T. Jones. *Fela!* tells the story of Nigerian musician and activist Fela Anikulapo Kuti.
2009	A remake of the movie *Fame,* about a performing arts high school in New York, opens in theatres.
2009	*Billy Elliot* wins the Tony Award for Best Musical.
2010	*Memphis* wins the Tony Award for Best Musical.
2011	*The Book of Mormon* wins the Tony Award for Best Musical.
2012	*Once* wins the Tony Award for Best Musical.
2013	*Kinky Boots* wins the Tony Award for Best Musical.
2013	Live musical theatre productions begin to be televised. The first one is *The Sound of Music.*
2014	*A Gentleman's Guide to Love and Murder* wins the Tony Award for Best Musical.
2014	A live performance of the musical *Peter Pan* is televised.
2015	The seventh annual National High School Musical Theatre Awards took place at the Minskoff Theatre on Broadway.
2015	The 29th annual Jazz & Tap Dance Festival featured live jazz, Broadway, tap, and hip-hop dance, and was held in Washington, DC.
2015	The *Phantom of the Opera* is the longest running musical on Broadway to date, with over 11,000 performances.
2015	A live performance of the musical *The Wiz* is televised.
2016	Live musical performances of *Grease, The Passion, The Rocky Horror Picture Show,* and *Hairspray* are televised.
2018	A live musical performance of *Jesus Christ Superstar* is televised.
2018	The *Phantom of the Opera* is still the longest running musical theatre production on Broadway.

Discussion Question

Discuss in class or provide written answers.

1. What is your definition of "style"? Also, do you think that having "style" is important to a jazz dancer? Why or why not?

2. What are some of the musical theatre productions that you have seen? Were they live performances or movie musicals? What do you think of the dance sequences in them?

3. How would you describe tap dance to a person who has never seen it before?

Figure 9.6

Contributed by Candice Kaminski, clikstudiosonline.com. ©Kendall Hunt Publishing Company.

MAJOR FIGURES IN JAZZ DANCE, MUSICAL THEATRE, AND TAP DANCE

Jazz dance, including tap and musical theatre, are art forms that had their beginnings in America. Here is a partial list of artists that have had a major impact on this vernacular dance.

Leading to the Minstrels and Beyond

John Durang (1768–1822)—Durang is known as one of America's first show dancers. Although he was white, he knew much about black dance. He was an expert at "hornpipe" dancing (a type of folk dance from England), although his version had many elements of African-American style. He was also the first white dancer to perform in blackface.

Thomas Rice (1808–1860)—Better known as Daddy "Jim Crow" Rice, this performer was another white dancer who borrowed from the black culture. He made the song and dance number "Jump Jim Crow" immensely popular and it became a fad dance of the time. His performances paved the way for the minstrel shows to come.

William Henry Lane (1825–1852)—Better known as "Master Juba," Lane combined Irish jig and African movements in his dancing during the 1840s. Because he was black, he was not allowed to perform on stage with white performers, and he performed for black audiences and Irish immigrants. He became more popular than most white minstrel performers and eventually toured with them. He is also said to have influenced the tap dance movements created during his era.

George Primrose (1852–1919)—A star of both the minstrel and vaudeville shows, Primrose popularized a style of tap dance known as the "soft shoe." The soft shoe is performed very gracefully, with the feet skimming, rather than loudly tapping, the floor.

The Vaudeville Era

Florenz Ziegfeld (1867–1932)—Ziegfeld was a producer who, in 1907, created the *Ziegfeld Follies*. The *Ziegfeld Follies* were a showcase of American "beauties," song and dance numbers, and comedy routines. These shows were similar to the revues of the French *Folies Bergere*. Ziegfeld produced a new follies each year until the Great Depression of the 1930s.

Ned Wayburn (1874–1942)—Wayburn was one of the most famous dance directors of the Vaudeville era. He also opened several dance studios that trained dancers for his shows. He focused on several types of show dancing, including musical comedy dancing, tap dance, ballroom, acrobats, and modern ballet.

Bill "Bojangles" Robinson (1878–1949, see Figure 9.7)—One of the great tap dancers of the Vaudeville era, Robinson may be best remembered as the person who danced with Shirley Temple in the 1935 movie *The Little Colonel* and the 1938 movie *Rebecca of Sunnybrook Farm*. He was also one of the first black performers who presented artistic dance on the vaudeville stage. He had a graceful and delicate style that he perfected throughout his career of sixty years, which included work on Broadway and in movie musicals.

Figure 9.7

Bill "Bojangles" Robinson and Shirley Temple in "Just Around the Corner."
© Twentieth Century Fox Film Corporation/Photofest.

Vernon Castle (1887–1918) and **Irene Castle** (1893–1969)—The Castles were a ballroom dance team introduced to the public by director Ned Wayburn. In addition to being dancers, they were also educators and introduced the public to ballroom dance through stage productions and classroom instruction. The Castles were immensely popular and set the standard for the way people dressed, behaved, and danced. They were in their heyday from 1912–1918. After Vernon's death, Irene continued to teach and even made educational dance films.

Ray Bolger (1903–1987)—Best known as the actor who played the scarecrow in *The Wizard of Oz*, Bolger was one of vaudeville's best-loved stars. His specialty was comic dance and his long, lanky frame added to his comic ability.

Margot Webb and **Harold Norton**—Known as Norton and Margot, this duo was one of the few African-American ballroom dance couples of the Vaudeville era. Although they adopted a traditional dance vocabulary (or a dance style "reserved" for white performers), they were not permitted to perform in the major vaudeville theatres. Nevertheless, their contribution to black dance and elevating the stature of the black artist has not gone unnoticed.

Broadway and the Movie Musical

Eubie Blake (1883–1983)—Blake was a composer and pianist who, together with other artists, created the Broadway musical *Shuffle Along* (considered to be the first African-American musical of note) in 1921. This production was popular with both white and black audiences and gave stature to the black Broadway artists.

Albertina Rasch (1891–1967)—Originally a ballet dancer, Rasch was a dance director who helped to popularize "fancy dancing." Originally, fancy dancing was comprised of acrobatic tricks, high kicks, splits, etc. Rasch, however, used ballet movements and syncopated dance steps that were set to modern music. She directed a company called the *Albertina Rasch Girls*, who performed worldwide.

Seymour Felix (1892–1961)—Felix was also a dance director who was concerned with the storyline of the musical. Beginning with the Rodgers and Hart musical *Peggy Ann*, produced in 1926, Felix was insistent that the dance numbers relate to or enhance the plot of the musical.

Busby Berkeley (1895–1976)—Berkeley was a dance director known for his use of "beautiful girls" in his productions. Often the women in a Berkeley number were costumed to look exactly alike, including wigs that were the same color and style. He moved them around on stage in intricate patterns and provided audiences with aerial shots that produced a kaleidoscope effect.

Bobby Connolly (1895–1944)—Another dance director of the 1920s, Connolly is best-known for his choreography in *The Wizard of Oz*. He is also credited with bringing "swing" dancing into popularity in musicals.

Robert Alton (1902–1957)—A popular dance director from the 1930s to the 1950s, Alton was fond of tap dance and employed it in several of his musicals, including *Anything Goes* and *Pal Joey*. Alton choreographed over thirty-two musicals.

Josephine Baker (1906–1975)—Baker began her career during the Vaudeville era and eventually became a protégée of Eubie Blake. In 1925, she performed in Paris and became an instant success. In 1926, she performed at the *Folies-Bergère* and brought the jazz craze in Paris to an all-time high. She is credited with introducing such dances as the Charleston and the Black Bottom to the European audience. During World War II, she volunteered for the French Red Cross. Due to her celebrity status, Baker found herself among German officers who attended her performances, and she began relaying information to the French Resistance that she had overheard. She wrote notes in invisible ink on her sheet music and smuggled them to the French authorities. For her actions, she was awarded the *Croix de Guerre* and the Medal of Resistance by the French government.

The Masters of Yesterday and Today

Several ballet and modern dance choreographers (previously discussed in ballet and modern *Major Figures*) have created some of our best-loved jazz, tap, and musical theatre choreography. For example: **George Balanchine** (*On Your Toes, I Married an Angel, Babes in Arms, The Boys from Syracuse, Song of Norway,* and *Where's Charley?*), **Agnes de Mille** (*Oklahoma!, Brigadoon, Carousel,* and *Allegro*), **Jerome Robbins** (*On the Town, Fiddler on the Roof, High Button Shoes, West Side Story,* and *The King and I*), **Katherine Dunham** (*Pins and Needles, Cabin in the Sky,* and *Stormy Weather*), **Helen Tamiris** (*Annie Get Your Gun, By the Beautiful Sea,* and *Fanny*), **Hanya Holm** (*Kiss Me Kate, Out of This World,* and *My Fair Lady*), **Valerie Bettis** (*Beggar's Holiday*), **Twyla Tharp** (remakes of *Hair, Singin' in the Rain,* and *Movin' Out*) and **Bill T. Jones** (*Spring Awakening* and *Fela!*).

Fred Astaire (1899–1987) and **Ginger Rogers** (1911–1995)—One of America's most popular dancing couples, Astaire and Rogers combined tap, ballroom, and ballet to create some of today's most memorable dance sequences. Rogers is said to have been a perfect partner to Astaire, as they both possessed a quality of grace and elegance in their movements. **Hermes Pan** (1910–1990), a Hollywood choreographer, frequently collaborated with Astaire to produce choreography for his dance sequences with Rogers, as well as his solo dances. The magic of Astaire and Rogers can be seen in such movies as *The Gay Divorcee* and *Top Hat.*

Gene Kelly (1912–1996, see Figure 9.8)—Kelly also combined tap, ballroom, and ballet in his dancing. But unlike Astaire, Kelly was much more of a "physical" and acrobatic dancer. One of the most famous tap dance sequences known today was performed by Kelly in the movie *Singin' in the Rain.*

Figure 9.8

Gene Kelly and Cyd Chiarisse on the set of "Brigadoon."
Sunset Boulevard/Corbis Historical/Getty Images

Eleanor Powell (1912–1982)—Powell began her career in tap dance as a performer in Atlantic City nightclubs, and eventually worked her way to Broadway and later Hollywood. Her tap dancing was defined as "machine-gun footwork." She was mainly a solo performer, but also danced with Fred Astaire. She was one of the many stars of the great MGM musicals of the 1930s.

Jack Cole (1913–1974)—Cole began his career as a dancer with Denishawn and Humphrey-Weidman. The exposure to East Indian dance, introduced to him by Ruth St. Denis, had a lasting effect on him and his choreography became a mixture of jazz and world dance. One example of this unique hybrid is *Kismet,* which is one of Cole's most popular musicals.

James "Buster" Brown (1913–2002)—Buster Brown's career spanned over seven decades, beginning as a tap dancer in vaudeville shows and ending as a dancer on Broadway and in movies. He is the 1998 recipient of the American Tap Dance Legend Award. He performed with Gregory Hines in the film *The Cotton Club,* and was also a beloved tap teacher and choreographer.

Frankie Manning (1915–2009)—Manning was a Harlem dancer noted for being one of the pioneers of the Lindy Hop, a social dance popular in the 1930s and 40s. Manning is credited with creating the "air step," in which the female partner was thrown in the air and landed in perfect timing with the music. In 1989, Manning co-choreographed the Broadway show *Black and Blue* (along with Fayard Nicholas, Cholly Atkins, and Henry LaTang), and won the Tony Award for Best Choreography. Manning went on to create dances for the Alvin Ailey American Dance Theatre and other companies.

Fayard Nicholas (1919–2006) and **Harold Nicholas** (1924–2000)—Better known as the Nicholas Brothers, they were a tap dancing act that performed many acrobatic movements in their dance routines. They performed in such movies as *The Pirates* and *Stormy Weather.*

Michael Kidd (1919–2007)—An outstanding musical theatre choreographer, Kidd won Tony Awards for his choreography in *Finian's Rainbow, Guys and Dolls,* and *Can-Can.* One of his best-loved movie musicals is *Seven Brides for Seven Brothers,* with choreography that combines square dance, folk, ballet, and modern with highly stylized acrobatic movements.

Gower Champion (1921–1980)—Before becoming a noted choreographer and director, Champion was a dancer and appeared in several musicals with his wife and dance partner, **Marge** (b. 1923). As a director, he was an expert at "musical staging," which linked the acting and the dancing. Some of America's best-loved musicals that Champion choreographed and directed include *Bye Bye Birdie, Carnival, Hello, Dolly!, I Do! I Do!,* and *42nd Street.*

Charles "Honi" Coles (1921–1992)—Coles is credited with creating high-speed rhythm tap and was known for his complex rhythmic patterns and movements. He was part-nered with **Charles "Cholly" Atkins** (1913–2003), who was known as a master of the soft shoe. Together they per-formed around the country for over twenty years, building their act into a comedy and dance routine. After their duet broke up, Coles and Atkins still performed sporadically for several years at benefits and reunion concerts. Atkins went on to become a choreographer for the groups at Motown Records. Coles was "rediscovered" in the late 1970s and choreographed on Broadway for performances such as *Bubbling Brown Sugar.*

Cyd Charisse (1922–2008, see Figure 9.8)—In the late 1930s, Charisse was a resident ballet dancer for MGM stu-dios and is known for her frequent pairings in movies with Fred Astaire and Gene Kelly. One of her most famous dance sequences appeared in the film *Singin' in the Rain* (1952), in a section known as the *Broadway Melody* finale. Fred Astaire referred to her as "beautiful dynamite."

Sammy Davis, Jr. (1925–1990)—Sammy Davis, Jr.'s career began as a young child, when he danced on the vaudeville stage. Davis became a famous singer, dancer, and actor and performed in all facets of the theatre on Broadway, in movies, nightclubs, etc. He is considered one of the best tap dancers and all-around entertainers ever known in this country.

Luigi (1925–2015)—Another master teacher, Luigi, who was based in New York City, developed a technique and style that was uniquely his own and is studied by students all over the world. It includes the use of specific arm and hand positions, as well as shoulder, upper torso, and hip movements.

Gwen Verdon (1925–2000)—Trained in ballet, Verdon came to jazz dance after seeing Jack Cole perform. She worked with Cole for many years and was his assistant. She also worked with Michael Kidd, as well as Bob Fosse, whom she married. Also an outstanding actor and singer, Verdon appeared in several plays and movie musicals, in-cluding *Can-Can, Damn Yankees, Redhead, Sweet Charity,* and *Chicago.*

Bob Fosse (1927–1987)—One of jazz dance's foremost choreographers, Fosse's choreography is recognizable by its angular shapes, undulating hip and shoulder move-ments, hip isolations, and turned-in legs. Fosse has pro-vided the choreography and direction for some of Ameri-ca's best-loved musicals: *Pippin, Cabaret, Chicago, Dancin',* and *Sweet Charity,* among others.

Jimmy Slide (1927–2008)—As a tap teacher, Slide stresses the importance of learning the foundational movements of tap and for also learning to slide the taps close to the floor. His innovative tap style that blended tap and jazz gave him the reputation of being an outstanding dancer and chore-ographer. In 2003, he won a Guggenheim Fellowship for Choreography. He danced in films and on Broadway, and received a Tony Award nomination for his role in *Black and Blue* (1989).

Gus Giordano (1930–2008)—A leading jazz teacher, Giordano developed the Jazz Dance World Congress, an organization created to preserve and expand the world of jazz dance. In 1962, Giordano developed a jazz company and school in Chicago, which is run by his daughter, Nan Giordano.

Chita Rivera (b. 1933)—Rivera has appeared in the chore-ography of Michael Kidd, Jerome Robbins, Gower Cham-pion, and Jack Cole, to name a few. Her outstanding sing-ing and acting ability has made her one of musical theatre's biggest stars. In 1992, she wowed audiences in the Broad-way musical *Kiss of the Spider Woman.*

Shirley MacLaine (b. 1934)—For many years MacLaine was a "chorus girl." She eventually became one of the most famous dancing and acting stars. One of her most popular roles was in the movie version of *Sweet Charity.*

Brenda Bufalino (b. 1937)—Bufalino is the artistic director of the American Tap Dance Foundation, one of the few dance companies that dedicate themselves exclusively to tap dance. Her choreography is complex, with movements that are syncopated and dynamic.

Tommy Tune (b. 1939)—Best known for his outstanding tap dance ability, Tune is also a choreographer and direc-tor, as well as a performer (one of the few artists who has been able to combine so many facets of the theatre into his working life). He has choreographed and directed some of Broadway's most popular shows, including *Best Little Whorehouse in Texas, A Day in Hollywood/A Night in the Ukraine, Cloud 9, My One and Only,* and the re-make of *Bye Bye Birdie.*

Lynn Dally (b. 1941)—Although she grew up studying tap, Dally began her career as a modern dancer, but eventually moved to Los Angeles and in 1979 founded the Jazz Tap Ensemble. This company is one of the leading jazz and tap companies in the country and features both dancers and jazz musicians. Dally is interested in showing different cultural influences in her choreography.

Michael Bennett (1943–1987)—One of America's most famous Broadway choreographers, Bennett created one of Broadway's most popular musicals, *A Chorus Line*. He began dancing as a child and at the young age of twenty-three won a Tony Award for his choreography in *A Joyful Noise*. Several more Tony Awards were awarded to him throughout his career. Among his choreography and directing accomplishments are *Company*, *Follies*, and *Dreamgirls*.

Gregory Hines (1946–2003)—Paired with his brother Maurice, Hines began tap dancing at a young age. Much of the resurgence of popularity that tap has enjoyed since the 1980s can be attributed to the many outstanding tap performances done by Hines. These performances can be seen in such movies as *White Nights* and *Tap*.

Lynne Taylor-Corbett (b. 1947)—Taylor-Corbett has created many dances for modern and ballet companies, but she is best known for her work in theatre and film. She choreographed the films *Footloose* and *My Blue Heaven*, as well as Disney's stage show *Aladdin*. In 2000, she received two Tony Award nominations and a Drama Desk nomination for her direction and choreography for Broadway's *Swing!*, and also choreographed *Chess* and *Titanic* for the Broadway stage.

Danny Buraczeski (b. 1949)—Buraczeski studied ballet and modern dance before landing on Broadway. His choreography is directly linked to his use of jazz music, in that both are rhythmically and dynamically complex.

Wayne Cilento (b. 1949)—Cilento has worked in national commercials, music videos, and on the concert stage. He is also one of Broadway's best choreographers, and created the movement for *Sweet Charity* (revival), *Wicked*, *Aida*, *The Who's Tommy*, among others. He has also done staging for pop and rock stars, such as Alicia Keys, Barry Manilow, Billy Joel, Donna Summer, and Pete Townshend.

Billy Siegenfeld (b. 1949)—As the artistic director and main choreographer for the Jump Rhythm Jazz Project, Siegenfeld is concerned with showing the strong connection between jazz dance and jazz music. His choreography depicts all of the rhythms, flavors, and complexities found in jazz music. He has choreographed on companies such as the José Limon Dance Company, Joffrey II, and Gus Giordano Jazz Dance Chicago.

Debbie Allen (b. 1950)—Best known for her role on the television series *Fame*, Allen is not only an outstanding dancer but also one of today's best-known jazz dance choreographers (also one of the few women recognized in this field). With both television and Broadway experience, Allen is also respected as a director.

Susan Stroman (b. 1954)—Stroman is one of the few women who both choreograph and direct for movies and live musicals. She is best known for her choreography and direction of the "dance play" *Contact*, which won the 2000 Tony Award for Best Musical. She has also collaborated with writer and actor Mel Brooks, and worked with him on the musical version of *The Producers*. In 2005, she made her directorial debut as a feature filmmaker with the big screen adaptation of the show. In 2007, she again collaborated with Brooks, as director and choreographer of the Broadway musical *Young Frankenstein*. She is also the director and choreographer of the musical *Happiness*.

Acia Gray (b. 1960)—A rhythm tap dancer and choreographer, Gray is also the co-founder and artistic director of Tapestry Dance Company. She works to bridge the gap between traditional and contemporary tap dance. She sees tap as a form of communication and has said that tap dancing is just another way of talking.

Rob Marshall (b. 1960)—Marshall began performing as a child and continued to dance as an adult until an injury (while performing in a production of *Cats*), made him make the decision to go into choreography and directing. He is best known for his choreography and direction of the movie version of *Chicago*, starring Renée Zellweger and Catherine Zeta-Jones, which received six Academy Awards including Best Picture. For Broadway, he has choreographed *Cabaret*, *Damn Yankees*, *Company*, and *Victor/Victoria*.

Kathleen Marshall (b. 1962)—Younger sister of Rob Marshall, she is also an outstanding choreographer and director. She has choreographed more than ten Broadway shows, and won two Tony Awards for *The Pajama Game* and *Wonderful Town*. She was seen as a judge on the reality show *Grease: You're the One That I Want*, which she choreographed and directed for Broadway after TV viewers selected the two lead characters.

Casey Nicholaw (b. 1962)—Nominated for Best Choreography for *Spamalot,* Nicholaw then went on to direct and choreograph the 2006 Broadway hit *The Drowsy Chaperone.* Before he began choreographing and directing, Nicholaw starred in eight Broadway shows, including *Thoroughly Modern Millie, Seussical: The Musical,* and *Saturday Night Fever.*

Adam Shankman (b. 1964)—Many people know Shankman as one of the judges on the television show *So You Think You Can Dance.* Shankman, however, has a long list of movie credits that includes bringing the Broadway hit *Hairspray* to the big screen. For many years, he was known as one of the best music video choreographers, creating music videos for such artists as Whitney Houston, the B-52's, and Stevie Wonder.

Herbin "Tamango" Van Cayseele (b. 1965)—Tamango is an award-winning tap dancer and the artistic director of Urban Tap, a company that performs tap, *capoeira,* African dance, and hip-hop. A former star of the show *Riverdance,* Tomango has gone on to thrill audiences with his diverse group of energetic dancers and unique choreography.

Napoleon D'umo (b. 1968) and **Tabitha D'umo** (b. 1973)—Tabitha and Napoleon are a married couple who choreograph together and are often said to have developed a new style of hip-hop known as lyrical hip-hop. Working together since 1996, they are best known for their choreography on the television show *So You Think You Can Dance.* Napoleon and Tabitha are also choreographers for MTV's *America's Best Dance Crew.*

Andy Blankenbuehler (b. 1970) is a choreographer who won the Tony Award and Drama Desk Award for his choreography for the Broadway musical *In the Heights.* He also created the choreography for *Nine to Five, The Wiz, Bring it On: The Musical,* and *Hamilton.*

Keith "Tyce" Diorio (b. 1970)—Diorio is best known for his work as a choreographer and guest judge on the television show *So You Think You Can Dance.* He has choreographed for and performed with some of the biggest names in pop music, such as Paula Abdul, Janet Jackson, and Jennifer Lopez. He also played a lead role in the Broadway production of *Fosse.*

Savion Glover (b. 1973, see Figure 9.9)—As a child, Glover starred in *The Tap Dance Kid* on Broadway, which led to parts in other plays such as *Black and Blue* and *Jelly's Last Jam.* He also starred in the movie *Tap,* with Gregory Hines and Sammy Davis, Jr. Glover has since starred in and choreographed *Bring in 'da Noise, Bring in 'da Funk* on Broadway for which he won a Tony Award for Best Choreography. This show depicts the African-American struggle through tap, rap, hip-hop, and funk. In 2016, he choreographed a revival of *Shuffle Along* for Broadway.

Alex Sanchez (b. 1974)—Originally a dancer on Broadway, Sanchez is now a sought-after musical theatre choreographer, creating dance sequences for many musical theatre productions around the country.

Ayodele Casel (b. 1976)—A dynamic tap dancer, Casel was the first female to dance with Savion Glover's company Not Your Ordinary Tappers. She was featured in a classical concerto written by composer Rob Kapilow, where she, as the tap dancer, was the "musical" soloist. She continually performs before sold-out audiences and is one of today's leading tap dancers.

Sonya Tayeh (b. 1978) is a dance teacher and jazz and contemporary choreographer, best known for her chor-

Figure 9.9

Savion Glover is a popular "rhythm tapper" who brings attention to intricate and percussive footwork.

eography on the television series *So You Think You Can Dance*. In 2013, she was nominated for an Emmy Award for her work on season nine. Tayeh has choreographed for pop stars such as Madonna, Florence and the Machine, and Kylie Minogue, as well as dance companies such as the Los Angeles Ballet, Martha Graham Dance Company, and the San Jose Repertory Theater.

Kaleena Miller (b. 1984)—Artistic director of Kaleena Miller Dance, this tap dancer also co-founded Rhythmic Circus, which was featured on *America's Got Talent*. Her mesmerizing footwork and advanced tap technique has made her one of today's most exciting tap performers.

Jumaane Taylor (b. 1986)—Born and raised in Chicago, Taylor is best known for his tap dance style in which he keeps the feet very close to the floor, producing intricate and quick sounds and rhythms. He is one of the rising stars of tap dance.

Social Dance

©AYAKOLEVdotCOM/Shutterstock, Inc.

Most of the discussion up to this point has focused on professional concert dance. But just as folk dances provided entertainment for people in the sixteenth century, every era possesses styles of dancing that are performed purely for pleasure and entertainment. These dances are reflective of the cultures in which they exist. Although categorized as social dance, some of these dance forms and styles have made their way to the concert stage, and many have had a profound impact on society.

. . . every era possesses styles of dancing that are performed purely for pleasure and entertainment. These dances are reflective of the cultures in which they exist.

Nearly every society has social dances that are a part of the culture. Each society has its own viewpoint about different aspects of social dance.

Ballroom and Popular Dance

Nearly every society has social dances that are a part of the culture. Each society has its own viewpoint about different aspects of social dance. For example, in some societies, social dance is a group activity meant to be enjoyed by an individual in conjunction with other people. In other societies, social dancing is meant to be enjoyed by two people—a couple (see Figure 10.1). Sometimes, social dance is seen as a completely individual activity. In some societies, strict rules apply to social dance with regard to males and females dancing together, appropriate physical contact, and dancing in public. In other societies, dance is an accepted means of expression, and people of all ages and genders are encouraged to participate. Today in

Figure 10.1

Vernon and Irene Castle, a
famous ballroom dance couple
of the early 1900s.
Courtesy of Photofest.

America, there are many different types of social dances (specifically ballroom, see Figure 10.2, and popular dances) and many different opinions regarding these dances.

Many social dances that were done in the past and are still done today in America came directly from the African-American communities and were adopted (and sometimes modified) by the white communities. For example, one of the most popular social dances ever developed was the Lindy Hop. The Lindy Hop was created in the Harlem nightclubs of the 1930s. Performed to swing music, it is a fast-paced, athletic dance done with a partner. When performed by the white community, this dance was usually done at a slower tempo and employed less of the daring lifts and tricks that were part of the original style. The Lindy Hop paved the way for other couple dances, including the Jitterbug of the 1940s and even the hustle of the late 1970s. It is interesting to note that dancers not trained in traditional techniques almost always created these dance forms.

Although each decade has seen the development of specific dances, the focus of this chapter is on the period between the 1950s and the present in America, a span of time in which a number of social dance styles emerged. For example, in the conservative 1950s, ballroom dancing, which included dances such as the waltz, foxtrot, and rumba, was a popular pastime for many Americans. Many of these styles of dance have their roots in European, African, and South American movements. For example, the waltz was created in the nineteenth century and danced by the elite in England and Germany and eventually all across Europe, before it reached the United States. Other dances, such as the rumba, samba, and tango, have their roots in movements created in the early 1900s in Africa and South America. In their original forms, these dances were considered to be too wild and sensual for the conservative communities (see Figure 10.3). Therefore, some of the movements (especially hip movements) were changed and instead, balletic lifts and turns were added. These "refined" ballroom dances were performed almost exclusively by white dancers.

With the advent of rock and roll in the 1950s, the younger generation abandoned the prevailing conservative attitude. This attitude change, as well as the popularity of rock and roll music, resulted in the development of many new dances. Many African-American singers began to gain popularity, such as Little Richard and Chuck Berry, and white youths began to listen to the music of these singers, as well as mimic their dance movements. The most popular artist of that time, Elvis Presley, was a white singer who had a "soulful" quality

Figure 10.2

Professional ballroom dancers.
©Shkvarko/Shutterstock, Inc.

to both his singing and his dancing. His hip-swaying movements were considered so offensive that he was only shown
from the chest up on the popular "Ed Sullivan Show."

In 1960, Chubby Checker recorded "The Twist," and a new
dance craze emerged. Other dances such as the Monkey,
Mashed Potato, and the Frug became popular with both black
and white teenagers. The mid-1960s introduced performers
such as Mick Jagger (of the Rolling Stones) and James Brown,
both of whom had a unique dance style that their fans adored.
In the late-1960s, a great change in dance styles occurred, which
was a direct reflection of the attitudes of that time. The Vietnam
War, the Civil Rights Movement, and an increased interest in il-
legal drugs created the era sometimes referred to as "radical."
Partner dancing, once the norm, was no longer the "in" thing to
do, and people danced alone or in groups. This type of dancing
was known as "free-style" dancing. People wanted to "do their
own thing," and this form reflected that feeling. A prime example of free-style dancing was captured in the film footage of
Woodstock, a three-day rock music event held on a farm in up-
state New York in the late 1960s. Here, people danced with ulti-

Figure 10.3

Tango, created and popularized in South America,
was considered wild and sensual when first seen in
the early 1900s. The "Tango Dip" is shown here.
©David Carreon/Shutterstock, Inc.

mate abandonment, due largely in part to the overwhelming feeling of freedom, as well as an abundant supply of drugs.

In the 1970s, rock music was still going strong. A new style of music emerged in the late 1970s, however, that would again change the course of social dance. Disco music became the craze and popularized such dances as the Hustle and the Bus Stop. Partner dancing was also popularized during this period, largely due to the 1977 movie *Saturday Night Fever,* which starred John Travolta. This movie set the trend for what was to occur in popular dance for most of the late 1970s and early 1980s. Nightclubs, glamour, and romance were the norm and looking fabulous was required of all who wanted to fit in.

Figure 10.4

Dancer performing a movement in a modern dance that comes from breaking vocabulary.
Copyright © 2004 by Bruce Davis.

Rap music was developed in the 1970s, but became popular in the 1980s as a voice for inner-city minority groups. This style of music helped to popularize a form of dance known as hip-hop, although hip-hop had begun long before the development of rap music. Hip-hop combines several movements from African and jazz dance vocabularies with newly created movements. It was developed by dancers who continue to create new steps and combinations today. Although this discussion is not about professional or concert dance, it is interesting to note how popular dances (which begin at a raw level) are taken into the professional dance world and incorporated into videos, musical theatre productions, and concert dance (see Figure 10.4). For example, there are many music videos that have incorporated hip-hop dancing and even popularized certain steps, such as the Running Man, the Roger Rabbit, the Jackie Chan, the Robocop, and the Spongebob.

Another example of the fusion between popular dance and concert dance can be found in the work of dancer and choreographer Rennie Harris (b. 1964). He is the artistic director of Rennie Harris Puremovement, a company based in Philadelphia that is dedicated to bringing hip-hop culture to the concert stage, as well as presenting workshops and classes for the public. One of the company's most critically acclaimed works is *Rome and Jewels* (2000), a hip-hop version of Shakespeare's *Romeo and Juliet.* This evening-length work uses actual Shakespearean text, as well as text developed by the cast, which is performed by a hip-hop poet. In this piece, Harris uses hip-hop to depict this tragic love story. *Rome and Jewels* has been wildly successful and has been performed across the United States and abroad.

The fast-paced 1980s brought breaking, more commonly known as break-dancing, to the mainstream and to the dance world.

> *The terminology used to refer to b-boying (breakdancing) changed after promotion by the mainstream media. Although widespread, the term "breakdancing" is looked down upon by those immersed in hip-hop culture. Purists consider "breakdancing" an ignorant term invented by the media that connotes exploitation of the art and is used to sensationalize breaking. The term "breakdancing" is also problematic because it has become a diluted umbrella term that incorrectly includes popping, locking, and electric boogaloo, which are not styles of "breakdance," but are funk styles that were developed separately from breaking in California. The dance itself is properly called "breaking," according to rappers such as KRS-One, Talib Kweli, Mos Def, and Darryl McDaniels of Run-DMC.[1]*

Breaking actually became popular in the inner cities during the 1970s, but did not receive widespread public attention until 1983, when the movie *Flashdance* featured a short breaking section. Before going into the mainstream, gangs had been using breaking as a form of competition. Emphasis was placed on virtuosity; the one who could do the most interesting and difficult movements was the best.

The dancers who performed this highly physical and acrobatic form were and are known as b-boys and b-girls. Some believe that the "B" stands for breaking, while others believe that it stands for the Bronx, where it is said that breaking (see Figure 10.5) first developed. The b-boys and b-girls from the East

Figure 10.5

Breaking became popular in the inner-cities during the 1970s and is still popular today.
© Stefanie van der Vinden/Shutterstock, Inc.

Figure 10.6

B-boy battle at a dance competition.
©de2marco/Shutterstock, Inc.

Coast perfected this dance style, while West Coast Funk dancers created movements such as "popping" and "locking."

A typical breaking session would be one where a circle is formed and each dancer enters the middle of the circle (known as a cypher, sometimes spelled cipher), one at a time. Once inside the circle, the dancer demonstrates his or her best breaking moves (see Figure 10.6). Each dancer would do a short demonstration, sometimes lasting only a few seconds to a few minutes. This short presentation, however, would be packed with fast and intricate footwork and amazing spins and flips.

Hip-hop dancing comes from and continues to inspire a contemporary culture. This culture has at its roots b-boying, graffiti writing, and the importance placed on the DJ/emcee, whose job it was (is) to provide the rhythms, mixes, scratching, and verbal "commands." This culture also inspired the development of rap music, a specific fashion trend, and a specific style of language/slang. Hip-hop dancing had an overall effect on the development of dance in the mainstream, particularly in music videos and in performances by pop and rap artists. Taking all this influence into consideration, hip-hop can be seen as more than a social dance form, but as an entire culture, with its own history, language, and major figures coming from both the East and West Coasts.

Another dance craze that was popularized in the early 1980s was slam dancing, in which the participants literally slammed into each other. Slam dancing was typically found in nightclubs that catered to the punk-rock crowd. This dance fad also began in the late 1970s (in England), but did not become popular with the mainstream in the United States until the 1980s (some feel as a direct revolt against the disco era). Later, there developed a small but dedicated crowd that took slam dancing one step further (by actually making it more violent). This dance craze, referred to as mosh dancing, was performed to heavy metal music. The participants referred to themselves as moshers, and religiously took part in this violent dance fad.

The early 1980s brought us music-television. At the time, these television stations devoted their entire programming to music videos and were extremely popular, two of which were MTV and VH-1. Michael Jackson (1958–2009) was the first artist to present dance in a way that people had never previously witnessed. Jackson's *Thriller* video (1984, choreographed by musical theatre choreographer Michael Peters [1948–1994]) was a sophisticated dance video that set a precedent for all other videos to follow. In order for a video to be popular, it had to contain unique, exciting, and creative dance sequences. Since then, there have been many artists who regularly present dance in their videos and live performances, including Janet Jackson, Madonna, Britney Spears, Jennifer

Lopez, Ricky Martin, Beyoncé, Lady Gaga, Usher, Bruno Mars, and the list goes on and on. Many of the movements seen in these videos come from social dance forms, particularly hip-hop.

Throughout the 1990s and into the twenty-first century, breaking and hip-hop have remained popular and are still going strong. Today, there are many active b-boy and b-girl groups. Also, since the media has kept these styles in the forefront—in television commercials, on YouTube, etc.—it is easy to see how it has remained so popular not only with the b-boys/girls but also in the mainstream (see Figure 10.7).

The influence that hip-hop has had on a global level also points to the major impact this dance genre has had. On every continent, hip-hop dance, music, and culture features prominently, even in some Middle Eastern countries where, by necessity, hip-hop is performed covertly. Hip-hop's far reaching impact can be clearly seen in a quick search on YouTube, which will feature several thousand hip-hop music and dance videos from all over the world.

Another dance craze to come into the twenty-first century is rave dancing, or raving. Danced to techno/electronic music, raving was for many years an underground dance style that began in the 1980s. Rave dancing is improvisational, with the participants strongly persuaded by the regular and hypnotic rhythm of the music. Many of the dance movements done at raves come directly from the hip-hop vocabulary, as does the use of the circle formation where the dancers "show their stuff." Also similar to hip-hop, there is a distinct style of dress that ravers wear, such as "phat pantz."

Figure 10.7

A b-girl in motion.
Contributed by dgarson.com. ©Kendall Hunt Publishing Company.

Although at the height of popularity in the 1990s, raves are still held in a number of places, including nightclubs. However, what some consider to be the "real" raves are the one-night, occasional parties set up in a warehouse or other space large enough to accommodate hundreds or even thousands of people. Although the mantra of most ravers is peace, freedom, and friendliness, there is a dark side to many rave parties. The use of drugs, particularly Ecstasy, has led to a number of overdoses at these events. Measures have been taken to make sure these events remain safe, such as promoters throwing drug-free raves and putting more of an emphasis on the music and the dancing, rather than the drug taking. The music and dancing, after all, are at the center of the raves and the main reasons why rave parties exist.

Social dance has once again been catapulted into the mainstream, largely due to the development of two reality television shows—*Dancing With the Stars* and *So You Think You Can Dance*. Although *So You Think You Can Dance* also focuses on genres such as contemporary, jazz, and hip-hop, both shows include a focus on ballroom dancing. Due to the popularity of these shows, ballroom dance studios report an increase in class attendance. Also, medical professionals have been reporting research findings that show that ballroom and other types of dancing can have both physical and mental benefits, such as lowering blood pressure, improving circulatory problems, fighting obesity, releasing stress, and providing a social outlet, particularly for older adults (see Figure 10.8). Given all of these factors, the number of people wanting to participate in some form of social dance has dramatically increased.

Figure 10.8

Older adults and their teacher in a jazz dance class.
©Robert Kneschke/Shutterstock, Inc.

It is pleasantly surprising to see how these two reality shows have taken off and the interest they have brought to dance in general. *Dancing With the Stars* reportedly has had up to twenty million viewers per episode, with *So You Think You Can Dance* following close behind. The nation-wide tours that have come after the season finales of both shows have been sold-out in every city. Although reality television is seen by some as banal entertainment, no one can deny the power and appeal of the dancing on these two programs.

Similar to hip-hop and breaking, krump dance, or krumping, is another dance form developed in the streets and taken into the mainstream. Krumping began as a street dance in South Central Los Angeles. With origins in the African-American community, this dance form was created to release anger and aggression, but in a nonviolent way. Although the movements are highly charged and aggressive, and the dancers even make contact with one another, all physical interactions are highly stylized (see Figure 10.9). In other words, the movements may look violent, but that is part of the aesthetic. Just as there are choreographers who took hip-hop out of the social dance setting and presented it as part of dance performances or concert dance, the same holds true for krumping. Television programs such as *So You Think You Can Dance* present krumping as a dance "category" and the contestants perform krumping routines. Therefore, krumping is another example of an urban social form whose status has been elevated in both commercial and artistic arenas.

Also similar to hip-hop and its inclusion of b-boys and b-girls and their crews, krumping has a social structure that includes groups known as "families" or "fams." The families have a leader (who is an advanced krump dancer) known as the "Big Homie," with additional members known as "Lil' Homies." There are also competitions among the respective families, and each dancer and family participates in order to achieve status and respect. In 2005, a documentary called *Rize* was a box office success that featured clowning and krumping. Clowning is different from krumping in that there is an element of comedy (joke telling or "dissing") included in the form, whereas krumping focuses on the aggressive and emotionally charged movements. *Rize* brought clowning and krumping into the mainstream, and they have been gaining popularity ever since.

Another social dance phenomenon that is seen worldwide is the increasingly popular flash mob. A flash mob occurs when a group of people begin to dance in a place where there are unsuspecting people going about their daily lives—at a train station, a shopping mall, or a museum, for example. The dances performed are usually pre-planned, and begin with one person or a small number of people and then gradually grow to include a large group. Although trained dancers perform some flash mobs, many incorporate people who love to dance and wish to be part of the flash mob experience. Flash mobs have been seen on nearly every continent, and a search on YouTube will result in hundreds of examples of these social dance events (see Figure 10.10). Over the years, flash mobs have gained so much popularity that they have been used for wedding proposals, to announce an upcoming birth, as a way to ask someone to a prom, and the list goes on and on. One popular occurrence is to get as many people as possible involved in specific flash mobs. In 2012, more than 50,000 people in 300 cities across North America engaged in a song and dance routine at the exact same time, setting the world record for the largest simultaneous flash mob.[2] There are even professional groups and companies that focus on creating flash mobs. For example, there is a group based in New York City called Improv Everywhere, whose mission it is to "cause scenes of chaos and joy in public places."[3] And, there are also flash mob companies that can be hired to perform a flash mob for a specific event.

Figure 10.9

Krumping is an aggressive, nonviolent street dance.
© Shutterstock, Inc.

Figure 10.10

Flash mob at *Palais Royal* square in Paris, France.
©Elena Dijour/Shutterstock, Inc.

Summary

Many people today, as in years past, enjoy social dancing. For example, there is now a tremendous interest in hip-hop and breaking. How long will emphasis on this dance form last? No one can know for sure. But one thing is certain: there will always be people who enjoy many aspects of social dancing and for a variety of reasons. Some feel that it is good exercise, while others say it makes them feel good on an emotional level. Many people dance to release their frustrations and negative energies and many people dance for the sheer fun of it. Whatever the reason people dance, the culture and society of the time to which they belong will certainly be reflected in the movements, style, and music that make up the dance. Table 10.1 outlines some events in social dance.

Table 10.1 *Outline of Social Dance Events*

1920s	Beginning of the Harlem Renaissance. Dances such as the Charleston and the Black Bottom became popular (as discussed in Chapter Nine).
1930s	The Lindy Hop began in the black communities and was then adopted and sometimes modified by the white communities.
1950s	Ballroom dancing came to the forefront. Dances such as the Waltz, Fox Trot, and Rumba became very popular (see Figure 10.11).
1950s	This decade saw the advent of rock and roll music. A new way of dancing was discovered.
1960s	Dances such as the Twist, Monkey and Mashed Potato emerged.
Late 1960s	Dance styles emerged that reflected turbulent times. Free-style dancing became the popular form of social dance.
1970	Disco music brought about such dances as the Hustle and the Bus Stop. Partner dancing once again became popular.
1980s	Breaking (see Figure 10.12), developed in the 1970s, became popular in the mainstream. Rap music gave rise to hip-hop culture. Slam dancing and mosh dancing were also seen in certain punk rock and heavy metal circles.
1980s	Music television (MTV, VH-1) popularizes the music video. Many social dance styles appeared in the videos of the music industry's most popular performers.
1990s–2000s	Rap music, hip-hop, and breaking remain popular. Rave dancing, which began in the 1980s as an underground dance craze, became the popular dance form leading into the twenty-first century. In 1995, David LaChapelle created the documentary *Rize*, which featured clowning and krumping, dance forms created in the African-American community of South Central Los Angeles.
2000–Present	Concert dance and social dance forms continue to be fused and create an exciting and unique aesthetic for many dance companies, including Rennie Harris Puremovement (founded in 1992), which focuses on hip-hop. Dance is brought to the mainstream by reality television shows such as *Dancing With the Stars* and *So You Think You Can Dance*. The medical profession reports on the significant health benefits of doing ballroom dance.
2010	Congresswoman Eleanor Holmes Norton introduces a National Dance Day resolution to promote dance and dance education. Celebrated on the last Saturday in July, this unofficial holiday was further introduced to the public by *So You Think You Can Dance* co-creator and *Dizzy Feet Foundation* co-president Nigel Lythgoe.
2011	National Dance Week Foundation was established as a non-profit institution. Originally formed in 1981 to bring greater awareness and recognition to dance, the organization has inspired thousands of events during the ten-day annual celebration, which occurs every April.
2011–2017	*Dancing With the Stars* and *So You Think You Can Dance* are still wildly popular television shows. Well-known dance styles and genres are featured, but unfamiliar dance styles, such as the New Orleans Bounce, are also introduced to the mainstream via these popular television shows. Choreographers such as Napoleon and Tabitha D'umo, who developed lyrical hip-hop, and Lil' C, also known as the King of Krump, are popular on the social dance as well as commercial and concert dance scenes. Interest in dance and taking dance lessons is still going strong.
Today	Popular music continues to be a catalyst for new fad dances, including the *Harlem Shake*, *Juju on that Beat*, *Whip/Nae Nae*, *The Dab*, *Shmoney Dance*, *Wobble*, and the *Walk it Out*. Television programs such as *Dancing With the Stars* and *So You Think You Can Dance* remain popular, while new shows such as *World of Dance* and the Netflix original series *We Speak Dance* bring more viewing options to the public.
	Scientific journals, such as the *New England Journal of Medicine* and *Scientific American*, publish articles and studies on the positive effects of dance. The articles focus not only on benefits for the body, but for the brain as well. In addition, dance is found to be beneficial for people with Parkinson's disease, and also lowers the risk of dementia.

Figure 10.11

Rumba is a ballroom dance of African and Cuban origin.
©TEA/Shutterstock, Inc.

Discussion Questions

Discuss in class or provide written answers.

1. What do you think were the most important issues during the 1980s and 1990s that might have had an impact on the social dances of those decades? How did these issues affect society?

2. What are some of the popular dances done today? What issues to date have had an impact on these dances? Make a prediction—what will social dances be like within the next few years? Why?

Figure 10.12

B-boys perform highly physical and acrobatic movements.
©AYAKOLEVdotCOM/Shutterstock, Inc.

part four

RELATED TOPICS

The following chapters discuss topics related to the art of dance: dance production, dance in education, and careers in dance. These topics hold great importance in the world of dance and serve specific and invaluable functions.

Dance Production: Behind the Scenes of a Dance Concert

When an audience takes their seats in a theatre and the lights go down, a magical hush fills the air. The curtain goes up, the lights display splashes of color and the dance begins. The audience, concerned only with what is happening in the present, rarely thinks about the long process that has brought the dancers to this moment.

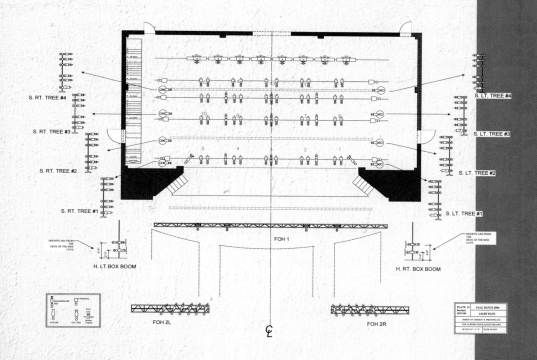

S. RT. TREE #4

S. RT. TREE #3

S. RT. TREE #2

S. RT. TREE #1

S. LT. TREE #4

S. LT. TREE #3

S. LT. TREE #2

S. LT. TREE #1

HEIGHTS ARE FROM THE DECK OF THE SIDE COVE

HEIGHTS ARE FROM THE DECK OF THE SIDE COVE

FOH 1

H. LT.BOX BOOM

H. RT. BOX BOOM

FOH 2L

FOH 2R

It would be surprising for some to realize exactly how much work and energy goes into mounting a dance production. An incredible amount of work has to be done in addition to creating the choreography and holding the rehearsals. This chapter discusses the steps that must be taken to produce a dance concert, and the people who play key roles in executing a production.

The Artistic Director

No matter what the size of the company or the company's budget, having an outstanding *artistic director* is *crucial* to the success and survival of any dance company. The artistic director is responsible for the overall aesthetic and artistic vision of the company and makes decisions relative to all artistic issues.

One of the many responsibilities of the artistic director is to choreograph for the company or invite guest choreographers to make dances that will be performed in the company's repertoire. Companies that perform dances choreographed by someone other than the artistic director are usually known as repertory companies. Once it is determined which dances will appear on a concert, the artistic director "programs" the dances so that they are performed in an appropriate concert order. For example, beginning a concert with a dance that has a dark and dramatic theme might be too much for the audience to view as soon as they sit down in their seats. It might be more appropriate to begin a concert with a lighter dance, to allow the audience time to adjust to the concert setting. Similarly, the final dance of a concert should be one that will send the audience away with a lasting impression.

In addition to making artistic decisions, artistic directors sometimes also make business decisions, or at least give input into certain business issues. For example, dealing with touring and teaching schedules, financial concerns, and fund-raising efforts are all a part of the artistic director's job. They are also usually responsible for hiring (and sometimes firing) the dancers.

Most artistic directors are the "founders" of their dance companies. For example, Paul Taylor founded the Paul Taylor Dance Company in 1961 and still serves as its artistic director. There are, however, many people who have taken over the artistic directorship of an already existing company. Judith Jamison, for example, took over the artistic directorship of the Alvin Ailey American Dance Theatre after Ailey's death in 1990. Before a new director takes over an already existing company, decisions must be made as to whether or not he or she will continue to direct the company in the same artistic manner that the previous director had. In Jamison's case, there was a commitment to keeping the artistic vision and legacy of Alvin Ailey alive. Therefore, she directed the company with that intent and priority in mind. Upon Jamison's retirement, Robert Battle became the artistic director, again with the intent of preserving Ailey's legacy. But for other companies, it might be determined (possibly by the Board members), that the new director should take the company in a different artistic direction that would benefit the dancers and the audience.

Steps in the Production Process

Properly planning and organizing a dance concert is of the utmost importance. It is crucial that the organizers have a well thought-out plan of action and adhere to the timing and schedule of that plan. Of course, certain adjustments might have to be made if an emergency should arise (for example, problems with lighting equipment). In these cases, every effort should be made to fix problems as soon as possible. It is important to remember that many items have to be accomplished that cannot be put off until the last moment.

The beginning point in the process of producing a dance concert is deciding where the program will be performed. Assuming that the dance company has an operating budget, securing a space to conduct the concert (theatre, gymnasium, senior center, museum, etc.) is obviously important. Some companies have agreements to perform their home seasons in the same theatre every year, but many smaller companies rent out space on a concert-to-concert basis. Sometimes dancers have to perform in spaces that are less than ideal and many are willing to compromise in order to get the chance to perform. Compromising with regard to an adequate dance floor, however, may not be wise. Having the right kind of dance floor (preferably a sprung, smooth, wood or vinyl floor) is important, since dancing on one that is not appropriate can be dangerous. For example, dancing on a floor that is too hard can lead to injuries such as shin splints, or ankle, knee, and lower back problems. Other considerations for securing a space include: the availability of dressing room space; the stage size; available lighting; location of the space and availability of parking and public transportation; the space's policies; and, of course, the cost.

Once a space is secured and rehearsals are underway, the artistic director, choreographer, or any other person who may be responsible for the concert, must direct their attention to factors including: publicity; designing and printing posters and programs; ticket sales; designing costumes; setting up lighting design(s); music (live or recorded); any sets and scenery; use of video or other technology; program order; and possibly renting equipment. In large, established companies, a number of people are responsible for accomplishing these tasks. Smaller dance companies who cannot afford to hire extra help are often left to take care of these details on their own. Therefore, in addition to creating the dances and running the rehearsals, the choreographer(s) or artistic director may also be responsible for most of the aforementioned tasks (with the dancers often pitching in as well). It is startling to see how many companies can successfully produce a concert, considering the enormous amount of work, effort, and finances it takes to achieve this goal.

People Behind the Production: The Support Staff

Few dance companies in the world can afford to have the ideal support and artistic staff. For the purposes of this discussion, let's create the ideal scenario and see who a dance company might employ if they had the funds to do so.

The ideal dance company would have a hard-working, dedicated *Board of Directors*. This group primarily consists of prominent members of the business and artistic community, most of whom dedicate their time to the company without receiving any pay. One of the Board's main functions is to conduct fund-raising activities. Other functions may include establishing rules, regulations, and policies regarding contracts, pay schedules, working conditions, etc.

Few dance companies in the world can afford to have the ideal support and artistic staff.

Figure 11.1

Dancer Ursula Payne during
a photo shoot.
Copyright © by Eduardo Patino.

In some instances, the Board has the power to hire, fire, and promote members of the artistic and support staff, including the dancers, choreographers, and the artistic director.

In an ideal situation, a dance company would have a *business manager* as well as a *company director.* The business manager is in charge of the company's budget and may write grants and help with fund-raising efforts. Of course, he or she is also responsible for paying the bills and staff salaries. The company manager is more directly involved with the dancers and artistic director than the business manager. He or she is responsible for designing rehearsal and production schedules and making sure everyone has the appropriate information to ensure that things run as smoothly as possible.

A well-known *public relations firm* can enhance the image of a dance company immensely, while at the same time build an audience for the company. This firm is usually responsible for developing advertisements for newspapers, radio, and television. They, along with a *graphics company*, also develop posters, flyers, and the concert program. So many of today's successful advertisements depend on flashy and provocative visual images in order to capture the potential audience's attention. Dance companies that use photography in their advertisements can greatly benefit from these professional services (see Figure 11.1).

A company needs a *box office manager*, who is in charge of reservations and ticket sales. A *house manager* is also required and is responsible for the ushers, seating arrangements, intermissions, and anything else that might occur in the "house" of the theatre (as opposed to backstage).

Backstage, the *technical director* is in charge of all of the equipment and technical aspects of the performance. Usually, this person has an *assistant technical director* and a *stage crew* to help with the technical work. The *stage manager* is responsible for "calling the show," or giving directions for the sound and lighting cues. This person works closely with the artistic director, technical director, and all the designers and assumes the majority of the responsibility once the performance gets underway. The stage manager's ability is crucial to the overall success of the performance. This person usually has an *assistant stage manager* who helps with details. The stage manager also works closely with the *lighting board operator(s), follow spot operator(s)* and *sound board operator(s),* who, under his or her direction, "run" the show, usually from the lighting and sound booths.

In addition to the above mentioned positions, some dance companies might also have *legal counsel; insurance agents; dance injury specialists, physical therapist* and *massage therapists; financial administrators; marketing directors; residency and workshop coordinators; rehearsal assistants; administrative assistants;* and *travel/booking agents.*

It is typical for many larger companies to have a school associated with the company, and therefore the following positions may be necessary: *school director; assistant director; administrative assistants; community outreach coordinators; accompanists; recruiting coordinator and recruiters; financial and budget managers; development personnel; on-site health professionals; a school board of directors*; and of course, *highly qualified faculty*. Some schools offer room and board to students from all over the world, such as the School of American Ballet, which is affiliated with the New York City Ballet. In these cases, all *residence life* activities such as housing, food, and round-the-clock supervision must be considered. These schools typically offer community, pre-professional, and professional dance classes. Some schools use their pre-professional classes as a training ground for dancers who might eventually dance with the professional company, and these students usually go through the process of being accepted into a trainee program, internship, or second or junior company before being hired by the professional company. Some schools might offer specialized classes, such as the Mark Morris Dance Center, which is affiliated with the Mark Morris Dance Group, and offers classes for children with disabilities called *Special Kids Dance*. They are also affiliated with *Dance for PD*, which is a collaboration between the Mark Morris Dance Group and the Brooklyn Parkinson Group, and offers dance classes to Parkinson's patients, as well as teacher training for this special population.

With the great variety of dance companies in the world, there are almost certainly some positions that have not even been mentioned that may in fact be a major part of some companies. It is striking, however, to look at the broad spectrum of dance companies—from the large, well-established companies to the small and struggling ones—and see how they are all committed to producing dance concerts and sharing them with the public.

The Artistic Collaborators

Several other people are important to the artistic development and production of a dance concert. In an ideal situation, a company would have a *lighting designer, costume designer, costume construction crew, hair and makeup artist,* and *set and scenic designer.* They might also have a *musical director* and *composer(s),* and even an *orchestra* associated with the company.

The Lighting Designer

In smaller, lower-budget companies, the collaboration with the lighting designer usually takes priority over all other factors, leaving the artistic director, dancers, etc., to design and make costumes, do their own hair and makeup, and work with previously recorded music. One of the main reasons why this collaboration is so important to the production is because the lights provide a theatrical feel to the dances that most choreographers desire. This statement does not imply that dances cannot be performed in natural light (or even under fluorescent lights!), but lighting can help transform the stage space and help chor-

... the collaboration with the lighting designer usually takes priority over all other factors ... because the lights provide a theatrical feel to the dances that most choreographers desire.

eographers "say" what they want. "Light itself is mysterious, inseparable from what it makes visible. In the natural world, though light fosters sight, it is neutral on matters of meaning. Theatrical light, entirely unnatural, fosters sight and insight; it is a subliminal whisper, providing emphasis, telling us what to make of what we see."[1]

Another reason why lighting designers are so valuable to most dance companies is because these designers not only have the artistic sense needed to create the designs, but they also possess the essential practical knowledge regarding electricity, lighting instruments, use of color, light plots, and the technical aspects of the theatre. Although some choreographers can design lights for their own dances, most have neither the time nor the knowledge of design, as well as the equipment, to properly light a concert.

Part of the knowledge that a lighting designer must have involves the different pieces of lighting equipment. A designer has many types of lighting instruments that he or she uses to create the desired effects on the stage (see Figure 11.2, which shows universal lighting symbols). Many lighting designers also utilize special software that have instrument and manufacturer specific symbols. For example, a *Fresnel* is a type of spotlight that features a lens with an edged or stepped pattern. This lens is a thick piece of glass patterned on the inside to resemble a series of steps. This design gives the light "a wide spread of illumination—which creates an even field with soft edges. . . ."[2] An *ellipsoidal reflector spotlight* (known as an ERS or by the trade name Leko), is used when the designer wishes to project a sharper, more focused beam of light. This instrument uses an "ellipsoidal reflector," a bowl-shaped apparatus that sits behind and around the bulb (or "lamp") "to gather light from one focal point and focus it on the second focal point."[3] Additionally, the ellipsoidal spotlight has metal shutters that can be manipulated to precisely control the spill of the light and the relative sharpness or softness of the beam's edge. There is also an *ellipsoidal reflector floodlight* (also known as an ERF or "scoop"), which can be used for ". . . throwing a broad wash of light over a wide area."[4] Often times, this instrument is used for lighting scenery. A *PAR can* or *PAR head* (parabolic aluminized reflector) provides an ". . . oval-shaped beam of light . . . [which] is uniquely harsh [intense], [while] the beam edge is fairly soft."[5] Designers use these four commonly known lighting instruments in different ways in order to produce certain "looks" on stage. The designer can use them separately or in conjunction with one another.

Lighting designers also use *striplights* to create a wash of light on a backdrop, cyclorama, or scrim (set pieces or pieces of material that hang in the upstage part of the stage). *Follow spots* are lighting instruments that are not found directly on the stage, but are projected onto the stage by an operator who is usually a far distance away (such as at the back of the theatre or in the lighting booth). The operator can move the beam of light all around the stage area. The follow spot can produce either a sharp or diffused light and the beam of light can be made very small or large. This instrument is usually used to highlight a person or object on stage. Another lighting instrument designers use is a *beam*

Figure 11.2

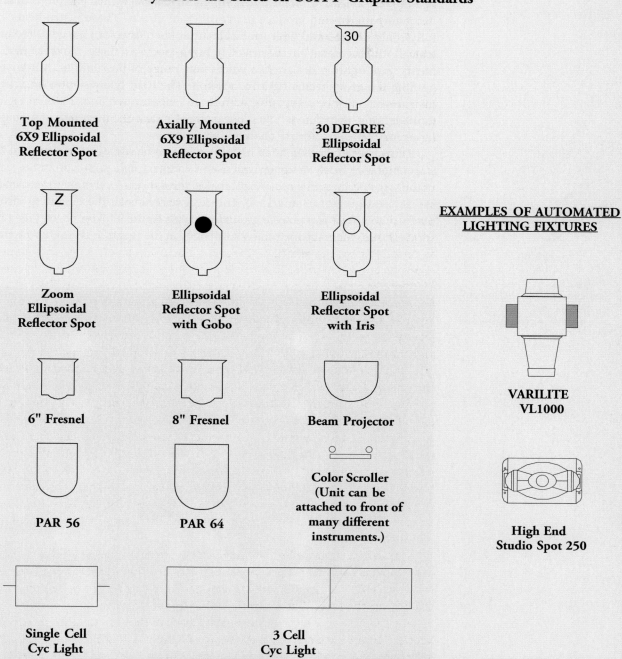

These symbols are recognized by the United States Institute for Theatre Technology (USITT) as universal lighting symbols.

projector, which throws a sharp beam of light and is often used to create special effects, such as sunlight coming in through a window.

There are also *automated lighting instruments* (also known as *movable lighting instruments* or *intelligent lighting instruments*), which can project many different patterns and produce many different effects. These instruments are fully computerized and have special features such as color changers. Technological advancements in theatrical lighting, such as these movable instruments, give lighting designers a whole new range of possibilities. Automated lighting requires specific lighting controls. The light board controlling these instruments must be compatible with these sophisticated lights. Where a standard lighting instrument takes one control channel to operate, automated lights may take up to thirty channels per instrument.

Of course, all these lighting instruments must be strategically placed on the stage. In dance, many designers will use the primary light source from the sides of the stage because this use of light makes the dancers look more three-dimensional (see Figures 11.3 and 11.4). The designer drafts all these lighting instruments onto a *light plot* (a scale ground plan, see Figure 11.8 on pages 178–179), which shows where the instruments will hang in the theatre). The lights are then

Side lights are used to illuminate the dancers.
Contributed by Ben Viatori. ©Kendall Hunt Publishing Company.

Figure 11.3

Figure 11.4

Side lighting is used specifically to highlight the dancers' bodies.
Contributed by Ben Viatori. ©Kendall Hunt Publishing Company.

hung and focused to specific areas on the stage. The lighting designer often uses different colored *gels* in front of the lighting instruments to produce certain effects. For example, if a dance depicted a person who is in a panicked state, the designer may choose to have an intense red glow over the stage. On the other hand, if the dance was about a mother's love for her child, the designer might illuminate the stage with a warm, pink, rosy color. Although both of these examples would use colors in the red spectrum, using different hues and intensities would evoke different emotions.

Designers may also incorporate the use of a *gobo,* which is a small, flat piece of metal with a cutout pattern in it. Gobos can produce many effects, such as a starry night, a cityscape, or a forest filled with trees, to name a few. High-quality glass gobos, called *lithos,* can accommodate precise, fine-detailed images, such as photographs or line drawings, and can also be in color or black and white. These *lithos* pass light very effectively and, depending on the pattern, can create everything from a beautiful, soft-shaded effect to multicolored projections.

Before the lighting designer begins to design the light plot, one or more meetings usually take place with the choreographer. The designer may also come to rehearsal(s) and watch the dance or dances that he or she will create designs for, or "light." Several items are usually discussed and taken into consideration when the designs are made, including: costume color; set design (if any); whether or not the dance will incorporate film or video; whether any special effects will be required; and, most important, the choreographer's concept of the dance. Although some choreographers and lighting designers work independently from each other, <u>many designers desire</u> the aforementioned information in order to <u>make the most effective lighting design</u> (see Figures 11.5, 11.6, and 11.7).

Figure 11.5

Lighting used to cast shadows and create a design on the stage floor.
Contributed by Ben Viatori. ©Kendall Hunt Publishing Company.

Figure 11.6

Dancers appearing in down pools of light, which isolate each performer in the stage space.
Contributed by Ben Viatori. ©Kendall Hunt Publishing Company.

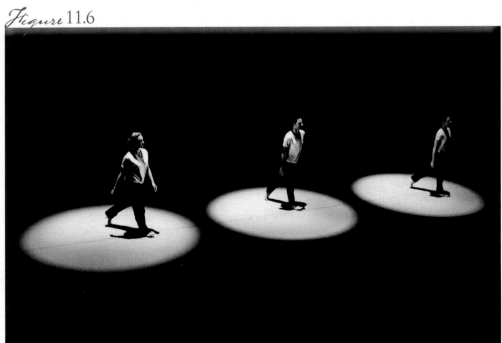

Figure 11.7

Dancers appear in stark white lighting, highlighting the emotional intensity during this section of the dance.

Contributed by Ben Viatori. ©Kendall Hunt Publishing Company.

One of today's most popular and sought-after lighting designers is Jennifer Tipton (b. 1938). She has designed lights for dance, theatre, and opera, and has worked with such choreographers as Paul Taylor, Twyla Tharp, and Jerome Robbins. She has won many awards for her designs, including two Tony Awards, two Drama Desks awards, and an Obie. What makes her such an outstanding designer is her ability to use light to ". . . [move] a piece along onstage. She knows how to punctuate movement in light, [and] create a narrative line for the action."[6] With her lighting designs, she is able to get the audience to see what she wants them to see. Although there are several different ways to light dance, Tipton relies on her intuition, stating, "There are many ideas. They're all light ideas. There's white light. There's colored light. There's light along the walls. There's light from the front. There's light from the side. There's light that lights the head. I'm playing with all of those things and I'm responding with my gut."[7]

The Costume Designer

Although many times dancers perform in typical dancewear, such as leotards and tights, costumes designed specifically for a dance can enhance the theatrical feel of that dance and also provide information to the audience regarding character, time period, and mood. The process that occurs between the choreographer and the costume designer is similar to the one that occurs between the choreographer and the lighting designer (i.e., meetings, discussions, viewing the dances). In addition, the choreographer usually has the opportunity to view sketches of the costumes before construction gets underway.

One of the most important issues concerning costumes has to do with mobility. The dancer(s) must be able to move comfortably in the costume.

Figure 11.8

Example of a light plot for a dance
concert.

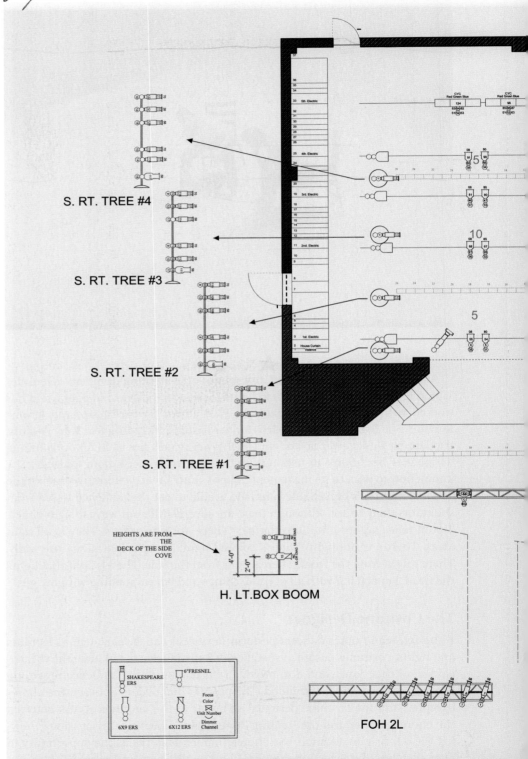

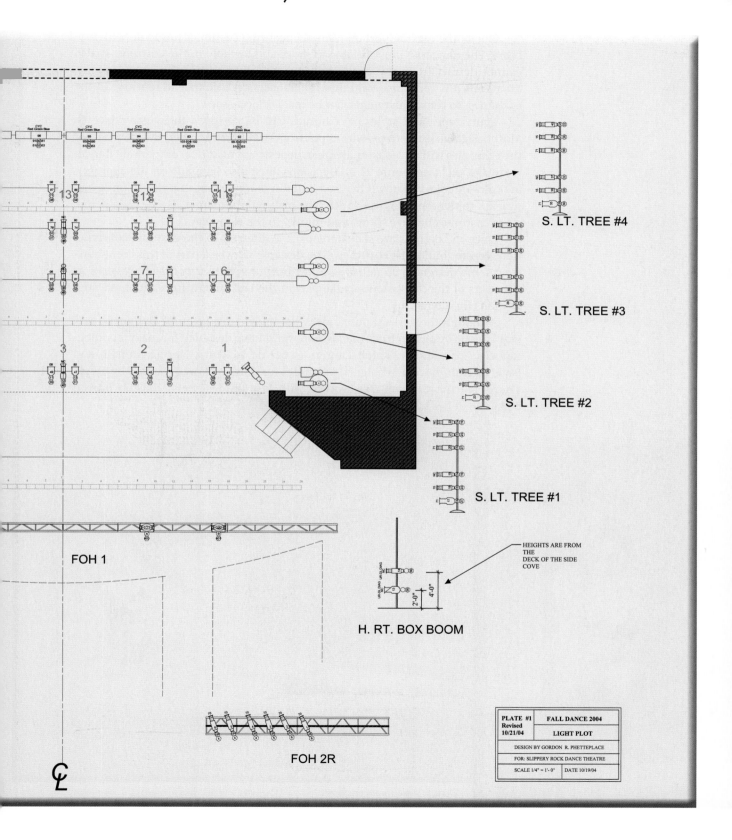

S. LT. TREE #4

S. LT. TREE #3

S. LT. TREE #2

S. LT. TREE #1

FOH 1

HEIGHTS ARE FROM
THE
DECK OF THE SIDE
COVE

H. RT. BOX BOOM

FOH 2R

PLATE #1 Revised 10/21/04	FALL DANCE 2004
	LIGHT PLOT
DESIGN BY GORDON R. PHETTEPLACE	
FOR: SLIPPERY ROCK DANCE THEATRE	
SCALE 1/4" = 1'- 0"	DATE 10/19/04

One of the most important issues concerning costumes has to do with mobility. The dancer(s) must be able to move comfortably in the costume. It also cannot detract from any of the movements found within the choreography. Therefore, it is very important that the dancers get a chance to rehearse in the costumes, so that adjustments can be made if necessary.

Many types and styles of costumes can be designed for dance concerts. Most designers (sometimes with input from the choreographer) decide whether the costumes will be realistic, abstract, pedestrian, historical or "period," dance-wear-like, etc. (see Figure 11.9). Decisions must also be made on the appropriate color or colors that will be used and if it is important that the color be significant to the theme of the dance. The material used must also be considered, since costumes have to "flow" and "move" in the right ways.

Once the designs are sketched out, it is often up to the costume construction crew to "build" the costumes. The designer may be a part of this crew, however, some designers do not even know how to sew. In this case they serve as overseers of the construction, take part in the costume fittings and make suggestions for alterations.

Although the general public does not know most costume designers, several famous designers from the fashion world have designed for major choreographers. For example, Ralph Lauren, Oscar de la Renta, Norma Kamali, and Isaac Mizrahi have all designed costumes for dances choreographed by Twyla Tharp. Martha Graham also worked with fashion designers; Halston having been one of her favorites.

Figure 11.9

Dancer in elaborate costume.
Contributed by Ben Viatori. ©Kendall Hunt Publishing Company.

The costume designer may also be responsible for determining how the dancers' hair will be worn and what makeup they will wear. In some companies hair and makeup artists assist the dancers, but in most companies the dancers are responsible for doing their own makeup and hairstyles.

The Set and Scenic Designer

Today, as in the past, artists from different genres collaborate on many projects that blend different art forms together in unique and interesting ways. For example, choreographers and visual artists have been collaborating on set designs since the court dances of the sixteenth century. As we have seen, classical ballet always employs the use of elaborate scenery. Similarly, choreographers in other dance genres have worked with set and scene designers and have produced outstanding works of art.

A long-term collaboration that has a place in modern dance history is the one between modern dance legend Martha Graham and the Japanese-American sculptor Isamu Noguchi (1904–1988). Graham and Noguchi collaborated on projects for more than fifty-three years. The ". . . process [they employed] was fairly uncomplicated. It would begin with Graham talking with the sculptor about the idea or theme for a piece. Noguchi would then make a tiny mock-up of the set. . . . The choreographer would seldom suggest any changes in the design; if something didn't quite work, she would make adjustments in her own work."[8] Obviously, these two artists had a wonderful working relationship, producing some of the most outstanding dances, set pieces, and designs known in the modern dance world. Some of Graham's dances that include set design and set pieces created by Noguchi are *Appalachian Spring, Night Journey,* and *Errand Into the Maze.*

Composers and Musicians

As stated earlier, some dance companies have a musical director and orchestra associated with it, although this association is usually found only in large ballet companies. Most dance companies that want to collaborate with musicians and perform with live music do so on special occasions, which usually means when money is available. It should be noted that grants are sometimes available for collaborative projects. In recent years, however, the dollar amount given by many grant organizations has been cut dramatically.

Throughout the history of dance, several collaborations between musicians and choreographers proved to be outstanding successes. Several have already been mentioned, such as the collaborations between composer Igor Stravinsky and ballet choreographers Vaslav Nijinsky and George Balanchine, and the many collaborations between composer John Cage and post-modern dance choreographer Merce Cunningham. The marriage of movement and music is a natural and important one, and many choreographers would prefer to work with musicians live in concert (as opposed to recorded music). Most choreographers, however, end up working with previously recorded music because of financial constraints.

Dance and Technology

With the advent of the video camera, choreographers and dancers widely used these devices to record and document choreography and dance events. For many years, equipment such as video cameras, computers, and some editing software were the only technologies available to dancers. Today, however, the vast amount of technological advances has opened up entirely new ways of creating. From the most basic use of technology to the most sophisticated, the possibilities for dance artists who create using dance and technology are endless.

Many choreographers are now choosing to create dances that utilize some of today's technological advancements (see Figure 11.10). With the advent of technology came the desire, for some choreographers, to go beyond "traditional" dance making and to experiment with the highly sophisticated film, video, computer systems, and lighting equipment that is available. Therefore, the demand for filmmakers, videographers, lighting designers, and computer experts has increased. Like everything else, however, finances are a great concern, especially since most of the equipment needed to do a multi-media (or

Many choreographers are now choosing to create dances that utilize some of today's technological advancements.

Figure 11.10

Vera's Body, created by Troika Ranch, a company that utilizes dance technology. The dancer is performing with live video feed, dancing with her virtual self in real time.

Copyright © by Tom Brazil.

mixed-media) project is very expensive. Some choreographers, in an attempt to save money, have learned how to use much of the equipment themselves and then rely on renting or borrowing it in order to complete their projects.

Although all uses of technology requires an advanced level of technical knowledge on the part of the user, there are a variety of ways that dance and technology come together for public performance (as well as dance and scientific research). For example, in performance, technology can be used to project a previously created video onstage while dancers perform live at the same time (see Figure 11.11). Dancers can also use live-feed projection, which happens in real time as the dancers are performing (see Figure 11.10). There are computer programs, such as one called Isadora that, ". . . is the perfect tool for artists, designers, [and] performers who want to add video and interactive media to their performance projects. The software is an interactive media playback platform that combines a media server, a visual programming environment, and a powerful video and audio processing engine."[9] There seems to be no end to the possibilities that technology can offer to dance creators, including the ability to dance with a virtual dancer(s), or to create virtual environments with which the dancers can interact.

There is also another use of technology with which dance makers can engage, but does not utilize live dance performance. Dance for the camera, or screen dance, can depict every dance genre and can be based on a strong narrative or storyline, or be abstract. Dance films can feature actual dancers, a manipulated version of the dancers, or even animation. A dance made for the camera can be seconds to hours in length, and requires significant knowledge of filming and editing in order to create a cohesive product. Some dancers and choreographers are becoming educated on the use of technology, while others must hire technology specialists to help bring the choreographer's vision to fruition.

While many people are used to attending dance concerts and seeing dancers live on stage, there are now dance for the camera events where only dance films are shown. These events, including conferences, workshops, and film festivals often times include dance films from around the globe, pointing to the international influence of technology on the dance field.

Although many see the use of technology as extending the possibilities of the body and the creativity of the dancer and choreographer, some feel that technology takes away from the live body moving in space. Whatever opinions people may have on this topic, it is clear that dance and technology will con-

Figure 11.11

The dancer is performing with a video created for the dance.
Contributed by Ben Viatori. ©Kendall Hunt Publishing Company.

tinue to be part of the landscape and culture of the dance world. As technology continues to progress, so will the artistic possibilities.

It should be mentioned that recording (videotaping) a dance, even at the most simplistic level, is important to most choreographers. For choreographers, recording their dances is the only way to truly preserve a dance. Because dance is an ephemeral art and is only alive at the moment that it is being performed, having a dance videotaped keeps a record of it, either for future use or merely to have in a choreographer's archives.

Summary

The task of producing a dance concert is an overwhelming and exhausting one, especially for smaller companies that have to do most of the work themselves. The process can be less complicated if the production efforts and the people involved are organized and stick to a clearly outlined plan. Of course, money is always a concern in dance production and keeping within a set budget is often difficult. Choreographers and artistic directors can sometimes supplement their budgets with grants from public and private sources, although the grant process can be a tedious and competitive one. Many dance companies, both large and small, have scaled down their production efforts (in terms of the amount of concerts done each year and the dollar amount allotted for each production), in order to save money and keep ticket prices reasonable. Some dance companies have even begun reaching dance audiences using the internet, posting their choreography to YouTube, Vimeo, and their web sites. One dance company, Online Dance Company, presents their work exclusively online. Many dance companies are recognizing that reaching audiences this way can be a powerful tool, and a way to bring new audiences to dance. As an example, American Ballet Theatre dancer Misty Copeland was the first African-American dancer in that company to be promoted to the level of principal dancer, and has appeared in advertisements for the athletic gear and apparel company Under Armor. Her first video with Under Armour received over nine million views (and counting). This number represents an amount much greater than the number of people who attend live dance performances during a given year. However, American Ballet Theatre has enjoyed an increase in attendance due to Copeland's visibility and popularity, and people are attending ballet who may never had attended before.[10] In this case, the wide reach of the internet, combined with an outstanding talent and excellent publicity, cannot be denied.

Although the future looks challenging for many dance companies, the passion and love for dance that most artistic directors and company members share has been the sustaining force that keeps many companies alive. One day, more value may be placed on the arts and substantial funding may be available for these outstanding artists.

The task of producing a dance concert is an overwhelming and exhausting one...

Discussion Questions

Discuss in class or provide written answers.

1. Some people feel that choreography should be able to stand on its own and does not necessarily need lighting, costumes, and set and scenery design in order to be effective. Do you think that lighting design is important to a dance? Why or why not? What about having costumes? Sets and/or scenery? Music? Discuss this issue.

2. What personal characteristics do you think are necessary for an artistic director to have? Why?

Figure 11.12

Contributed by Candice Kaminski, clikstudiosonline.com. ©Kendall Hunt Publishing Company.

Dance in Education and Careers in Dance

Much of this text has served as an introduction to dance as an art form and to those people who have helped shape the world of dance. In this chapter, the focus is on dance in education and also on the careers that a person can have in the dance field.

Contributed by dgarson.com.
©Kendall Hunt Publishing Company.

Today, many dance educators present the argument that teaching and learning dance as an art form is conspicuously absent from the American student's education.

Dance in Education

Historically, dance has been a part of the K–12 education system and colleges and universities for many years, although the relationship between dance and many educational institutions has not always been positive. In past years (as well as today), dance, when offered in grades K–12, was taught through physical education departments. The majority of this teaching focused on folk and square dance, because these genres were usually the ones that physical education instructors could teach. Today, many dance educators present the argument that teaching and learning *dance as an art form* is conspicuously absent from the American student's education. There are approximately 38 states where dance teachers can become certified to teach in the public schools, therefore more dance professionals are being hired by school districts. However, not all schools can afford to hire a dance specialist.

This discussion focuses mostly on dance education in grades K–12 of public institutions and dance at the university or college level. There are, however, many places where people of all ages and abilities can go to study dance. Some of the places that offer dance classes are private studio schools; professional studio schools; recreation centers; public and private elementary, junior high and high schools; and public and private colleges and universities. Although there are many places where a person could study dance, most require the participants to pay for their lessons. This requirement is one of the reasons why dance educators feel passionate about having dance in the public education system—so that every child, regardless of financial ability, can participate in this artistic activity. Dance educators feel that it is the right of every child to experience dance—not just the privileged few.

Most dance educators know the benefits that all children can gain from taking dance (as outlined in the "Creative Movement" section of *Chapter Seven: Improvisation and Creative Movement*). Through dance, children have the potential to become more aware and in-tune with their bodies; develop a positive sense of self-esteem (there are no "winners" or "losers" in dance); socialize with other children; learn to cooperate with other children; use critical thinking skills; use problem-solving skills; improve balance and coordination; increase strength and flexibility; and become aesthetically aware.

Due to severe budget cuts, a lack of knowledge regarding dance, and an overall apathy for the arts that seems to be common in some areas of public education, the future of dance in K–12 education looks grim for some school districts. However, for other school districts, dance is valued and a priority, which may have to do with the expectations of parents who insist on arts inclusion in school curricula. As parents become more informed and realize that their children have the right to study all the arts, we may see dance become a common offering in all public schools. It is encouraging to witness the inclusion of dance certification in many states, thus enabling dance instructors to teach in public schools. But not all states have such certification, and the fear that dance programs could be cut at any moment is quite alarming.

Charter schools, which are publicly funded, are another place where students can study dance, as there are many performing arts charter schools throughout the country. Like public schools, some charter schools require that the students who attend live within the district, although there are charter schools who will bus students from outside the charter school's home district.

Within private schools, there is often access to dance lessons that students receive as part of their tuition. Many times these schools are equipped with dance studios and theatres that are appropriate for dance performances. For those students who are focused on careers in dance and show promise and talent, there are performing arts boarding schools throughout the country, where students study dance and academics. These schools are highly competitive and usually accept students who demonstrate the ability to dance at a pre-professional and professional level. Students who study at these boarding schools,

Dance educators feel that it is the right of every child to experience dance—not just the privileged few.

which are usually grades 9–12, often move far away from their homes in order to receive this kind of focused education, including international students who come to the United States to study dance and the other arts.

Dance in higher education has a much more stable and respected history than dance in K–12 education. Budget cuts, however, negatively affect many dance programs (as well as other programs) in colleges and universities. Often dance departments are asked to do more with less. Many dance departments have had to turn to grant writing and fund-raising in order to provide students with a quality education. On the other hand, some dance departments in this country that are the centerpieces of their institutions have healthy budgets and outstanding resources. What factors contribute to the health and well-being of a college or university dance department? Certainly the priorities determined by an institution's administrators are a major factor in the success of any dance program. Excellent leadership by the department chairperson or dance director is also crucial to the success of the unit. But ultimately, having outstanding faculty is the most important aspect in the success or demise of a program, since they are the ones who have the most effect on the students.

Dance educator and writer Margaret H'Doubler is credited with being one of the first people to bring dance into higher education. She did so through the physical education department at the University of Wisconsin, beginning in the late 1920s. Martha Hill, another dance educator, established the first bachelor of arts degree in dance in 1932 at Bennington College in Bennington, Vermont. Although dance instruction has made great strides since that time (specifically because of information in dance science and kinesiology, dance injuries, and dance technology), the efforts of H'Doubler and Hill have not gone unnoticed.

In addition to these two women, many outstanding dance educators have had major influences on dance in education. Some have been influential because they were (or are) active in national organizations that establish policies related to dance in higher education, while others have contributed to the field by presenting scholarly and artistic work that is considered an important part of the dance world. There are also, however, the people "in the trenches"; the many outstanding dance educators who unselfishly give their time, effort, and energy to their departments and to their students. There have always been and always will be people who have a love, desire, and passion to teach and learn the art of dance. This fact will ensure an important place for dance in higher education.

Figure 12.1

Contributed by dgarson.com. ©Kendall Hunt Publishing Company.

There have always been and always will be people who have a love, desire, and passion to teach and learn the art of dance. This fact will ensure an important place for dance in higher education.

Figure 12.2

Careers in Dance

Throughout this text, we have examined the roles of the choreographer and dancer, although these are not the only career options for people who are involved in the world of dance. Becoming a dance educator is a popular profession in dance, although it takes much skill, patience, and dedication to be an effective one. Different age groups, levels of talent, etc., have to be considered with regard to teaching. For example, not everyone who teaches dance will be able to work well with young children. On the other hand, not all teachers are equipped to teach advanced dancers. Some teachers can effectively teach a number of different age groups, levels, and dance genres, although these people are rare. It is more common to find dance teachers who have specialty areas and excel in teaching in those areas of expertise.

Other dance and dance-related professions include: dance therapist, dance science or medicine specialist, dance kinesiologist, dance historian and writer, dance critic, dance notator, dance captain, rehearsal director, dance administrator, dance company manager, artistic director, dance videographer, dance technology specialist, massage or body therapists, fitness and wellness instructor, somatics practitioner, Pilates instructor, and liturgical dance specialist. There are also related fields such as costume designer, lighting designer, set designer, and stage manager.

Regardless of the area of focus or professional path a dancer wishes to follow, there is much to be said about the value of a dance education. When a person studies dance, they embark on a course of study that requires discipline, passion, commitment, the ability to work long, demanding hours, and the ability to receive critical feedback. Serious dance students are required to think critically and creatively as well as communicate effectively and present themselves in a professional manner at all times. The argument can be made that an education in dance is as valuable, viable, and reputable as any other course of study, academic or otherwise. Many agree that studying dance gives a person the life skills that are necessary and required for any profession. Therefore, it is effective training for many career paths that a person may choose.

The Final Word

The purpose of this text is to introduce students to dance as an art form, as well as a popular form of entertainment. The information is an overview of specific subject areas. It must be stressed that there is a wealth of information, specific and general, on all the topics covered in this text. For those students wishing to delve more deeply into certain topics, the information is at your fingertips—at computer terminals and in the DVD collection of your school or local library, on the internet, and at local, regional, and national theatres.

Seeing as much dance as possible is also an important step in learning about dance. Viewing dances on DVDs and on the internet can be valuable, but viewing dance these ways does not provide the same experience as seeing a live performance. Of course, the best way to learn about dance is to actually *do it.* Making the decision to take a dance class may be difficult for some, but the vast majority of people who take a dance class find it to be a wonderful experience. Many dance artists, educators, and enthusiasts believe that if people would allow themselves the opportunity to experience dance (by participating and viewing), they would certainly find a love and appreciation for the art form.

Discussion Question

Discuss in class or provide written answers.

1. Other than the ones mentioned in this chapter, what are some additional dance and dance-related careers?

Figure 12.3

part five

ADDITIONAL RESOURCES

The following section contains important resources pertaining to reading materials, films, DVDs, digital downloads, and dance information on the internet.

Contributed by Ben Viatori. ©Kendall Hunt Publishing Company.

Suggested Readings

The following lists contain examples of some of the excellent books written about dance and dance-related subjects. Some of the books have been cross-referenced under more than one category. Several lists, however, might be referred to when looking up a particular subject area. For example, if the subject "modern dance" or "contemporary dance" was being explored, the reader might also want to look under Biographies and Autobiographies, Philosophy and Aesthetics, etc., in addition to looking under the Modern and Contemporary Dance heading. Similarly, several of the dance criticism books listed under Modern Dance also contain information on ballet and vice versa.

Ballet: History and Criticism

Amberg, George. *Ballet in America*. New York: Duel, Sloan and Pearce, 1949.

Anderson, Jack. *Ballet and Modern Dance: A Concise History*. Princeton, NJ: Princeton Book Company, 1986.

Anderson, Zoe. *Ballet Lover's Companion*. New Haven: Yale University Press, 2015.

Balanchine, George, and Francis Mason. *Balanchine's Complete Stories of the Great Ballets*. (second ed.) New York: Doubleday & Co., 1977.

_____. *Ballets of Today: Being a Supplement to the Complete Book of Ballets*. London: Beaumont, 1954.

_____. *Ballets Past and Present: Being a Third Supplement to the Complete Book of Ballets*. London: Beaumont, 1955.

_____. *Complete Book of Ballets: A Guide to the Principal Ballets of the 19th and 20th Centuries*. New York: G.P. Putnam's Sons, 1938.

Beaumont, C.W. *A Short History of Ballet*. London: Beaumont, 1944.

_____. *Supplement to the Complete Book of Ballets*. London: Beaumont, 1942.

_____. *The Cecchetti Method of Classical Ballet Theory and Technique*. Mineola: Dover Publications, 2003.

Becker, Rob. *Ballet in the Studio*. Amsterdam: Lecturis, 2016.

Bellow, Juliet. *Modernism on Stage: The Ballets Russes and the Parisian Avant-Garde*. Burlington, VT: Ashgate, 2013.

Bingham, Jane. *Ballet*. Chicago: Heinemann-Raintree, 2008.

Bland, Alexander. *A History of Ballet and Dance in the Western World*. New York: Praeger Co., 1976.

Brinson, Peter, and Clement Crisp. *The International Book of Ballet*. New York: Stein and Day Co., 1971.

Bruhn, Erik, and Lillian Moore. *Bournonville and Ballet Technique*. London: A. & C. Black Co., 1961.

Caddy, Davinia. *Ballets Russes and Beyond: Music and Dance in Belle-Epoque Paris*. New York: Cambridge University Press, 2012.

Chazin-Bennahum, Judith. *Rene Blum and the Ballets Russes: In Search of a Lost Life*. New York: Oxford University Press, 2011.

Clarke, Mary, and Clement Crisp. *Ballet: An Illustrated History*. New York: Universe Books, 1978.

_____, and David Vaughn (Eds.). *The Encyclopedia of Dance and Ballet*. New York: G.P. Putnam's Sons, 1977.

Cowart, Georgia J. *The Triumph of Pleasure: Louis XIV and the Politics of Spectacle*. Chicago: University of Chicago Press, 2008.

Crippa, Valeria. *Nureyev*. New York: Rizzoli, 2003.

Crisp, Clement, and Edward Thorp. *The Colorful World of Ballet*. London: Octopus Books, 1977.

Crosland, Margaret. *Ballet Carnival: A Companion to Ballet*. London: Arco Co., 1957.

Danilova, Nina. *Eight Female Classical Ballet Variations*. New York: Oxford University Press, 2016.

Delman, Gregg. *Misty Copeland*. New York: Rizzoli, 2016.

Duberman, Martin B. *The Worlds of Lincoln Kirstein*. Evanston, IL: Northwestern University Press, 2008.

Duerden, Rachel S. *The Choreography of Anthony Tudor: Focus on Four Ballets*. Madison: Fairleigh Dickinson University Press, 2004.

Edwards, Leslie. *In Good Company: Sixty Years With the Royal Ballet*. Alton: Dance Books, 2003.

Eliot, Karen. *Albion's Dance: British Ballet During the Second World War*. New York: Oxford University Press, 2016.

Ellison, Nancy, Kevin Mckenzie and Rachel S. Moore. *In Classic Style: The Splendor of American Ballet Theatre*. New York: Rizzoli, 2008.

Ezrahi, Christina. *Swans of the Kremlin: Ballet And Power in Soviet Russia*. Pittsburgh: University of Pittsburgh Press, 2012.

Fairfax, Edmund. *The Styles of Eighteenth Century Ballet*. Lanham, MD: Rowman & Littlefield Publishers, 2003.

Franchi, Christine (Ed.). *Kenneth MacMillan at the Royal Opera House*. New York: Oberon Books, 2006.

Garafola, Lynn. *Diaghilev's Ballet Russes*. New York: Oxford University Press, 1989.

_____ (Ed.). *Rethinking the Sylph: New Perspectives on the Romantic Ballet*. Hanover, NH: Wesleyan University Press, 1997.

Goldner, Nancy. *More Balanchine Variations*. Gainesville: University Press of Florida, 2011.

Grace, Robert. *The Borzoi Book of Ballets*. New York: Knopf Publishers, 1947.

Grant, Gail. *Technical Manual and Dictionary of Classical Ballet*. Internet: Editorial Benei Noaj, 2008.

Greskovic, Robert. *Ballet 101: A Complete Guide to Learning and Loving the Ballet*. New York: Hyperion, 1998.

Gruen, John. *The Private World of Ballet*. New York: Viking Press, 1975.

Guest, Ivor Forbes. *Paris Opera Ballet*. Pennington, NJ: Princeton Book Company, 2006.

_____. *The Dancer's Heritage: A Short History of Ballet*. London: The Dancing Times, 1960.

Hager, Bengt. *Ballet Suedois*. New York: Harry N. Abrams, Inc., Publishers, 1990.

Haggin, B.H. *Ballet Chronicle*. New York: Horizon Books, 1970.

Hamilton, Linda H. *Dancer's Way: The New York City Ballet Guide to Mind, Body, and Nutrition*. New York: St. Martin's Press, 2008.

Harris, Andrea. *Making Ballet American: Modernism Before and Beyond Balanchine*. New York: Oxford University Press, 2018.

Haskell, Arnold. *Ballet*. Revised. New York: Pelican Books, 1949.

_____. *Balletomania; Then and Now*. New York: Knopf Publishers, 1977.

Homans, Jennifer. *Apollo's Angels: A History of Ballet*. New York: Random House, 2010.

Joseph, Charles M. *Stravinsky's Ballets*. New Haven: Yale University Press, 2011.

Jurgensen, Kurt A. (Comp. and Ed.). *The Bournonville Ballets: A Photographic Record*. London: Dance Books, Ltd., 1987.

Kelly, Deirdre. *Ballerina: Sex, Scandal, and Suffering Behind the Symbol of Perfection*. Vancouver: Greystone Books, 2014.

Kirstein, Lincoln. *Dance: A Short History*. New York: Putnam, 1935. Reprint: Princeton Book Co., 1987.

_____. *Movement and Metaphor: Four Centuries of Ballet*. New York: Preager Co., 1970.

Krokover, Rosalyn. *New Borzoi Book of Ballets*. New York: Knopf Publishers, 1956.

Lawrence, Robert. *The Victor Book of Ballets and Ballet Music*. New York: Simon & Schuster, 1950.

Lee, Carol. *Ballet in Western Culture*. Boston: Allyn and Bacon, 1999.

Maynard, Olga. *The American Ballet*. Philadelphia: Macrae Smith Co., 1959.

Meylac, Michael (Ed.). *Behind the Scenes at the Ballets Russes: Stories from a Golden Age*. London: I B Tauris, 2018.

Morrison, Simon Alexander. *Bolshoi Confidential: Secrets of the Russian Ballet from the Rule of the Tsars to Today*. New York: Liveright Publishing Corporation, 2016.

Norton, Leslie. *Leonide Massine and the 20th Century Ballet*. Jefferson, NC: McFarland & Company, 2004.

Noverre, Jean Georges. *Letters on Dancing and Ballet*. London: Cyril Beaumont, 1951. Reprint: New York: Dance Horizons, 1981.

Palmer, Winthrop. *Theatrical Dancing in America*. New York: Ackerman Co., 1945.

Paskevska, Anna. *Ballet Beyond Tradition*. New York: Routledge, 2004.

_____. *Both Sides of the Mirror: The Science and Art of Ballet*. Princeton, NJ: Princeton Book Company, 2008.

Paskevska, Anna. *Getting Started in Ballet: A Parent's Guide to Dance Education*. New York: Oxford University Press, 2016.

Pawlick, Catherine E. *Vaganova Today: The Preservation of Pedagogical Tradition*. Gainesville: University Press of Florida, 2011.

Persson, Johan. *Royal Ballet: 161 Images*. London: Oberon Books Ltd., 2003.

Pritchard, Jane (Ed.). *Diaghilev and the Golden Age of the Ballets Russes: 1909–1929*. London: Victoria & Albert Museum, 2010.

_____. *Diaghilev and the Ballets Russes, 1909–1929: When Art Danced with Music*. London: Victoria & Albert Museum, 2013.

Reynolds, Nancy, and Susan Reimer-Torn. *Dance Classics: A Viewer's Guide to the Best-Loved Ballets and Modern Dances*. Pennington, NJ: a capella books, 1991.

Rommet, Zena, and Lisa Jo Sagolla. *Zena Rommett: the Art of Floor Barre: Ballet Class on the Floor: A Conditioning Program for Dancers, Athletes, the Injured, and the Elderly*. Princeton, NJ: Princeton Book Company, 2009.

Scholl, Tim. *From Petipa to Balanchine: Classical Revival and the Modernization of Ballet*. London/New York: Routledge, 1996.

_____. *Sleeping Beauty: A Legend in Progress*. New Haven: Yale University Press, 2004.

Schonberg, Bent. *World Ballet and Dance 1989–90*. London: Dance Books Ltd., 1989.

Shay, Anthony. *Dancing Across Borders: The American Ballet Theatre*. Jefferson, NC: McFarland & Company, 2008.

Siegel, Marcia B. *Mirrors & Scrims: The Life and Afterlife of Ballet*. Middletown, CT: Wesleyan University Press, 2010.

Souritz, Elizabeth. *Soviet Choreographers of the 1920s*. Translated by Lynn Visson (Ed.) with additional translation by Sally Banes. Durham, NC: Duke University Press, 1990.

Swinson, Cyril. *Guidebook to the Ballet*. New York: Macmillan, 1961.

Volynsky, Akim. *Ballet's Magic Kingdom: Selected Writings on Dance in Russia, 1911–1925*. New Haven: Yale University Press, 2008.

Walczak, Barbara. *Balanchine, the Teacher: Fundamentals That Shaped the First Generation of New York City Ballet Dancers*. Gainesville: University Press of Florida, 2008.

White, John Jr. *Advanced Principles in Teaching Classical Ballet*. Gainesville: University Press of Florida, 2009.

Whittier, Cadence Joy. *Creative Ballet Teaching: Technique and Artistry for the 21st Century Ballet Dancer*. New York: Routledge, 2018.

Woodward, Ian. *Ballet*. London: Hodder and Soughton Co., 1977.

Young, Laura. *Boston Ballerina: A Dancer, a Company, an Era*. Lebanon, NH: University Press of New England, 2018.

Ballroom and Social Dance

Aletti, Vince. *The Disco Files 1973–78: New York's Underground, Week by Week*. Internet: DJhistory.com, 2009.

Barlow, Jeremy. *Dance Through Time: Images of Western Social Dancing from the Middle Ages to Modern Times*. Oxford: Bodleian Library, 2012.

Bottomer, Paul. *Ballroom Dancing: Step-by-Step*. Eatontown, NJ: Anness Publishing, 2007.

Buckland, Theresa. *Society Dancing: Fashionable Bodies in England, 1870–1920*. New York: Palgrave Macmillan, 2011.

Dodds, Sherril. *Dancing on the Canon: Embodiments of Value in Popular Dance*. New York: Palgrave Macmillan, 2011.

Ericksen, Julia A. *Dance with Me: Ballroom Dancing and the Promise of Instant Intimacy*. New York: New York University Press, 2011.

Garcia, Cindy. *Salsa Crossings: Dancing Latinidad in Los Angeles*. Durham: Duke University Press, 2013.

Giordano, Ralph G. *Social Dancing in America, Vol. 1: A History and Reference Fair Terpsichore to the Ghost Dance, 1607–1900.* Santa Barbara, CA: Greenwood Publishing Group, 2006.

——————. *Social Dancing in America, Vol. 2: A History and Reference Lindy Hop to Hip-Hop, 1901–2000.* Santa Barbara, CA: Greenwood Publishing Group, 2006.

——————. *Social Dancing in America: A History and Reference.* Santa Barbara, CA: Greenwood Publishing Group, 2006.

Guzman-Sanchez, Thomas. *Underground Dance Masters: Final History of a Forgotten Era.* Santa Barbara, CA: Praeger, 2012.

Hodge, Susie. *Latin and Ballroom.* Chicago: Heinemann-Raintree, 2008.

Hutchinson, Sydney (Ed.). *Salsa World: A Global Dance in Local Contexts.* Philadelphia: Temple University Press, 2014.

Knowles, Mark. *The Wicked Waltz and Other Scandalous Dances: Outrage at Couple Dancing in the 19th and Early 20th Centuries.* Jefferson, NC: McFarland & Company, 2009.

Malnig, Julie. *Ballroom, Boogie, Shimmy Sham, Shake: A Social and Popular Dance Reader.* Champaign, IL: University of Illinois Press, 2008.

Manning, Frankie, and Cynthia R. Millman. *Frankie Manning: Ambassador of Lindy Hop.* Philadelphia: Temple University Press, 2008.

Mccarren, Felicia M. *French Moves: The Cultural Politics of Le Hip Hop.* New York: Oxford University Press, 2013.

Merritt, Carolyn. *Tango Nuevo.* Gainesville: University Press of Florida, 2012.

Monteyne, Kimberly. *Hip Hop on Film: Performance Culture, Urban Space, and Genre Transformation in the 1980s.* Jackson: University Press of Mississippi, 2013.

Nelson, Tom L. *Swing Dance Encyclopedia.* Bloomington, IN: Authorhouse, 2008.

——————. *1000 Novelty and Fad Dances.* Bloomington, IN: Authorhouse, 2009.

Sagolla, Lisa Jo. *Rock 'N' Roll Dances of the 1950s.* Porthsmouth, NH: Greenwood Press, 2011.

Schloss, Joseph. *Foundation: B-Boys, B-Girls, and Hip-Hop Culture in New York.* New York: Oxford University Press, Incorporated, 2009.

Silvester, Victor. *Theory and Technique of Ballroom Dancing.* Internet: Read Books, 2008

Viladrich, Anahi. *More than Two to Tango: Argentine Tango Immigrants in New York City.* Tucson: University of Arizona Press, 2013.

Biographies and Autobiographies

Acocella, Joan. *Mark Morris.* New York: Farrar, Straus, Giroux, 1993.

Albright, Ann Cooper. *Traces of Light: Absence and Presence in the Work of Loie Fuller.* Middleton, CT: Wesleyan University Press, 2007.

Aria, Barbara. *Misha: The Mikhail Baryshnikov Story.* New York: St. Martin's Press, 1989.

Armitage, Merle (Ed.). *Martha Graham.* CA: privately printed, 1937. Reprint: New York: Dance Horizons, 1966.

Blair, Frederika. *Isadora: Portrait of the Artist as a Woman.* New York: McGraw-Hill, 1986.

Bradley, Karen K. *Rudolph Laban.* New York: Routledge, 2008.

Bremser, Martha (Ed.). *Fifty Contemporary Choreographers.* London: Routledge, 1999.

Brown, Carolyn. *Chance and Circumstance: Twenty Years with Cage and Cunningham.* Evanston, IL: Northwestern University Press, 2009.

Candelario, Rosemary. *Flowers Cracking Concrete: Eiko & Koma's Asian/American Choreographies.* Middletown, CT: Wesleyan University Press, 2016.

Cano, Nan Deane. *Acts of Light: Martha Graham in the Twenty-first Century.* Gainesville: University Press of Florida, 2006.

Cheng, Anne Anlin. *Second Skin: Josephine Baker and The Modern Surface.* New York: Oxford University Press, 2011.

Chin, Elizabeth (Ed.). *Katherine Dunham: Recovering an Anthropological Legacy, Choreographing Ethnographic Futures.* Santa Fe: School for Advanced Research Press, 2014.

Climenhaga, Royd. *Pina Bausch.* New York: Routledge, 2009.

Cohen, Selma Jeanne. *Doris Humphrey: An Artist First*. Middletown, CT: Wesleyan University Press, 1972.

Conrad, Christine. *Jerome Robbins: That Broadway Man, That Ballet Man*. London: Booth-Clibborn Editions, 2000.

Copeland, Misty. *Life in Motion: An Unlikely Ballerina*. New York: Simon & Schuster, 2014.

Cunningham, Merce. *The Dancer and the Dance*. In conversation with Jacqueline Lesschaeve. New York: Marion Boyars Inc., 1985.

Current, Richard Nelson. *Loie Fuller, Goddess of Light*. Boston: Northeastern University Press, 1997.

D'amboise, Jacques. *I Was a Dancer: A Memoir*. New York: Alfred A Knopf, 2011.

Daneman, Meredith. *Margot Fonteyn*. New York: Viking, 2004.

de Mille, Agnes. *Martha*. New York: Random House, 1991.

Dee Das, Joanna. *Katherine Dunham: Dance and the African Diaspora*. New York: Oxford University Press, 2017.

Desti, Mary. *The Untold Story: The Life of Isadora Duncan 1921–1927*. New York: Horace Liveright, 1929.

Dreier, Katherine Sophie. *Shawn the Dancer*. London: J.M. Dent & Son, Ltd., 1933.

Duberman, Martin. *The Worlds of Lincoln Kirstein*. New York: Knopf Publishing, 2007.

Duncan, Irma. *Duncan Dancer*. Middletown, CT: Wesleyan University Press, 1966.

——————. *Isadora Duncan: Pioneer in the Art of Dance*. New York: The New York Public Library, 1958.

Duncan, Isadora. *My Life*. New York: Horace Liveright, 1927.

Dunning, Jennifer. *Alvin Ailey: A Life in Dance*. Boston: Addison-Wesley, 1996.

Evans, Bill. *Reminiscences of a Dancing Man: A Photographic Journey of a Life in Dance*. Reston, VA: AAPHERD, 2006.

Farrell, Suzanne. *Holding on to the Air*. With Tony Bentley. New York: Summit Books, 1990.

Fokine, Vitale. *Fokine: Memoirs of a Ballet Master*. Boston: Little, Brown and Company, 1961.

France, Charles Engell (Ed.). *Baryshnikov at Work*. New York: Alfred A. Knopf, 1979.

Franceschina, John Charles. *Hermes Pan: The Man Who Danced with Fred Astaire*. New York: Oxford University Press, 2012.

Franko, Mark. *Martha Graham in Love and War: The Life in the Work*. New York: Oxford University Press, 2012.

Freedman, Russell. *Martha Graham: A Dancer's Life*. New York: Clarion Books, 1998.

Garafola, Lynn (Ed.). *José Limón: An Unfinished Memoir*. Hanover, NH: University Press of New Hampshire, 1998.

Garelick, Rhonda K. *Electric Salome: Loie Fuller's Performance of Modernism*. Princeton, NJ: Princeton University Press, 2009.

Garfunkel, Trudy. *Letter to the World: The Life and Dances of Martha Graham*. New York: Little, Brown and Company, 1995.

Gitelman, Claudia (Ed.). *Liebe Hanya: Mary Wigman's Letters to Hanya Holm*. Madison: University of Wisconsin Press, 2003.

Gitelman, Claudia, and Randy Martin (Eds.). *The Returns of Alwin Nikolais: Bodies, Boundaries and the Dance Canon*. Middletown, CT: Wesleyan University Press, 2007.

Gottlieb, Robert. *George Balanchine: The Ballet Maker*. New York: HarperCollins, 2004.

Graham, Martha. *Blood Memory: An Autobiography*. New York: Doubleday, 1991.

——————. *The Notebooks of Martha Graham*. Introduction by Nancy Wilson Ross. New York: Harcourt, Brace, & Jovanovich, 1973.

Guterl, Matthew Pratt. *Josephine Baker and the Rainbow Tribe*. Cambridge, MA: Belknap Harvard, 2014.

Hammond, Bryan, comp. *Josephine Baker*. Biography by Patrick O'Connor. London: Random House UK, 1991.

Hasday, Judy L. *Agnes de Mille: Dancer and Choreographer*. Topeka: Sagebrush Educational Resources, 2004.

Haskell, Arnold. *Diaghieff*. London: Victor Gollancz, 1935.

Haskins, James. *Katherine Dunham*. New York: Coward, McCann & Geoghegan, 1982.

——————— and N.R. Mitgang. *Mr. Bojangles: The Biography of Bill Robinson*. New York: William Morrow and Co., 1988.

Hill, Constance Valis. *Brotherhood in Rhythm: The Jazz Tap Dancing of the Nicholas Brothers*. New York: Oxford University Press, 2000.

Hilton, Wendy. *Wendy Hilton: A Life in Baroque Dance and Music*. Hillsdale, NY: Pendragon, 2010.

Horosko, Marian (Ed.). *Martha Graham: The Evolution of Her Dance Theory and Training*. Gainesville: University Press of Florida, 2002.

Jones, Bill T. *Last Night on Earth*. With Peggy Gillespie. New York: Pantheon Books, 1995.

Jones, Sabrina. *Isadora Duncan*. New York: Farrer, Straus & Giroux, 2008.

Jowitt, Deborah. *Jerome Robbins: His Life, His Theater, His Dance*. New York: Simon and Schuster, 2004.

——————— (Ed.). *Meredith Monk*. Baltimore, MD: Johns Hopkins University Press, 1997.

Kavanagh, Julie. *Nureyev: The Life*. New York: Knopf Doubleday Publishing, 2008.

Kendall, Elizabeth. *Balanchine and the Lost Muse: Revolution and the Making of a Choreographer*. New York: Oxford University Press, 2013.

Klosty, James (Ed.). *Merce Cunningham*. New York: Saturday Review Press, E.P. Dutton & Co., 1975.

Knowles, Mark. *Man who Made the Jailhouse Rock: Alex Romero, Hollywood Choreographer*. Jefferson, NC: McFarland & Company, 2013.

Koner, Pauline. *Solitary Song: An Autobiography*. Durham, NC: Duke University Press, 1989.

Kostelanetz, Richard (Ed.). *Merce Cunningham: Dancing in Space and Time*. Pennington, NJ: a capella books, 1992.

Lambert-Beatty, Carrie. *Being Watched: Yvonne Rainer and the 1960s*. Cambridge, MA: MIT Press, 2008.

Leatherman, Leroy. *Martha Graham: Portrait of the Lady as an Artist*. New York: Alfred A. Knopf, 1966.

Livingston, Lili Cockerille. *American Indian Ballerinas*. Norman: University of Oklahoma Press, 1997.

MacDougall, Allan Ross. *Isadora: A Revolutionary in Art and Love*. New York: Thomas Nelson & Sons, 1960.

Magriel, Paul David. *Isadora Duncan*. New York: Henry Holt & Co., 1947.

Maynard, Olga. *Judith Jamison: Aspects of a Dancer*. New York: Doubleday & Co., 1982.

McDonagh, Don. *Martha Graham*. New York: Praeger Publishers, 1974.

Meade, Fionn (Ed.). *Merce Cunningham: Co:mm:on Ti:me* New York: Artbook D.A.P, 2017.

Morse, Meredith. *Soft is Fast: Simone Forti in the 1960s and After*. Cambridge, MA: MIT Press, 2016.

Newhall, Mary Anne Santos. *Mary Wigman*. New York: Routledge, 2018.

Nijinsky, Vaslav. *The Diary of Vaslav Nijinsky*. Joan Acocella (Ed.). New York: Farrar, Straus, Giroux, 1999.

O'Conner, Barbara. *Barefoot Dancer: The Story of Isadora Duncan*. Minneapolis: Lerner Publishing Group, 2003.

Panov, Valery. *To Dance*. With George Feifer. New York: Avon Books, 1978.

Percival, John. *The World of Diaghilev*. Revised ed. New York: Harmony Books, 1979.

Perlmutter, Donna. *Shadowplay: The Life of Anthony Tudor*. New York: Viking Press, 1991.

Rose, Phyllis. *Jazz Cleopatra: Josephine Baker in Her Time*. New York: Doubleday, 1991.

Rainer, Yvonne. *Feelings are Facts: A Life*. Cambridge, MA: MIT Press, 2006.

Riley, Kathleen. *Astaires: Fred & Adele*. New York: Oxford University Press, 2012.

Rosenberg, Susan. *Trisha Brown: Choreography as Visual Art*. Middletown, CT: Wesleyan University Press, 2017.

Ross, Janice. *Anna Halprin: Experience as Dance*. Berkeley: University of California Press, 2009.

Scheijen, Sjeng. *Diaghilev: A Life*. Translated by Jane Hedley-Prole. New York: Oxford University Press, 2010.

Schneider, Ilya Ilyich. *Isadora Duncan: The Russian Years*. Translated by David Magershack. London: MacDonald, 1968.

Schwartz, Peggy. *Dance Claimed Me: A Biography of Pearl Primus*. New Haven: Yale University Press, 2011.

Seed, Patricia. *José Limón and la Malinche: The Dancer and the Dance*. Austin, TX: University of Texas Press, 2008.

Seroff, Victor. *The Real Isadora*. London: Hutchinson, 1972.

Servos, Norbert. *Pina Bausch Wuppertal Dance Theatre: Or the Art of Training a Goldfish—Excursions Into Dance*. Cologne: Ballett-Bühnen Verlag, 1984.

Shawn, Ted. *One Thousand and One Night Stands*. With Gray Poole. New York: Doubleday, 1960.

——————— . *Ruth St. Denis*. CA: J. H. Nash, 1920.

Sherman, Jane, and Barton Mumaw. *Barton Mumaw, Dancer: From Denishawn to Jacob's Pillow and Beyond*. Hanover, NH: Wesleyan University Press, 2000.

Siegel, Marcia B. *Howling Near Heaven: Twyla Tharp and the Reinvention of Modern Dance*. New York: St. Martin's Press, 2006.

Soares, Janet Mansfield. *Louis Horst: Musician in a Dancer's World*. Durham, NC: Duke University Press, 1992.

Sokolova, Lydia. *Dancing for Diaghilev: The Memoirs of Lydia Sokolova*. Richard Buckle (Ed.). San Francisco: Mercury House, 1989.

Sorell, Walter. *Hayna Holm: Biography of an Artist*. Middletown, CT: Wesleyan University Press, 1969.

Soto, Jock. *Every Step You Take: A Memoir.* New York: Harpercollins, 2011.

Spivak, Jeffrey. *Buzz: The Life and Art of Busby Berkeley.* Lexington: University Press of Kentucky, 2011.

St. Denis, Ruth. *An Unfinished Life.* New York: Harper and Brothers, 1939. Reprint: New York: Dance Horizons, 1969.

Steegmuller, Francis (Ed.). *Your Isadora: The Love Story of Isadora Duncan and Gordon Craig.* New York: Random House and the New York Public Library, 1974.

Stodelle, Ernestine. *Deep Song: The Dance Story of Martha Graham.* New York: Schirmer Books, 1984.

Strom, Robert. *Lady of Burlesque: The Career of Gypsy Rose Lee.* Jefferson, NC: McFarland & Company, 2011.

Sutton, Tina. *Making of Markova: Diaghilev's Baby Ballerina to Groundbreaking Icon.* New York: Pegasus Books, 2014.

Taper, Bernard. *Balanchine: A Biography.* New York: Times Books, 1982. Reprint: Berkeley: University of California Press, 1987.

Tchernichova, Elena. *Dancing on Water: A Life in Ballet, from the Kirov to the ABT.* Evanston, IL: Northeastern University Press, 2013.

Teachout, Terry. *All in the Dances: A Brief Life of George Balanchine.* New York: Harcourt Trade, 2004.

Terry, Walter. *Frontiers of Life: The Life of Martha Graham.* New York: Thomas Y. Crowell Co., 1975.

——————————. *Isadora Duncan: Her Life, Her Art, Her Legacy.* New York: Dodd, Mead & Co., 1963.

——————————. *Miss Ruth: The More Living Life of Ruth St. Denis.* New York: Dodd, Mead & Co., 1969.

——————————. *Ted Shawn, Father of American Dance.* New York: Dial Press, 1977.

Tharp, Twyla. *Push Comes to Shove: An Autobiography.* New York: Bantam Books, 1992.

Thoms, Victoria. *Martha Graham: Gender and the Haunting of a Dance Pioneer.* Wilmington, NC: Intellect Books, 2013.

Vaill, Amanda. *Somewhere: The Life of Jerome Robbins.* New York: Broadway Books, 2008.

Vaughan, David. *Frederick Ashton.* New York: Alfred A. Knopf, 1977.

——————————. *Merce Cunningham: Fifty Years.* New York: Aperature, 1997.

Vaughan, David (Ed.). *Merce Cunningham: Creative Elements.* New York: Routledge, 2016.

Warren, Larry. *Anna Sokolow: The Rebellious Spirit.* Princeton, NJ: Dance Horizons/Princeton Book Co., 1990.

——————————. *Lester Horton: Modern Dance Pioneer.* New York: Marcel Dekker Press, 1977.

Wasson, Sam. *Fosse.* New York: Houghton Mifflin Harcourt, 2013.

Wigman, Mary. *The Mary Wigman Book.* Edited and translated by Walter Sorell. Middletown, CT: Wesleyan University Press, 1975.

Yudkoff, Alvin. *Gene Kelly: A Life of Dance and Dreams.* New York: Watson-Guptil Publications, 2000.

Choreography

Albright, Ann Cooper. *Choreographing Difference: The Body and Identity in Contemporary Dance.* Hanover, NH: University Press of New England, 1997.

Bartel, Maya. *The 1960s Body Through Sculptural Movement and Static Dance—the Works of George Segal, Allan Kaprow, and Yvonne Rainer.* Internet: VDM Verlag Dr. Mueller e.K, 2008.

Blom, Lynne Anne, and Tarin L. Chaplin. *The Intimate Act of Choreography.* Pittsburgh: University of Pittsburgh Press, 1982.

Butterworth, Jo, and Liesbeth Wildschut. *Contemporary Choreography: A Critical Reader.* New York: Routledge, 2009.

Cass, Joan. *The Dance: A Handbook for the Appreciation of the Choreographic Experience.* Jefferson, NC: McFarland & Company, 1999.

Cunningham, Merce. *Changes: Notes on Choreography.* New York: Something Else Press, 1968.

Defrantz, Thomas F. (Ed.). *Choreography and Corporeality: Relay in Motion.* London: Palgrave Macmillan, 2016.

Duerden, Rachel, and Neil Fisher (Eds.). *Dancing Off the Page: Integrating Performance, Choreography, Analysis and Notation/Documentation.* Pennington, NJ: Princeton Book Company, 2007.

Eichenbaum, Rose. *Masters of Movement: Portraits of America's Great Choreographers.* New York: W.W. Norton & Company, 2004.

Ellfeldt, Lois. *A Primer for Choreographers.* Mountain View, CA: Mayfield Publishing Co., 1967.

Fisher, Jennifer, and Anthony Shay. *When Men Dance: Choreographing Masculinities Across Borders*. New York: Oxford University Press, Incorporated, 2009.

Foster, Susan Leigh. *Choreographing Empathy: Kinesthesia in Performance*. New York: Routledge, 2011.

Gere, David. *How to Make Dances in an Epidemic: Tracking Choreography in the Age of AIDS*. Madison: University of Wisconsin Press, 2004.

Gotman, Kelina. *Choreomania: Dance and Disorder*. New York: Oxford University Press, 2018.

Grody, Svetlana McLee, and Dorothy Daniels Lister (Eds.). *Conversations with Choreographers*. Portsmouth, NH: Heinemann, 1996.

Hawkins, Alma. *Creating Through Dance*. Upper Saddle River, NJ: Prentice-Hall, 1966. Revised. Princeton, NJ: Princeton Book Co., 1988.

_____. *Moving from Within: A New Method for Dance Making*. Pennington, NJ: a capella books, 1991.

Hodes, Stuart. *A Map of Making Dances*. New York: Ardsley House Publishers, 1998.

Humphrey, Doris. *The Art of Making Dances*. Barbara Pollack (Ed.). New York: Rinehart & Co., 1959. Reprint: Princeton, NJ: Princeton Book Co., 1990.

Joy, Jenn. *Choreographic*. Cambridge, MA: MIT Press, 2014.

Kloetzel, Melanie, and Carolyn Pavlik. *Site Dance: Choreographers and the Lure of Alternative Spaces*. Gainesville: University Press of Florida, 2009.

Lansdale, Janet. *Decentring Dancing Texts: The Challenge of Interpreting Dances*. New York: Pelgrave Macmillan, 2008.

Lavendar, Larry. *Dancers Talking Dance: Critical Evaluation in the Choreography Class*. Champaign, IL: Human Kinetics, 1996.

Lerman, Liz. *Hiking the Horizontal: Field Notes from A Choreographer*. Middletown, CT: Wesleyan University Press, 2011.

McGreevy-Nichols, Susan, and Helene Scheff. *Building Dances: A Guide to Putting Movements Together*. Champaign, IL: Human Kinetics, 1995.

Minton, Sandra. *Choreography: A Basic Approach Using Improvisation*. Champaign, IL: Human Kinetics, 2007.

Morris, Gay (Ed.). *Choreographies of 21st Century Wars*. New York: Oxford University Press, 2016.

Pomer, Janice. *Dance Composition: An Interrelated Arts Approach*. Champaign, IL: Human Kinetics, 2008.

Popat, Sita. *Invisible Connections: Dance, Choreography and Internet Connections*. London: Routledge, 2006.

Portanova, Stamatia. *Moving Without a Body: Digital Philosophy and Choreographic Thoughts*. Cambridge, MA: MIT Press, 2013.

Reynolds, Dee. *Rhythmic Subjects: Uses of Energy in the Dances of Mary Wigman, Martha Graham, and Merce Cunningham*. Pennington, NJ: Princeton Book Company, 2007.

Rosenthal, Stephanie. *Move: Choreographing You: Art and Dance Since the 1960s*. Cambridge, MA: MIT Press, 2012.

Schrader, Constance A. *A Sense of Dance: Exploring Your Movement Potential*. Champaign, IL: Human Kinetics, 1996.

Smith, Jacqueline M. *Dance Composition: A Practical Guide for Teachers*. Pennington, NJ: Princeton Book Co., 1976.

Turner, Margaret J. *New Dance: Approaches to Nonliteral Choreography*. With Ruth Grauert and Arlene Zallman. Pittsburgh: University of Pittsburgh Press, 1971.

Wong, Yutian. *Choreographing Asian America*. Middletown, CT: Wesleyan University Press, 2010.

Dance Education/Dance Pedagogy

Amans, Diane (Ed.). *Introduction to Community Dance Practice*. (second ed.) London: Palgrave Macmillan, 2017.

Ashley, Linda. *Dancing with Difference: Culturally Diverse Dances in Education*. Rotterdam: Sense, 2012.

Ashley, Linda. *Intersecting Cultures in Music and Dance Education: An Oceanic Perspective*. New York: Springer, 2016.

Bales, Melanie, and Rebecca Nettl-Fiol. *The Body Eclectic: Evolving Practices in Dance Training*. Champaign, IL: University of Illinois Press, 2008.

Barringer, Janice. *Pointe Book: Shoes, Training and Technique*. (second ed.) Pennington: Princeton Book Company, 2004.

Benzwie, T. *More Moving Experiences: Connecting Arts, Feelings and Imagination (Grades K–12)*. Tucson, AZ: Zephyr Press, 1996.

Brehm, Mary Ann, and Lynne McNett. *Making Kinesthetic Sense: Creative Dance as a Tool for Learning*. New York: McGraw-Hill Higher Education, 2007.

Brodie, Julie A. *Dance and Somatics: Mind-Body Principles of Teaching and Performance*. Jefferson, NC: McFarland & Company, 2012.

Camilleri, Vanessa A. *Healing the Inner-City Child Creative Arts–Therapies with at-Risk Youth*. Philadelphia: Jessica Kingsley Limited, 2007.

Carline, Sally. *Lesson Plans for Creative Dance: Connecting with Literature, Arts, and Music*. Champaign, IL: Human Kinetics, 2011.

Cone, Theresa Purcell. *Teaching Children Dance*. Champaign, IL: Human Kinetics, 2012.

Dow, Connie Bergstein. *Dance, Turn, Hop, Learn!: Enriching Movement Activities for Preschoolers*. St. Paul, MN: Redleaf Press, 2006.

Dunkin, Anne. *Dancing in Your School: A Guide for Preschool and Elementary School Teachers*. Pennington, NJ: Princeton Book Company, 2006.

Ellison, Nancy. *Ballet Book: Learning and Appreciating the Secrets of Dance*. New York: Universe, 2003.

Erkert, Jan. *Harnessing the Wind: The Art of Teaching Modern Dance*. Champaign, IL: Human Kinetics, 2003.

Franklin, Eric N. *Dynamic Alignment Through Imagery*. Champaign, IL: Human Kinetics, 2012.

Forbes, Harriet. *Creative Movement for 3–5 Year Olds*. Clinton Township: First Steps Press, 2003.

Fraser, Diane. *Play Dancing: Discovering and Developing Creativity in Young Children*. Chicago: Independent Publishers Group, 2003.

Gilbert, Anne Green. *Brain-Compatible Dance Education*. Reston, VA: AAPHERD, 2006.

——————. *Creative Dance for all Ages: A Conceptual Approach*. Reston: AAPHERD, 2003.

Gray, Judith A. *Dance Instruction: Science Applied to the Art of Movement*. Champaign, IL: Human Kinetics, 1989.

Hagood, Thomas K. *A History of Dance in American Higher Education*. Lewiston, NY: The Edwin Mellen Press, 2000.

——————. *Legacy in Dance Education: Essays and Interviews on Values, Practices, and People: An Anthology*. Amherst, NY: Cambria Press, 2008.

Hammond, Sandra Noll. *Ballet Basics*. New York: McGraw-Hill, 2004.

Hanna, Judith Lynne. *Partnering Dance and Education: Intelligent Moves for Changing Times*. Champaign, IL: Human Kinetics, 1999.

Hawkins, Alma. *Creating Through Dance*. Pennington, NJ: Dance Horizons, 1988.

H'Doubler, Margaret N. *Dance: A Creative Art Experience*. (second ed.) Madison: University of Wisconsin Press, 1957.

——————. *The Dance*. New York: Harcourt, Brace and Co., 1925.

——————. *The Dance and Its Place in Education*. New York: Harcourt, Brace and Co., 1925.

Joyce, Mary. *First Steps in Teaching Creative Dance to Children*. (second ed.) Mountain View, CA: Mayfield Publishing Company, 1980.

Kassing, Gayle. *Dance Teaching Methods and Curriculum Design*. Champaign, IL: Human Kinetics, 2003.

Kimmerle, Marliese. *Teaching Dance Skills: A Motor Learning and Development Approach*. Andover: Michael J. Ryan Publishing, 2003.

Kramer, Susan. *Rhythms and Dances for Toddlers and Preschoolers*. Internet: Lulu.com, 2007.

Li, Zihao. *Dancing Boys: High School Males in Dance*. Canada: University of Toronto Press, 2016.

Louis, Murray. *The Nikolais/Louis Dance Technique*. New York: Routledge, 2004.

McCutchen, Brenda Pugh. *Teaching Dance as Art in Education*. Champaign, IL: Human Kinetics, 2006.

McPherson, Elizabeth, and Joseph W. Polisi. *The Contributions of Martha Hill to American Dance and Dance Education, 1900–1995*. Lewiston, NY: The Edwin Mellen Press, 2008.

Minton, Sandra. *Using Movement to Teach Academics: The Mind and Body as One Entity*. Lanham, MD: Rowman and Littlefield Education, 2008.

Preston-Dunlop, Valerie. *Modern Educational Dance*. Boston: Plays, Inc., 1990.

Purcell, Theresa M. *Teaching Children Dance: Becoming a Master Teacher*. Champaign, IL: Human Kinetics, 1994.

Sansom, Adrienne N. *Movement and Dance in Young Children's Lives: Crossing the Divide*. New York: Peter Lang, 2011.

Shapiro, Sherry B. (Ed.). *Dance, Power, and Difference: Critical and Feminist Perspectives on Dance Education.* Champaign, IL: Human Kinetics, 1998.

Sofras, Pamela Anderson. *Dance Composition Basics.* Champaign, IL: Human Kinetics, 2006.

Speer, Dean. *On Technique.* Gainesville: University Press of Florida, 2010.

Sprague, Marty, Helen Scheff, and Susan McGreevy-Nichols. *Dance About Anything.* Champaign, IL: Human Kinetics, 2006.

Stinson, Susan W. *Embodied Curriculum Theory and Research in Arts Education: A Dance Scholar's Search for Meaning.* New York: Springer, 2016.

Williams, Drid. *Teaching Dancing with Ideokinetic Principles.* Champaign, IL: University of Illinois Press, 2011.

Zeller, Jessica. *Shapes of American Ballet: Teachers and Training Before Balanchine.* New York: Oxford University Press, 2016.

Dance in World Cultures

Allenby Jaffé, Nigel. *Folk Dance of Europe.* North Yorkshire, England: Folk Dance Enterprises, 1990.

Ambrose, Kay. *Classical Dances and Costumes of India.* London: A&C Black, 1950.

Anoop, Maratt Mythili (Ed.). *Scripting Dance in Contemporary India.* New York: Lexington Books, 2016.

Axtmann, Ann. *Indians and Wannabes: Native American Powwow Dancing in the Northeast and Beyond.* Gainesville: University Press of Florida, 2013.

Beamann, Patricia Leigh. *World Dance Cultures: From Ritual to Spectacle.* New York: Routledge, 2018.

Boas, Franziska (Ed.). *The Function of Dance in Human Society.* Revised. New York: Dance Horizons, 1973.

Bowers, Faubian. *The Dances of India.* New York: Columbia University Press, 1953.

_____. *Theatre in the East: A Survey of Asian Dance and Drama.* New York: Grove Press, Inc., 1956.

Brandon, James R. *The Cambridge Guide to Asian Theatre.* Cambridge, England: Cambridge University Press, 1993.

_____, William P. Malm, and Donald H. Shively. *Studies in Kabuki: Its Acting, Music, and Historical Context.* Honolulu: East-West Center, 1978.

Buonaventura, Wendy. *Serpent of the Nile: Women and Dance in the Arab World.* Northampton, MA: Interlink Publishing Group, Incorporated, 2009.

Byrom, Franklin. *The Complete Folkdance Notebook.* Bloomington, IN: Xlibris Corporation, 2009.

Campbell, Joseph. *The Masks of God: Primitive Mythology.* New York: Viking Press, 1959.

Casey, Betty. *International Folk Dancing.* New York: Doubleday and Co., 1981.

Castaldi, Francesca. *Choreographies of African Identities: Negritude, Dance and the National Ballet of Senegal.* Urbana, IL: University of Illinios Press, 2006.

Chakravorty, Pallabi. *Dance Matters: Performing India.* New York: Routledge, 2010.

Changnon, Napoleon. *Yanomamo: The Fierce People.* (third ed.) New York: CBS Publishing, 1983.

Charsley, Simon R., and Laxmi Narayan Kadekar (Eds.). *Performers and Their Arts in India.* New York: Routledge, 2007.

Chasteen, John Charles. *National Rhythms, African Roots: The Deep History of Latin American Popular Dance.* Albuquerque: University of New Mexico Press, 2004.

Coast, John. *Dancing Out of Bali.* Berkeley: Periplus Editions, 2004.

Condit, Jonathan. *Music of the Korean Renaissance: Songs and Dances of the Fifteenth Century.* New York: Cambridge University Press, 2009.

Dagan, Esther A. (Ed.). *The Spirit's Dance in Africa: Evolution, Transformation, and Continuity in Sub-Sahara.* Canada: Galerie Amrad African Arts Publications, 1997.

Daniel, Yvonne. *Caribbean and Atlantic Diaspora Dance: Igniting Citizenship.* Champaign, IL: University of Illinois Press, 2011.

Davida, Dena (Ed.). *Fields in Motion: Ethnography in the Worlds of Dance.* Waterloo, ON: Wilfrid Laurier University Press, 2011.

Davis, Kathy. *Dancing Tango: Passionate Encounters in A Globalizing World.* New York: New York University Press, 2015.

Delamont, Sara. *Embodying Brazil: An Ethnography of Diasporic Capoeira*. New York: Routledge, 2017.

Delgado, Celest Frases (Ed.). *Everynight Life: Culture and Dance in Latin America*. Durham, NC: Duke University Press, 1997.

Denniston, Christine. *The Meaning of Tango: The History and Steps of the Argentinean Dance*. London: Anova Books, 2008.

Descutner, Janet. *Asian Dance*. Langhorne, PA: Chelsea House Publishers, 2004.

Drake-Boyt, Elizabeth. *Latin Dance*. Portsmouth, NH: Greenwood, 2011.

Dunham, Katherine. *Journey to Accompong*. New York: Henry Holt, 1946.

Ellfeldt, Lois. *Folk Dance*. Dubuque, IA: Wm. Brown Publishers, 1969.

Ernst, Earle. *The Kabuki Theatre*. New York: Oxford University Press, 1956.

Essien, Aniefre. *Capoeira Beyond Brazil: From a Slave Tradition to an International Way of Life*. Berkeley: North Atlantic Books, 2008.

Foley, Catherine E. *Step Dancing in Ireland: Culture and History*. Burlington, VT: Ashgate, 2013.

Fraleigh, Sondra Horton. *Butoh Metamorphic Dance and Global Alchemy*. Champaign, IL: University of Illinois Press, 2010.

Fraser, Kathleen W. *Before They Were Belly Dancers: European Accounts of Female Entertainers in Egypt, 1760–1870*. Jefferson, NC: McFarland & Company, 2015.

Forrest, John. *The History of Morris Dancing, 1458–1750*. Studies in Early English Drama, 5. Toronto: University of Toronto Press, 1999.

Fraleigh, Sondra. *Dancing into Darkness: Butoh, Zen, and Japan*. Pittsburgh: University of Pittsburgh Press, 1999.

——————. *Hijikata Tatsumi and Ohno Kazuo*. London: Routledge, 2006.

Gibson, John G. *Gaelic Cape Breton Step-Dancing: An Historical and Ethnographic Perspective*. Kingston, Canada: Mcgill-Queens University Press, 2017.

Ginn, Victoria. *The Spirited Earth: Dance, Myth, and Ritual from South Asia to the South Pacific*. New York: Rizzoli, 1990.

Goldberg, Meira K. (Ed.). *Global Reach of the Fandango in Music, Song and Dance: Spaniards, Indians, Africans and Gypsies*. United Kingdom: Cambridge Scholars Publishing, 2016.

Gonzalez, Anita. *Jarocho's Soul: Cultural Identity and Afro-Mexican Dance*. Lanham, MD: University Press of America, 2004.

Gonzalez, Varela, and Sergio Armando. *Power in Practice: The Pragmatic Anthropology of Afro-Brazilian Capoeira*. New York: Berghahn Books, 2017.

Greene, Hank (Ed.). *Square and Folk Dancing: A Complete Guide for Students, Teachers, and Callers*. New York: Harper and Row, 1984.

Griffith, Lauren Miller. *In Search of Legitimacy: How Outsiders Become Part of an Afro-Brazilian Tradition*. New York: Berghahn Books, 2016.

Groppa, Carlos. *Tango in the United States: A History*. Jefferson, NC: McFarland & Company, 2009.

Hahn, Tomie. *Sensational Knowledge: Embodying Culture through Japanese Dance*. Lebanon, NH: University Press of New England, 2007.

Hobin, Tina. *Belly Dance: The Dance of Mother Earth*. London: Marion Boyars, 2003.

Hughes, Russell Meriwether ("La Meri"). *Dance as an Art Form*. New York: Barnes, 1933.

——————. *Hindu Dance*. New York: Benjamin Bolm, 1963.

——————. *Spanish Dancing*. (second ed.) Pittsfield, MA: Eagle Printing & Binding Co., 1968.

Imada, Adria L. *Aloha America: Hula Circuits Through the U.S. Empire*. Durham, NC: Duke University Press, 2012.

John, Suki. *Contemporary Dance in Cuba: Tecnica Cubana as Revolutionary Movement*. Jefferson, NC: McFarland & Company, 2012.

Kaschl, Elke. *Dance and Authenticity in Israel and Palestine: Performing the Nation*. Leiden: Brill, 2003.

Kothari, Sunil (Ed.). *New Directions in Indian Dance*. New York: Marg Publications, 2006.

Krystal, Matthew. *Indigenous Dance and Dancing Indian: Contested Representation in the Global Era*. Boulder: University Press of Colorado, 2011.

Liska, Maria Mercedes. *Argentine Queer Tango: Dance and Sexuality Politics in Buenos Aires*. Translated by Peggy Westwell. Lanham, MD: Lexington Books, 2017.

Looper, Matthew G. *To Be Like Gods: Dance in Ancient Maya Civilization*. Austin, TX: University of Texas Press, 2009.

Lyons, Renee Critcher. *Revival of Banned Dances: A Worldwide Study*. Jefferson, NC: McFarland & Company, 2012.

McDonald, Caitlin E. *Belly Dance Around the World: New Communities, Performance and Identity*. Jefferson, NC: McFarland & Company, 2013.

McGowan, Margaret M. *Dance in the Renaissance: European Fashion, French Obsession*. New York: Routledge, 2008.

McKee, Eric. *Decorum of the Minuet, Delirium of the Waltz: A Study of Dance-Music Relations in 3/4 Time*. Bloomington, IN: Indiana University Press, 2012.

McLean, Mervyn. *Weavers of Song: Polynesian Music and Dance*. Chicago: Independent Publishers Group, 2003.

Meftahi, Ida. *Gender and Dance in Modern Iran: Biopolitics on Stage*. New York: Routledge, 2016.

Morcom, Anna. *Illicit Worlds of Indian Dance: Cultures of Exclusion*. New York: Oxford University Press, 2013.

Munsi, Urmimala Sarkar (Ed.). *Traversing Tradition: Celebrating Dance in India*. New York: Routledge, 2011.

Nair, Sreenath (Ed.). *Natyasastra and the Body in Performance: Essays on Indian Theories of Dance and Drama*. Jefferson, NC: McFarland & Company, 2015.

Nakamura, Matazo. *Kabuki: Backstage, Onstage, An Actor's Life*. New York: Kodansha International/USA Ltd., 1988.

Neveu Kringelbach, Helene. *Dance Circles: Movement, Morality and Self-Fashioning in Urban Senegal*. New York: Berghahn Books, 2013.

Ohno, Kazuo. *Kazuo Ohno's World from Without and Within*; Trans. Middletown: Wesleyan University Press, 2004.

Ojrzynska, Katarzyna. *Dancing as if Language no Longer Existed: Dance in Contemporary Irish Drama*. New York: Peter Lang Ltd, 2014.

O'Shea, Janet. *At Home in the World: Bharata Natyam on the Global Stage*. Lebanon, NH: University Press of New England, 2007.

Pittman, Anne M. *Dance A While: Handbook for Folk, Square, Contra and Social Dance*. (ninth ed.) Redwood City: Benjamin-Cummings, 2005.

Ponchianinho, Mastre. *Essential Capoeira: The Guide to Mastering the Art*. Berkeley: North Atlantic Books, 2007.

Reed, Susan Anita. *Dance and the Nation: Performance, Ritual, and Politics in Sri Lanka*. Madison: University of Wisconsin Press, 2010.

Richards, Tazz (Ed.). *The Belly Dance Book: Rediscovering the Oldest Dance*. Concord, CA: Backbeat Press, 2000.

Rowe, Nicholas. *Raising Dust: A Cultural History of Dance in Palestine*. London: IB Tauris, 2010.

Sachs, Curt. *World History of the Dance*. New York: W.W. Norton & Co., 1937.

Seiden, Allan. *The Art of the Hula*. Waipahu, Hawaii: Island Heritage Publishing, 2008.

Sellers, Julie A. *Merengue and Dominican Identity: Music as National Unifier*. Jefferson, NC: McFarland & Company, 2004.

Sellers-Young, Barbara. *Belly Dance, Pilgrimage and Identity*. London: Palgrave Macmillan, 2016.

Sharif, Keti. *Bellydance: A Guide to Middle Eastern Dance, Its Music, Its Culture and Costume*. St. Leonard's: Allen and Unwin, 2004.

Shay, Anthony. *Choreographing Identities: Folk Dance, Ethnicity and Festival in the United States and Canada*. Jefferson, NC: McFarland & Company, 2006.

Shay, Anthony. *Ethno Identity Dance for Sex, Fun and Profit: Staging Popular Dances Around the World*. London: Palgrave Macmillan, 2016.

Shresthova, Sangita. *Is it all about Hips?: Around the World with Bollywood Dance*. Thousand Oaks, CA: Sage Publications, 2011.

Sikand, Nandini. *Languid Bodies, Grounded Stances: The Curving Pathway of Neoclassical Odissi Dance*. New York: Berghahn Books, 2017.

Sloat, Susanna (Ed.). *Making Caribbean Dance: Continuity and Creativity in Island Cultures*. Gainesville: University Press of Florida, 2010.

Snodgrass, Mary Ellen. *Encyclopedia of World Folk Dance*. Lanham, MD: Rowman & Littlefield, 2016.

Solway, Andrew. *African and Asian Dance*. Chicago: Heinemann-Raintree, 2008.

_____. *Country and Folk Dance*. Chicago: Heinemann-Raintree, 2008.

Stillman, Amy K. *Sacred Hula: The Historical Hula 'Ala' apapa*. Honolulu: Bishop Museum Press, 1998.

Talmon-Chvaicer, Maya. *The Hidden History of Capoeira: A Collision of Cultures in the Brazilian Battle Dance*. Austin, TX: University of Texas Press, 2007.

Taylor, Gerard. *Capoeira 100: An Illustrated Guide to the Essential Movements and Techniques*. Berkeley: North Atlantic Books, 2006.

Thobani, Sitara. *Indian Classical Dance and the Making of Postcolonial National Identities: Dancing on Empire's Stage*. New York: Routledge, 2017.

Vaughan, Umi. *Rebel Dance, Renegade Stance: Timba Music and Black Identity in Cuba*. Ann Arbor: University of Michigan Press, 2012.

Walkowitz, Daniel J. *City Folk: English Country Dance and the Politics of the Folk in Modern America*. New York: New York University Press, 2010.

Waring, Rob. *Capoeira: The Fighting Dance*. Boston: Cengage Heinle, 2008.

——————. *The Story of the Hula*. Boston: Cengage Heinle, 2008.

Welsh-Asante, Kariamu. *The African Aesthetic: Keeper of the Tradition*. Westport, CT: Greenwood Press, 1993.

——————. *African Dance*. Langhorne, PA: Chelsea House Publishers, 2004.

——————. *Umfundalai: An African Dance Technique*. Lawrenceville, NJ: African World Press, 1995.

——————. *Zimbabwe Dance: Rhythmic Forces, Ancestral Voices—An Aesthetic Analysis*. Trenton, NJ: Africa World Press, 2000.

Yarber, Angela. *Embodying the Feminine in the Dances of the World's Religions*. New York: Peter Lang, 2011.

Zubko, Katherine C. *Dancing Bodies of Devotion: Fluid Gestures in Bharata Natyam*. Lanham, MD: Lexington Books, 2014.

Jazz Dance, Musical Theatre, and Tap Dance

Berkson, Robert. *Musical Theatre Choreography*. New York: Watson Gupstill Publishers, 1990.

Briggeman, Jane. *Burlesque: Legendary Stars of the Stage*. Berkeley: Ten Speed Press, 2004.

Bufalino, Brenda. *Tapping the Source: Tap Dance Stories, Theory and Practice*. Great Barrington, MA: SteinerBooks, 2004.

Cohen-Solal, Annie. *New York Mid-Century: 1945–1965; Art, Architecture, Design, Dance, Theater, Nightlife*. New York: Vendome, 2014.

Decker, Todd R. *Music Makes Me: Fred Astaire and Jazz*. Oakland: University of California Press, 2011.

DiMeglio, John E. *Vaudeville U.S.A.* Bowling Green, OH: Bowling Green University Popular Press, 1973.

Emery, Lynne Fauley. *Black Dance from 1619 to Today*. (second ed.) Princeton, NJ: Princeton Book Company, 1988.

Gallafent, Edward. *Astaire and Rogers*. New York: Columbia University Press, 2004.

Gardner, Kara Anne. *Agnes de Mille: Telling Stories in Broadway Dance*. New York: Oxford University Press, 2016.

Garofoli, Wendy, and Jon Lehrer. *Jazz Dance*. Mankato, MN: Capstone Press, Incorporated, 2008.

Glover, Savion, and Bruce Weber. *Savion! My Life in Tap*. New York: William Morrow, 2000.

Haskins, James. *Black Dance in America*. New York: HarperCollins Publishers, 1990.

——————. *Break Dancing*. Minneapolis: Lerner Publications Co., 1985.

——————. *The Cotton Club*. New York: New American Library, 1984.

Hill, Constance Valis. *Tap Dancing America: A Cultural History*. New York: Oxford University Press, 2010.

Kislan, Richard. *Hoofing on Broadway*. New York: Prentice Hall Press, 1987.

Knowles, Mark. *Tap Dance Dictionary*. Jefferson, NC: McFarland & Company, 2012.

——————. *The Early History of Tap Dancing*. Jefferson, NC: McFarland & Company, 2007.

Kraines, Minda Goodman, and Esther Kan. *Jump Into Jazz*. Mountain View, CA: Mayfield Publishing Co., 1983. Reprint, 1990.

La Pointe-Crump, Janice, and Kimberly Staley. *Discovering Jazz Dance: America's Energy and Soul*. Dubuque, IA: Brown and Brechmark, 1992.

Leczkowski, Jennifer. *The Art of Tap Dancing*. Philadelphia: Running Press Book Publishers, 2006.

Long, Robert Emmet. *Broadway, The Golden Years: Jerome Robbins and the Great Choreographer-Directors 1940 to the Present.* New York: Continuum International Publishing Group, 2003.

McWaters, Debra. *The Fosse Style.* Gainesville: University Press of Florida, 2008.

Rees, Heather. *Tap Dancing: Rhythm in Their Feet.* Marlborough: Crowood Press, 2003.

Sampson, Henry T. *Blacks in Blackface: A Source Book on Early Black Musical Shows.* Metuchen, NJ: Scarecrow Press, 1980.

Smith, Bill. *The Vaudevillians.* New York: Macmillan, 1976.

Sobel, Bernard. *Pictorial History of Vaudeville.* New York: Citadel Press, 1961.

Stearns, Jean, and Marshall Stearns. *Jazz Dance.* New York: Da Capo Press, 1994.

Sunderland, Margot, and Kenneth Pickering. *Choreographing the Stage Musical.* Studio City, CA: Players Press, 2009.

Symonds, Dominic (Ed.). *Gestures of Music Theatre: The Performativity of Song and Dance.* New York: Oxford University Press, 2014.

Van Gyn, Geraldine, and Donne Van Sant O'Neill. *Jazz Dance.* Champaign, IL: Human Kinetics Publishers, 1987.

Modern and Contemporary Dance: History and Criticism

Albright, Ann Cooper (Ed.). *Taken By Surprise: A Dance Improvisation Reader.* Hanover: Wesleyan University Press, 2003.

Adair, Christy. *British Dance: Black Routes.* New York: Routledge, 2017.

Anderson, Jack. *The American Dance Festival.* Durham, NC: Duke University Press, 1987.

—————. *Art Without Boundaries: The World of Modern Dance.* Iowa City: University of Iowa Press, 1997.

—————. *Ballet and Modern Dance: A Concise History.* Princeton, NJ: Princeton Book Co., 1986.

—————. *Dance.* New York: Newsweek Books, 1974.

Anderson, Janet. *Modern Dance.* Langhorne, PA: Chelsea House Publishers, 2004.

Armitage, Merle. *Dance Memoranda.* Edwin Corle (Ed.). New York: Duell, Sloan and Pearce, 1949.

Au, Susan. *Ballet and Modern Dance.* New York: Thames and Hudson, 2012.

Banes, Sally. *Democracy's Body: Judson Dance Theatre 1962–1964.* Durham, NC: Duke University Press, 1993.

Basualdo, Carlos. *Dancing Around the Bride: Cage, Cunningham, Johns, Rauschenberg, and Duchamp.* New Haven: Yale University Press, 2012.

—————. *Reinventing Dance in the 1960s: Everything Was Possible.* Madison: University of Wisconsin Press, 2003.

—————. *Terpsichore in Sneakers.* Revised. Middletown, CT: Wesleyan University Press, 1987.

Battock, Gregory (Ed.). *The New Art: A Critical Anthology.* New York: E.P. Dutton & Co., 1966.

Bennahum, Ninotchka (Ed.). *Radical Bodies: Anna Halprin, Simone Forti, and Yvonne Rainer in California and New York, 1955–1972.* Berkeley, CA: University of California Press, 2017.

Brooks, Lynn M. *Women's Work: Making Dance in Europe Before 1800.* Madison: University of Wisconsin Press, 2008.

Brown, Jean Morrison (Ed.). *The Vision of Modern Dance.* Princeton, NJ: Princeton Book Co., 1979.

—————, Naomi Mindlin, and Charles H. Woodford (Eds.). *The Vision of Modern Dance in the World of Its Creators.* Hightstown, NJ: Princeton Book Company, 1998.

Burt, Ramsay. *The Judson Dance Theatre: Performative Traces.* New York: Routledge, 2006.

Burt, Ramsay. *Ungoverning Dance: Contemporary European Theatre Dance and the Commons.* New York: Oxford University Press, 2017.

Cass, Joan. *Dancing Through History.* Englewood Cliffs, NJ: Prentice Hall, 1993.

Chujoy, Anatole, and P.W. Manchester. *The Dance Encyclopedia.* New York: Simon & Schuster, 1967.

Cohen, Selma Jeanne (Ed.). *Dance as a Theatre Art.* (second ed.) Princeton, NJ: Princeton Book Co., 1992.

—————. *Modern Dance: Seven Statements of Belief.* Middletown, CT: Wesleyan University Press, 1966.

—————. *Next Week, Swan Lake.* Middletown, CT: Wesleyan University Press, 1982.

Cohen, Marshall, and Roger Copeland (Eds.). *What Is Dance?* New York: Oxford University Press, 1983.

Conner, Lynne. *Spreading the Gospel of Modern Dance: Newspaper Dance Criticism in the United States, 1850–1934.* Pittsburgh: University of Pittsburgh Press, 1997.

Copeland, Roger. *Merce Cunningham and the Modernizing of Modern Dance*. New York: Routledge, 2004.

Croce, Arlene. *Afterimages*. New York: Alfred A. Knopf, 1978.

Davies, Jenefer. *Aerial Dance: A Guide to Dance with Rope and Harness*. New York: Routledge, 2018.

Defrantz, Thomas. *Dancing Revelations: Alvin Ailey's Embodiment of African American Culture*. New York: Oxford University Press, 2004.

de Mille, Agnes. *America Dances*. New York: Macmillan, 1980.

——————. *The Book of Dance*. New York: The Golden Press, 1963.

Denby, Edwin. *Dancers, Buildings and People in the Streets*. New York: Horizon Press, 1965.

——————. *Dance Writings*. Gainesville: University Press of Florida, 2007.

——————. *Looking at the Dance*. New York: Horizon Press, 1968.

Dickinson, Edward Ross. *Dancing in the Blood: Modern Dance and European Culture on the Eve of the First World War*. United Kingdom: Cambridge University Press, 2017.

Drake-Boyt, Elizabeth. *Dance as a Project of the Early Modern Avantgarde*. Internet: VDM Verlag Dr. Mueller e.K, 2008.

Duncan, Irma. *The Technique of Isadora Duncan*. New York: Kamin Publishers, 1937. Reprint: New York: Dance Horizons, 1970.

Duncan, Isadora. *The Art of the Dance*. New York: Theatre Arts Books, 1970.

Ekstein, Modris. *Rites of Spring*. Boston: Houghton Mifflin, 1989.

Ellfeldt, Lois. *Dance: From Magic to Art*. Dubuque, IA: Wm. Brown Publishers, 1976.

Ellis, Havelock. *Dance of Life*. Boston: Houghton Mifflin, 1923.

Emery, Lynne Fauley. *Black Dance from 1619 to Today*. (second ed.) Princeton NJ: Princeton Book Co., 1988.

Forti, Simone. *Handbook in Motion*. Halifax, Canada: The Press of the Nova Scotia College of Art and Design, 1973.

George-Graves, Nadine. *Urban Bush Women: Twenty Years of African American Dance Theater, Community Engagement, and Working it Out*. Madison: University of Wisconsin Press, 2010.

Gitelman, Claudia (Ed.). *On Stage Alone: Soloists and the Modern Dance Canon*. Gainesville: University Press of Florida, 2014.

Glass, Barbara S. *African American Dance, An Illustrated History*. Jefferson, NC: McFarland & Company, 2007.

Greenfield, Lois. *Airborn: The New Dance Photography of Lois Greenfield*. San Francisco: Chronicle Books, 1998.

Hawkins, Erick. *The Body Is a Clear Place and Other Statements on Dance*. Princeton, NJ: Princeton Book Co., 1992.

Hay, Deborah. *Using the Sky: A Dance*. New York: Routledge, 2016.

H'Doubler, Margaret. *Dance: A Creative Art Experience*. Reprint: Madison: University of Wisconsin Press, 1957.

Hering, Doris. *Twenty-Five Years of American Dance*. Revised. New York: Rudolf Orthwine, 1954.

Hodgson, Moira. *Quintet: Five American Dance Companies*. Photographs by Thomas Victor. New York: William Morrow, 1976.

Horst, Louis, and Carroll Russell. *Modern Dance Forms*. San Francisco: Impulse Publications, 1961. Reprint: Princeton, NJ: Princeton Book Co., 1987.

——————. *Pre-Classic Dance Forms*. New York: The Dance Observer, 1937. Reprint: Princeton, NJ: Princeton Book Co., 1987.

Jackson, Naomi. *Converging Movements: Modern Dance and Jewish Culture at the 92nd Street Y*. Hanover, NH: University Press of New England, 2000.

Johnston, Jill. *Marmalade Me*. New York: E.P. Dutton & Co., 1971.

Jowitt, Deborah. *Dance Beat: Selected Views and Reviews, 1967–76*. New York: Marcel Dekker, 1977.

——————. *Time and the Dancing Image*. New York: William Morrow, 1988.

Katan, Einav. *Embodied Philosophy in Dance: Gaga and Ohad Naharin's Movement Research*. London: Palgrave Macmillan, 2016.

Kosstrin, Hannah. *Honest Bodies: Revolutionary Modernism in the Dances of Anna Sokolow*. New York: Oxford University Press, 2017.

Kowal, Rebekah J. *How to do Things with Dance: Performing Change in Postwar America*. Middletown, CT: Wesleyan University Press, 2010.

Kraus, Richard. *History of the Dance*. Englewood Cliffs, NJ: Prentice-Hall, 1969.

Kreemer, Connie. *Further Steps: Fifteen Choreographers on Modern Dance*. New York: Harper & Row, 1987.

Laban, Rudolf von. *Choreutics*. Lisa Ullman (Ed.). London: MacDonald & Evans, 1966.

_____. *A Life for Dance*. New York: Theatre Arts Books, 1975.

_____. *The Mastery of Movement*. (fifth ed.) Plymouth, U.K.: Northcote House, 1989.

_____. *Principles of Dance and Movement Notation*. London: MacDonald & Evans, 1956.

Lewis, Daniel. *The Illustrated Dance Technique of José Limon*. New York: Harper & Row, 1980.

Livet, Anne (Ed.). *Contemporary Dance: An Anthology of Lectures, Interviews and Essays with Many of the Most Important Contemporary American Choreographers, Scholars and Critics*. New York: Abbeville Press, 1978.

Lloyd, Margaret. *The Borzoi Book of Modern Dance*. New York: Alfred A. Knopf, 1949. Reprint: Princeton, NJ: Princeton Book Co., 1987.

Long, Richard A. *The Black Tradition in American Dance*. New York: Smithmark, 1995.

Louis, Murray. *Inside Dance*. New York: St. Martin's Press, 1981.

_____. *On Dance*. Pennington, NJ: a capella books, 1992.

Magriel, Paul David. *A Bibliography of Dancing*. New York: M.W. Wilson, 1936. Reprint: New York: Benjamin, 1966.

_____. *Chronicles of the American Dance*. New York: Henry Holt, 1948. Reprint: New York: Da Capo, 1975.

Main, Lesley. *Directing the Dance Legacy of Doris Humphrey: The Creative Impulse of Reconstruction*. Madison: University of Wisconsin Press, 2012.

Manning, Susan. *Modern Dance, Negro Dance: Race in Motion*. Minneapolis: University of Minnesota Press, 2006.

Martin, John. *America Dancing*. New York: Dodge, 1936.

_____. *The Dance in Theory*. Princeton, NJ: Princeton Book Co., 1989.

_____. *Introduction to the Dance*. New York: A.S. Barnes, 1933. Reprint: New York: Dance Horizons, 1965.

_____. *John Martin's Book of the Dance*. New York: Tudor Publishing Co., 1963.

_____. *The Modern Dance*. New York: A.S. Barnes, 1933. Reprint: Princeton, NJ: Princeton Book Co., 1989.

Maynard, Olga. *American Modern Dancers: The Pioneers*. Boston: Little, Brown, 1965.

Mazo, Joseph. *Prime Movers: The Makers of Modern Dance in America*. New York: William Morrow, 1977. Reprint: Princeton, NJ: Princeton Book Co., 1984.

McDonagh, Don. *The Complete Guide to Modern Dance*. New York: Doubleday & Co., 1976. Reprint: New York: Popular Library, 1977.

_____. *The Rise and Fall of Modern Dance*. New York: Outerbridge and Dienstfrey, 1970. Reprint: New York: New American Library, Inc., 1971.

McGrath, Aoife (Ed.). *Dance Matters in Ireland: Contemporary Dance Performance and Practice*. London: Palgrave Macmillan, 2018.

McPherson, Elizabeth. *Bennington School of the Dance: A History in Writings and Interviews*. Jefferson, NC: McFarland & Company, 2013.

Moore, Lillian. *Artist of the Dance*. New York: Crowell, 1938. Reprint: New York: Dance Horizons, 1976.

Morris, Gay. *A Game for Dancers: Performing Modernism in the Postwar Years, 1945–1960*. Middletown, CT: Wesleyan University Press, 2006.

Morgenroth, Joyce. *Speaking of Dance: Twelve Contemporary Choreographers on Their Craft*. New York: Routledge, 2004.

Nadel, Myron Howard, and Constance Nadel Miller (Eds.). *The Dance Experience: Readings in Dance Appreciation*. New York: Universe Books, 1978.

Palmer, Winthrop. *Theatrical Dancing in America*. (second ed.) New York: A.S. Barnes and Co., 1978.

Percival, John. *Experimental Dance*. New York: Universe Books, 1971.

Perron, Wendy. *Through The Eyes of a Dancer: Selected Writings*. Middletown, CT: Wesleyan University Press, 2013.

Ramsey, Burt. *Alien Bodies: Representations of Modernity, "Race," and Nation in Early Modern Dance*. New York: Routledge, 1998.

Reynolds, Nancy, and Susan Reimer-Torn. *Dance Classics: A Viewer's Guide to the Best-Loved Ballets and Modern Dances*. Pennington, NJ: a capella books, 1991.

Rochlein, Harvey. *Notes on Contemporary American Dance 1964*. Baltimore, MD: University Extension Press, 1964.

Sachs, Curt. *World History of the Dance*. New York: W.W. Norton and Company, 1937.

Schlundt, Christine. *The Professional Appearances of Ruth St. Denis and Ted Shawn.* New York: The New York Public Library, 1962.

Selden, Elizabeth. *The Dancer's Quest.* Berkeley: University of California Press, 1935.

_____. *Elements of the Free Dance.* New York: A.S. Barnes and Co., 1930.

Shawn, Ted. *Every Little Movement.* New York: Ted Shawn, 1954. Reprint: New York: Dance Horizons, 1968.

_____. *33 Years of American Dance.* Pittsfield, MA: Eagle Printing & Binding Co., 1959.

Sherman, Jane. *The Drama of Denishawn Dance.* Middletown, CT: Wesleyan University Press, 1979.

_____. *Soaring.* Middletown, CT: Wesleyan University Press, 1976.

Siegel, Marcia B. *At the Vanishing Point.* New York: Saturday Review Press, 1972.

_____. *Days on Earth.* New Haven: Yale University Press, 1987.

_____. *The Shapes of Change: Images of American Dance.* Boston: Houghton Mifflin Co., 1979.

_____. *Watching the Dance Go By.* Boston: Houghton Mifflin Co., 1977.

Soloman, John, and Ruth Soloman (Eds.). *East Meets West in Dance: Voices in the Cross-Cultural Dialogue.* Philadelphia: Harwood Academic Publishers, 1995.

Solway, Andrew. *Modern Dance.* Chicago: Heinemann-Raintree, 2008.

Sorell, Walter (Ed.). *The Dance Has Many Faces.* (second ed.) New York: Columbia University Press, 1966.

_____. *Dance in Its Time.* New York: Doubleday, 1981 Reprint: New York: Columbia University Press, 1986.

_____. *The Dance Throughout the Ages.* New York: Grosset and Dunlap, 1967.

_____. *The Dancer's Image: Points and Counterpoints.* New York: Columbia University Press, 1981.

_____. *The Duality of Vision: Genius and Versatility in the Arts.* New York: Bobbs-Merrill Co., 1970.

_____. *Looking Back in Wonder.* New York: Columbia University Press, 1986.

Steinberg, Stephen Cobbett. *The Dance Anthology.* New York: New American Library, 1980.

Stewart, Virginia, and Merle Armitage (Eds.). *The Modern Dance.* New York: E. Weyhe, 1935. Reprint: New York: Dance Horizons, 1970.

Stodelle, Ernestine. *The Dance Technique of Doris Humphrey and Its Creative Potential.* (second ed.) Princeton, NJ: Princeton Book Co., 1990.

Strauss, Marc Raymond. *Looking at Contemporary Dance: A Guide for the Internet Age.* Princeton, NJ: Princeton Book Company, 2011.

Streb, Elizabeth. *Streb: How to Become an Extreme Action Hero.* New York: Feminist Press, 2010.

Strohschein, Heather. *Between Modern Dance and Intercultural Performance.* Internet: VDM Verlag Dr. Mueller e.K, 2008.

Terry, Walter. *The Dance in America.* Revised ed. New York: Harper & Row, 1973.

_____. *I Was There: Selected Dance Reviews and Articles, 1930–1976.* New York: Marcel Dekker, 1978.

Tracy, Robert. *Ailey Spirit: The Journey of an American Dance Company.* Boston: Time Warner Group, 2004.

Tonkin, Maggie. *Fifty: Half a Century of Australian Dance Theatre.* Cambridge, MA: Wakefield Press, 2016.

van Tuyl, Marian (Ed.). *Anthology of Impulse.* New York: Dance Horizons, 1970.

Wigman, Mary. *The Language of Dance.* Translated by Walter Sorell. Middletown, CT: Wesleyan University Press, 1975.

Philosophy and Aesthetics

Abra, Allison. *Dancing in the English Style: Consumption, Americanisation and National Identity in Britain, 1918–50.* United Kingdom: Manchester University Press, 2017.

Adair, Christy. *Women and Dance: Sylphs and Sirens.* New York: New York University Press, 1994.

Albright, Ann Cooper. *Engaging Bodies: The Politics and Poetics of Corporeality.* Middletown, CT: Wesleyan University Press, 2013.

Aloff, Mindy. *Dance Anecdotes: Stories From the Worlds of Ballet, Broadway, the Ballroom and Modern Dance.* New York: Oxford University Press, 2006.

Arnheim, Rudolf. *Toward a Psychology of Art.* Berkeley: University of California Press, 1967.

Banes, Sally. *Before, Between, and Beyond: Three Decades of Writing Dance*. Madison: University of Wisconsin Press, 2007.

_____. *Dancing Women: Female Bodies on Stage*. New York: Routledge, 1998.

_____. *Writing Dancing in the Age of Postmodernism*. Hanover, NH: University Press of New England, 1994.

Briginshaw, Valerie A. *Dance, Space and Subjectivity*. New York: Palgrave Macmillan, 2009.

Brown, Benita. *Myth Performance in the African Diasporas: Ritual, History, and Dance*. Lanham, MD: Scarecrow, 2014.

Buckland, Theresa Jill (Ed.). *Dancing From the Past to the Present: Nation, Culture, Identities*. Madison: University of Wisconsin Press, 2006.

Buonaventura, Wendy. *Something in the Way She Moves: Dancing Women From Salome to Madonna*. New York: Da Capo Press, 2004.

Burridge, Stephanie (Ed.). *Dance, Access and Inclusion: Perspectives on Dance, Young People and Change*. New York: Routledge, 2018.

Cage, John. *Silence*. Middletown, CT: Wesleyan University Press, 1961.

Carter, Alexandra. *Rethinking Dance History*. New York: Routledge, 2004.

Claid, Emilyn. *Yes? No! Maybe . . .: Seductive Ambiguity in Dance*. New York: Routledge, 2006.

Croft, Clare (Ed.). *Queer Dance: Meanings and Makings*. New York: Oxford University Press, 2017.

DeFrantz, Thomas F. *Dancing Revelations: Alvin Ailey's Embodiment of African American Culture*. New York: Oxford University Press, Incorporated, 2006.

Dils, Ann, Robin Gee, and Matthew Brookoff. *Intersections: Dance, Place, and Identity*. Dubuque, IA: Kendall Hunt Publishing Company, 2006.

Dutt, Bishnupriya. *Engendering Performance: Indian Women Performers in Search of an Identity*. Thousand Oaks, CA: Sage Publications, 2010.

Fancher, Gorden, and Gerald Meyers (Eds.). *Philosophical Essays on Dance*. New York: Dance Horizons, 1981.

Farnell, Brenda (Ed.). *Human Action, Signs in Cultural Context: The Visible and the Invisible in Movement and Dance*. Metuchen, NJ: Scarecrow Press, 1995.

Foster, Susan Leigh. *Choreographing History*. Bloomington: Indiana University Press, 1995.

_____ (Ed.). *Corporealities: Dancing Knowledge, Culture and Power*. New York: Routledge, 1996.

_____. *Worlding Dance*. New York: Palgrave Macmillan, 2009.

Fraleigh, Sondra. *Dance and the Lived Body: A Descriptive Aesthetic*. Pittsburgh: University of Pittsburgh Press, 1987.

_____. Sondra. *Dancing Identity: Metaphysics in Motion*. Pittsburgh: University of Pittsburgh Press, 2004.

Gard, Michael. *Men Who Dance: Aesthetics, Athletics and the Art of Masculinity*. New York: Peter Lang, 2006.

Geollner, Ellen W., and Jacqueline Shea Murphy (Eds.). *Bodies of the Text: Dance as Theory, Literature as Dance*. New Brunswick, NJ: Rutgers University Press, 1995.

Ghiselin, Brewster (Ed.). *The Creative Process*. Berkeley: University of California, 1952.

Giersdorf, Jens Richard. *Body of the People: East German Dance Since 1945*. University of Wisconsin Press, 2013.

Gill, Sam D. *Dancing Culture Religion*. Lanham, MD: Lexington Books, 2012.

Gottlieb, Robert. *Reading Dance: A Gathering of Memoirs, Reportage, Criticism, Profiles, Interviews, and Some Uncategorizable Extras*. New York: Knopf Doubleday Publishing Group, 2008.

Gottschild, Brenda Dixon. *Digging the Africanist Presence in American Performance: Dance and Other Contexts*. Westport, CT: Greenwood Press, 1996.

Hamera, Judith. *Dancing Communities: Performance, Difference, and Connection in the Global City*. New York: Palgrave MacMillan, 2006.

Hanna, Judith Lynne. *The Performer-Audience Connection*. Austin, TX: University of Texas Press, 1983.

Highwater, Jamake. *Dance Rituals of Experience*. New York: Oxford University Press, 1996.

Jackson, Naomi M., and Toni Samantha Phim. *Dance, Human Rights, and Social Justice: Dignity in Motion*. Lanham, MD: Scarecrow Press, 2008.

King-Dorset, Rodreguez. *Black Dance in London, 1730–1850: Innovation, Tradition and Resistance*. Jefferson, NC: McFarland & Company, 2008.

Kinney, Troy. *The Dance: Its Place in Art and Life*. New York: F.A. Stokes Co., 1924.

Kodat, Catherine Gunther. *Don't Act, Just Dance: The Metapolitics of Cold War Culture*. New Brunswick: Rutgers University Press, 2015.

Kolb, Alexandra. *Performing Femininity: Dance and Literature in German Modernism*. New York: Peter Lang AG, 2009.

Kolcio, Katja Pylyshenko. *Movable Pillars: Organizing Dance, 1956–1978*. Middletown, CT: Wesleyan University Press, 2010.

Kowal, Rebekah J. (Ed.). *Oxford Handbook of Dance and Politics*. New York: Oxford University Press, 2017.

Kwan, Sansan. *Kinesthetic City: Dance and Movement in Chinese Urban Spaces*. New York: Oxford University Press, 2013.

Langer, Susanne. *Feeling and Form*. New York: Charles Scribner's Sons, 1953.

_____. *Philosophy in a New Key*. New York: Mentor Books, 1951.

_____. *Problems of Art*. New York: Charles Scribner's Sons, 1957.

_____. *Reflections on Art*. Baltimore, MD: Johns Hopkins University Press, 1959.

Lepecki, Andre. *Dance*. Cambridge, MA: MIT Press, 2012.

_____. *Exhausting Dance: Performance and the Politics of Movement*. New York: Routledge, 2006.

_____. *Of the Presence of the Body: Essays on Dance and Performance Theory*. Middletown: Wesleyan University Press, 2004.

_____ and Jenn Joy. *Planes in Composition: Dance, Theory and the Global*. London: Seagull Books, 2009.

Manning, Erin. *Politics of Touch: Sense, Movement, Sovereignty*. Minneapolis: University of Minnesota Press, 2006.

Margolis, Joseph (Ed.). *Philosophy Looks at the Arts*. (third ed.) Philadelphia: Temple University Press, 1987.

Martin, Rosemary. *Dance, Diversity and Difference: Performance and Identity Politics in Northern Europe and the Baltic*. London: I B Tauris, 2018.

May, Rollo. *The Courage to Create*. New York: W.W. Norton and Co., 1975.

Mills, Dana. *Dance and Politics: Moving Beyond Boundaries*. Manchester, UK: Manchester University Press, 2017.

Minton, Sandra. *Dance, Mind and Body*. Champaign, IL: Human Kinetics, 2003.

Morris, Geraldine (Ed.). *Rethinking Dance History: Issues and Methodologies*. New York: Routledge, 2018.

Nadel, Myron (Ed.). *Dance Experience: Insights Into History, Culture and Creativity*. Pennington: Princeton Book Company, 2003.

Neveu Kringelbach, Helene. *Dancing Cultures: Globalization, Tourism and Identity in the Anthropology of Dance*. New York: Berghahn Books, 2012.

Nevile, Jennifer. *Dance, Spectacle, and the Body Politick, 1250–1750*. Bloomington, IN: Indiana University Press, 2008.

Oliver, Wendy (Ed.). *Dance and Gender: An Evidence-Based Approach*. Gainesville, FL: University Press of Florida, 2017.

Picart, Caroline Joan. *From Ballroom to Dancesport: Aesthetics, Athletics, and Body Culture*. Albany: State University of New York Press, 2006.

Pine, Adam (Ed.). *Geographies of Dance: Body, Movement, and Corporeal Negotiations*. Lanham, MD: Lexington Books, 2014.

Puma, Fernando (Ed.). *7 Arts*. New York: Doubleday & Co., 1953.

Reynolds, Nancy. *No Fixed Points: Dance in the Twentieth Century*. New Haven: Yale University Press, 2003.

Rodrigues, Graziela. *Dancer–Researcher–Performer: A Learning Process*. New York: Peter Lang, 2017.

Shay, Anthony (Ed.). *Oxford Handbook of Dance and Ethnicity*. New York: Oxford University Press, 2016.

Shapiro, Sherry. *Dance in a World of Chance*. Champaign, IL: Human Kinetics, 2008.

Shawn, Ben. *The Shape of Content*. Cambridge, MA: Harvard University Press, 1957.

Sheets, Maxine. *Phenomenology of Dance*. Madison: University of Wisconsin Press, 1966.

Simonson, Mary. *Body Knowledge: Performance, Intermediality, and American Entertainment at the Turn of the Twentieth Century*. New York: Oxford University Press, 2013.

Strauss, Marc Raymond. *Dance Criticism of Arlene Croce: Articulating a Vision of Artistry, 1973–1987*. Jefferson, NC: McFarland & Company, 2005.

Thomas, Helen. *Dance, Modernity and Culture: Explorations in the Sociology of Dance*. New York: Routledge, 1995.

_____. *The Body, Dance and Cultural Theory*. New York: Palgrave Macmillan, 2003.

Thomas, Kenneth. *The Religious Dancing of American Slaves, 1820–1865: Spiritual Ecstasy at Baptisms, Funerals, and Sunday Meetings*. Lewiston, NY: The Edwin Mellen Press, 2008.

Thompson, Katrina Dyonne. *Ring Shout, Wheel About: The Racial Politics of Music and Dance in North American Slavery.* Champaign, IL: University of Illinois Press, 2014.

Tompkins, Calvin. *The Bride and the Bachelors.* New York: Viking Press, 1965. Reprint: New York: Penguin Books, 1976.

Udall, Sharyn Rohlfsen. *Dance and American Art: A Long Embrace.* Madison: University of Wisconsin Press, 2012.

Related Topics

Anker, Verena. *Digital Dance.* Internet: VDM Verlag Dr. Mueller e.K, 2008.

Arendell, Telory D. (Ed.). *Dance's Duet with the Camera: Motion Pictures.* London: Palgrave Macmillan, 2016.

Barber, E.J.W. *Dancing Goddesses: Folklore, Archaeology, and the Origins of European Dance.* New York: WW Norton, 2013.

Beeler, Stan. *Dance, Drugs and Escape.* Jefferson, NC: McFarland & Company, 2007.

Beradi, Gigi. *Finding Balance: Fitness, Health and Training for a Lifetime in Dance.* (second ed.) New York: Routledge, 2004.

Bernasconi, Jayne, and Nancy Smith. *Aerial Dance.* Champaign, IL: Human Kinetics, 2008.

Bleeker, Maaike (Ed.). *Transmission in Motion: The Technologizing of Dance.* New York: Routledge, 2017.

Chazin-Bennahum, Judith. *The Lure of Perfection: Fashion and Ballet, 1780–1830.* New York: Routledge, 2004.

Clark, Heather. *Dance as the Spirit Moves: A Practical Guide to Worship and Dance.* Shippensburg, PA: Destiny Image Publishers, 2009.

Cohen, Selma Jeanne (Ed.). *International Encyclopedia of Dance* (6 vols.). New York: Oxford University Press, 1998.

DeFrantz, Thomas F. (Ed.). *Dancing Many Drums: Excavations in African American Dance.* Madison: University of Wisconsin Press, 2002.

Dodd, Sherril. *Bodies of Sound: Studies Across Popular Music and Dance.* Burlington, VT: Ashgate, 2013.

Ellfeldt, Lois, and Edwin Carnes. *Dance Production Handbook.* Palo Alto, CA: National Press Books, 1971.

Enters, Angna. *On Mime.* Middletown, CT: Wesleyan University Press, 1965.

Fine, Elizabeth. *Soulstepping: African American Step Shows.* Champaign, IL: University of Illinois Press, 2003.

Flaum Cruz, Robyn. *Dance/Movement Therapists in Action: A Working Guide to Research Options.* Springfield, IL: Charles C. Thomas, 2012.

Forsythe, William, and Roslyn Sulcas. *William Forsythe: Improvisation Technologies.* New York: Hatje Cantz Verlag GmbH & Co KG, 2009.

_____. *William Forsythe: Suspense.* Zurich, Switzerland: JRP Ringier Kunstverlag AG, 2008.

Franco, Mark (Ed.). *Oxford Handbook of Dance and Reenactment.* New York: Oxford University Press, 2017.

Franklin, Eric. *Conditioning For Dance.* Champaign, IL: Human Kinetics, 2004.

_____. *Dance Imagery for Technique and Performance.* Champaign, IL: Human Kinetics, 1996.

_____. *Dynamic Alignment Through Imagery.* Champaign, IL: Human Kinetics, 1996.

Gerrow, Maurice, and Paul Tanner. *A Study of Jazz.* Dubuque, IA: Wm. Brown Publishers, 1973.

Gottschild, Brenda Dixon. *Digging the Africanist Presence in American Performance: Dance and Other Contexts.* Westport, CT: Greenwood Press, 1996.

Hanna, Judith Lynne. *Dancing for Health: Conquering and Preventing Stress.* Walnut Creek: Altamira, 2006.

Harrison, Mary Kent. *How to Dress Dancers: Costuming Techniques for Dance.* Pennington, NJ: Princeton Book Co., 1979.

Hayes, Elizabeth R. (Ed.). *A Guide to Dance Production.* Reston, VA: American Alliance for Health, Physical Education, Recreation and Dance, 1981.

Hayes, Jill. *Soul and Spirit in Dance Movement Psychotherapy: A Transpersonal Approach.* Philadelphia: Jessica Kingsley, 2013.

Hazzard-Gordon, Katrina. *Jookin': The Rise of Social Dance Formations in African-American Culture.* Philadelphia: Temple University Press, 1990.

Horst, Louis. *Pre-Classic Dance Forms.* Pennington, NJ: Princeton Book Co., 1937.

Huntington, Carla Stalling. *Hip Hop Dance.* Jefferson, NC: McFarland & Company, 2007.

Hutchinson, Ann. *Labanotation*. New York: New Directions, 1954. Reprint: New York: Theatre Arts Books, 1977.

Karkou, Vassiliki (Ed.). *Oxford Handbook of Dance and Wellbeing*. New York: Oxford University Press, 2017.

King, Kenneth. *Writing in Motion: Body, Language, Technology*. Hanover: Wesleyan University Press, 2003.

Klippinger, Karen. *Dance Anatomy and Kinesiology*. Champaign, IL: Human Kinetics, 2007.

Kolosek, Lisa Schlansker. *National Museum of Dance and Hall of Fame: Celebrating 30 Years*. New York: State University of New York Press, 2017.

Kuppers, Petra. *Disability Culture and Community Performance: Find A Strange and Twisted Shape*. New York: Palgrave Macmillan, 2011.

Larasati, Rachmi Diyah. *Dance That Makes You Vanish: Cultural Reconstruction in Post-Genocide Indonesia*. Minneapolis: University of Minnesota Press, 2013.

Laws, Kenneth, and Arleen Sugano. *Physics and the Art of Dance: Understanding Movement*. New York: Oxford University Press, 2008.

Lust, Annette. *Bringing the Body to The Stage and Screen: Expressive Movement for Performers*. Lanham, MD: Scarecrow Press, 2012.

Main, Lesley (Ed.). *Transmissions in Dance: Contemporary Staging Practices*. London: Palgrave Macmillan, 2017.

Menear, Pauline, and Terry Hawkins. *Stage Management and Theatre Administration*. London: Phaidon Press, 1995.

Mitoma, Judy, and Elizabeth Zimmer (Ed.). *Envisioning Dance on Film and Video*. New York: Routledge, 2003.

Morgan, Barbara. *Martha Graham: Sixteen Dances in Photographs*. New York: Duel, Sloan and Pearce, 1941.

Nakajima, Nanako (Ed.). *Aging Body in Dance: A Cross-Cultural Perspective*. New York: Routledge, 2017.

Nettl, Paul. *The Story of Dance Music*. New York: Philosophical Library, 1947.

Pallant, Cheryl. *Contact Improvisation: An Introduction to a Vitalizing Dance Form*. Jefferson, NC: McFarland & Company, 2006.

Pecal, Lynn. *Costume Design: Techniques of Modern Masters*. New York: Watson-Guptill Publications, 1999.

Perkins, William Eric (Ed.). *Droppin' Science: Critical Essays on Rap Music and Hip-Hop Culture*. Philadelphia: Temple University Press, 1996.

Ray, Ollie. *Encyclopedia of Line Dances: The Steps That Came and Stayed*. Charleston, IL: Siddall and Ray Research Foundation, 1997.

Rochberg, George. *The Aesthetics of Survival: A Composer's View of Twentieth-Century Music*. Ann Arbor: University of Michigan Press, 1984.

Rosenberg, Douglas (Ed.). *Oxford Handbook of Screendance Studies*. New York: Oxford University Press, 2016.

Russell, Tilden A. *Theory and Practice in Eighteenth-Century Dance: The German-French Connection*. Newark, DE: University of Delaware Press, 2018.

Schlaich, Joan, and Betty Dupont (Eds.). *Dance: The Art of Production*. (second ed.) Princeton, NJ: Princeton Book Co., 1988.

Schott-Billmann, France. *Primitive Expression and Dance Therapy: When Dancing Heals*. Translated by Terence Holden. New York: Routledge, 2015.

Stebbins, Genevieve. *The Delsarte System of Expression*. New York: Dance Horizons, 1978.

Steele, Valerie. *Dance & Fashion*. New Haven: Yale University Press, 2013.

Taylor, Cici, and Jim Taylor. *Psychology of Dance*. Champaign, IL: Human Kinetics, 1995.

Trowbridge, Charlotte. *Dance Drawings of Martha Graham*. Foreword by Martha Graham, preface by James Johnson Sweeney. New York: Dance Observer, 1945.

White, Shane, and Graham White. *Stylin': African American Expressive Culture From Its Beginnings to the Zoot Suit*. Ithaca, NY: Cornell University Press, 1998.

Williams, Drid. *Anthropology and the Dance: Ten Lectures*. Urbana: University of Illinois Press, 2003.

Wilmer, S.E. *Native American Performance and Representation*. Tucson, AZ: University of Arizona Press, 2009.

Young, Harvey. *Black Theater is Black Life: An Oral History of Chicago Theater and Dance, 1970–2010*. Evanston, IL: Northwestern University Press, 2014.

Zehr, Leslie. *The Alchemy of Dance: Sacred Dance as a Path to the Universal Dancer*. Internet: iUniverse, Incorporated, 2008.

Magazines, Periodicals, and Newspapers

The following is a partial list of magazines, periodicals, newspapers, and newsletters (from the United States and abroad) that currently write about dance, either regularly or periodically, or feature articles on dance.

American Dance Guild Newsletter, American Dance Guild, New York. www.americandanceguild.org
American Journal of Dance Therapy, New York. www.adta.org
American Theatre, Theatre Communications Group, New York. www.tcg.org
Attitude, Dance Giant Steps, Inc., Brooklyn, NY. www.attitudedancermag.org
Ballet Review, Dance Research Foundation, Inc., New York. www.balletreview.com
Ballett International, Cologne, Germany. www.ballet-tanz.de
Ballroom Dancing Times, Dancing Times, Ltd., London, England. https://www.dancing-times.co.uk
Choreography and Dance (back issues only), Newark, NJ. http://www.periodicals.com/html/ihp_e.html?ec52461
Contact Quarterly, Contact Collaborations, Inc., Northampton, MA. www.contactquarterly.com
CORD Newsletter, Congress on Research in Dance, Brockport, NY. www.cordance.org
Dance Australia, Yaffa Publishing Group, Australia. www.danceaustralia.com.au
Dance Chronicle, Marcel Dekker Journals, New York. www.jstor.org
Dance Magazine, Dance Magazine, Inc., New York. www.dancemagazine.com
Dance Research Journal, Congress on Research in Dance, Brockport, NY. www.cordance.org
Dance Teacher, International Dance Teachers' Association, Ltd., Brighton, England. www.idta.co.uk
Dance Teacher, Lifestyle, Venture, NY. www.dance-teacher.com
Dance/USA Journal, Washington, DC. www.danceusa.org
Dancing Times, Dancing Times, Ltd., London, England. http://www.dancing-times.co.uk
Journal of Dance Education, Michael Ryan Publishing, Inc., Andover, NJ. www.jmichaelryan.com
Journal of Dance Science and Medicine, Michael Ryan Publishing, Inc., Andover, NJ. www.iadms.org
Journal of Physical Education, Recreation and Dance, Reston, VA. www.tandfonline.com
Movement Research Performance Journal, New York. www.movementresearch.org
The New York Times, New York. www.nytimes.com
The New Yorker, New York. www.newyorker.com
Performing Arts Resources, New York. www.brown.edu
Smithsonian, Washington, DC. www.smithsonianmagazine.com
Soho Weekly News, New York. www.sohoweeklynews.com
Studies in Dance History, a capella books, Pennington, NJ. www.sdhs.org
Village Voice, New York. www.villagevoice.com
Washington Post, Washington, DC. www.washingtonpost.com

Dance DVD and Digital Distributors

Today, much of what is viewed of dance can be seen on the internet. For some, however, DVDs or digital downloads are still a convenient way to view dance. Many dance DVDs are still available for viewing, and new danced films are coming out on the market all the time. Monthly subscription companies such as Nexflix and Hulu usually carry many musical theatre options, as well as some of the more popular ballets (many examples have been listed in the text). There are, however, several media companies that carry a great variety of videos and DVDs (some even carry eight-millimeter films). (Note: as of the publishing of this text, all the companies listed were in the business of selling and/or renting DVDs, digital downloads, and films). Of course, dance clips are readily available on the internet at **www.youtube.com, www.danceinteractive.jacobspillow.org** and **www.vimeo.com**.

Amazon. Has many popular dance titles. **www.amazon.com**

American Alliance for Health, Physical Education, Recreation and Dance, Reston, VA. Includes videos and DVDs on dance instruction, biographies, folk dance, ballroom, and world dances. Also includes film rentals of the "Dance Design" series, among others. **www.pgpedia.org**

ARC Videodance, New York. (212) 206-6492. Includes dances on the minstrel shows and vaudeville.

Artfilms, Australia. Includes a large selection of DVD, especially contemporary dance of European and Austrailian artists. **www.artfilms.com.au**

Bullfrog Films, Oley, PA. Includes a wonderful collection of dance videos and DVDs. **www.bullfrogfilms.com**

Columbia Tristar Home Video, Culver City, CA. Includes many musical theatre videos and DVDs. **www.sonypictures.com**

Merce Cunningham Trust, New York. Includes videos, films, and DVDs of the choreography of Merce Cunningham. **www.mercecunningham.org**

Dance Films Association, Inc., New York. **www.dancefilms.org**

Dance Heritage, Washington, D.C. Includes a significant collection of dance films. **www.danceheritage.org/treasures/html**

Dance Horizons Videos, Pennington, NJ. Includes: dance instruction (for adults and children), dance history, performances, biographies, and fitness and health. **www.dancehorizons.com**

Dancetime Publications, Kentfield, CA. Includes: videos and DVDs that cover 500 years of social dance. **www.DancetimePublications.com**

Educational Video Network, Huntsville, TX. Includes many educational videos and DVDs. **www.evndirect.com**

Film and Video Distributors (American Dance Festival Videos), Madison. Includes videos and DVDs by Douglas Rosenberg of some of modern dance's leading choreographers and dance companies. **www.adfvideo.com**

Films for Humanities and Sciences, Princeton, NJ. **www.films.com**

First Light Video Publishing, Venice, CA. Includes videos and DVDs on television production and media arts. **www.firstlightvideo.com**

Great Performances: Dance in America, New York. Has many dance videos and DVDs that are seen on public television. *www.pbs.org*

Insight Media, New York. Includes many world dance videos and DVDs, as well as other topics. *www.insightmedia. info*

Instructional Support Services, Indiana University, Bloomington. Includes a large selection of dance videos and films (sales and rentals). (800) 552-8620. *www.indiana.edu*

International Film Bureau, Inc., Chicago. (312) 427-4545.

Kultur Video, West Long Branch, NJ. Includes a large selection of dance videos and DVDs. *www.kulturvideo.com*

MGM/UA Home Entertainment, Santa Monica, CA. Includes many musical theatre videos and DVDs. *www.mgm.com*

Michael Blackwood Productions, Inc., New York. Includes excellent videos and DVDs on post-modern choreographers and other contemporary choreographers. *www.michaelblackwoodproductions.com*

Paramount Home Video, Hollywood, CA. (323) 956-8090. *www.imdb.com*

Rize, Lions Gate Films, 2005.

Teacher's Video Company, Scottsdale, AZ. Includes videos and DVDs on ballet, jazz and swing, and ballroom. *www. smavideo.com*

Twentieth Century Fox Home Entertainment, Beverly Hills, CA. Sells many musical theatre videos and DVDs. *www. foxconnect.com*

V.I.E.W. Video, New York. *www.view.com/*

Videoda, East Charleston, VT. Has several contact improvisation videos. *www.contactquarterly.com*

Warner Reprise Video, New York. *http://timewarner.com/*

Dance on the Internet

*There is a wealth of information on the internet regarding any and all aspects of dance. Doing a web search can lead to hundreds, even thousands, of internet sites devoted to dance. Here is a listing of some excellent dance sites, many of which contain a links page that will lead to additional dance sites. YouTube (**www.youtube.com**), and Vimeo (**www.vimeo.com**) have thousands of video clips, both professional and amateur.*

Artslynx International Dance Resources. www.artslynx.org/dance/
BalletCompanies.com. www.balletcompanies.com
Contemporary/Modern Dance Companies. www.contemporary-dance.org
Criticaldance.com. www.criticaldance.com/index.html
Dance USA. www.danceusa.org/
Dance.Com. http://dance.com
Dance Films Association. www.dancefilmsassn.org/
Dance Heritage. www.danceheritage.org/treasures.html
Dance Insider. www.danceinsider.com
Dance Magazine. www.dancemagazine.com
Dance Wire. www.dancewirepdx.org
Educational Technology Clearinghouse. www.etc.usf.edu
Gaynor Minden. http://www.dancer.com
Library of Congress. www.loc.gov/
National Dance Educators Association. www.ndeo.org
New York Public Library Jerome Robbins Dance Division. www.nypl.org/about/divisions/jerome-robbins-dance-division
Premiere Dance Network. http://www.premierdancenetwork.com
Voice of Dance. www.voiceofdance.net

Suggested Videos and DVDs

Chapter 1

The Creative Process. Huntsville, TX: Educational Video Network, 1995.

Dance as Art, Dance as Entertainment with Daniel Nagrin. Tempe, AZ: Daniel Nagrin Theatre, Film and Dance Foundation, 1975.

Dancing. Program 1: The Power of Dance and *Program 4: Dance at Court.* West Long Branch, NJ: Kultur, 1993.

Early Dance. Part I: From Greeks to Renaissance and *Part II: The Baroque Era.* Pennington, NJ: Dance Horizons, 1995.

Why Man Creates. Santa Monica, CA: Pyramid Media, 1968.

Chapter 2

Dance as an Art Form. Five-part series including videos on *Body, Motion, Shape, Space* and *Time.* New York: Chimera Foundation for the Arts, 1972–1973.

Dancing Bodies. New York: Insight Media, 2012.

The Creative Process. Huntsville, TX: Educational Video Network, 1995.

Chapter 3

Ballet Russe. NY: Zeitgeist Films.

Baryshnikov: The Dancer and the Dance. West Long Branch, NJ: Kultur, 1983.

Dance and Body-Mind Centering: A Workshop with Bonnie Bainbridge Cohen. Brussels: Contredanse, 2006.

Jiri Kylián's Black and White Ballets. Chatsworth, CA: Image Entertainment, 1997.

Three by Duato. Chatsworth, CA: Image Entertainment, 2000.

Turning Point. 20th Century Fox Home Entertainment, 1997.

White Nights. Columbia Tristar, 1985.

Chapter 5

American Ballet Theatre at the Met: Mixed Bill. West Long Branch, NJ: Kultur, 1984.

Billboards. New York: NVC Arts, Warner Reprise Video, 1993.

Choreography by Balanchine. New York: Nonesuch, Warner Vision Entertainment, 1995.

Dancing for Mr. B.: Six Balanchine Ballerinas. West Long Branch, NJ: Kultur, 1989.

Dancing—Program Four—Dance at Court. West Long Branch, NJ: Kulture, 1993.

Dancing—Program Six—Dance Centerstage. West Long Branch, NJ: Kulture, 1993.

Glory of the Bolshoi. West Long Branch, NJ: Kultur, 1995.

Glory of the Kirov. West Long Branch, NJ: Kultur, 1995.

How Ballet Began. New York: Insight Media, 1975.

Il Ballarino: The Art of Renaissance Dance. Pennington, NJ: Dance Horizons, 1991.

La Sylphide. West Long Branch, NJ: Kultur, 1971.

Nureyev. New York: Insight Media, 2009.

Paris Dances Diaghilev. New York: Electra Entertainment, 1991.

Pavlova. West Long Branch, NJ: Kultur, 1983.

Romantic Era. NVC Arts International/ABC Video, 1980.

Rudolf Nureyev in Giselle. West Long Branch, NJ: Kultur, 1979.

Sleeping Beauty. West Long Branch, NJ: Kultur, 1965.

Swan Lake. West Long Branch, NJ: Kultur, 1982.

Swan Lake by Matthew Bourne. Rest of World: BBC and NVC, 1996.

Turning Point. 20th Century Fox Home Entertainment, 1997.

Video Dictionary of Classical Ballet. West Long Branch, NJ: Kultur, 1991.

White Nights. Columbia Tristar, 1985.

William Forsythe: Just Dancing Around. West Long Branch, NJ: Kultur, 1996.

Note: Many contemporary ballet dance companies have videos of their dances available on their company's websites or YouTube channel. Netflix and other video streaming companies also offer a wide array of contemporary dance films.

Chapter 6

A Tribute to Alvin Ailey. West Long Branch, NJ: Kultur, 1990.

Ailey Dances. West Long Branch, NJ: Kultur, 1982.

Anna Sokolow. Pennington, NJ: Dance Horizons, 1980.

Bill T. Jones: Dancing to the Promise Land. New York: V.I.E.W. Video, 1994.

Butoh: Body on the Edge of Crisis. New York: Michael Blackwood Productions, 1997.

Cage/Cunningham. New York: Cunningham Dance Foundation, 1991.

Catherine Wheel. West Long Branch, NJ: Kultur, 1981.

Charles Weidman: On His Own. Pennington, NJ: Dance Horizons, 1990.

Dance Black America. Pennington, NJ: Dance Horizons, 1984.

Dancing—Program Seven: The Individual and Tradition. West Long Branch, NJ: Kultur, 1993.

Denishawn: The Birth of Modern Dance. West Long Branch, NJ: Kultur, 1988.

Dido and Aeneas: Mark Morris Dance Company. Chatsworth, CA: Image Entertainment, 1995.

European Dance Theatre: Tanztheatre. Pennington, NJ: Dance Horizons, 1997.

Falling Down Stairs: Yo-Yo Ma and Mark Morris. PA: Bullfrog Films, 1995.

Flickers. WI: ADF Video, 1996.

German Lineage in Modern Dance: Wigman Through Nikolais. New York: Insight Media, 2011.

History of Modern Dance. New York: Insight Media, 2008.

Isadora Duncan: Movement From the Soul. CA: Direct Cinema, 1989.

Limón: A Life Beyond Words. NJ: Dance Conduit/Antidote Films, 2003.

Making Dances: Seven Postmodern Choreographers. New York: Michael Blackwood Productions, 1980.

Mark Morris Dance Group: The Hard Nut. New York: Electra Entertainment, 1992.

Martha Graham. New York: Video Arts International, 1984.

Men Who Danced: Ted Shawn and His Male Dancers. Pennington, NJ: Dance Horizons, 1986.

Merce Cunningham—A Lifetime of Dance. New York: Thirteen/WNET, 2000.

Merce Cunningham: Points in Space. West Long Branch, NJ: Kultur, 1986.

Paul Taylor Dance Company. New York: Nonesuch: Warner Vision Entertainment, 1977.

Paul Taylor: Dancemaker. New York: New Video, 1998.

Retracing Steps: American Dance Since Postmodernism. New York: Michael Blackwood Productions, 1988.
The Enduring Essence: The Technique and Choreography of Isadora Duncan. MA: Images, 1990.
The Shakers. NJ: Dance Horizons Video, 1998.
Tribute to Alvin Ailey. IL: Home Vision, 1990.
Trisha Brown. WI: ADF Video, 1996.
Understanding Pina: The Legacy of Pina Bausch. New York: Insight Media, 2010.
Water Study. Pennington, NJ: Dance Horizons, 1998.
With My Red Fires/New Dance (Doris Humphrey). Pennington, NJ: Dance Horizons, 1978.
The World of Alwin Nikolais. New York: Nikolais/Louis Foundation for Dance, 1996.

Note: Many contemporary modern dance companies have videos of their dances available on their company's websites or YouTube channel. Netflix and other video streaming companies also offer a wide array of contemporary dance films.

Chapter 7

Contact Improvisation/Fall After Newton. VT: Videoda, 1987.
Creative Movement: A Step Toward Intelligence. West Long Branch, NJ: Kultur, 1973.
Dance Improvisation, Parts I–IV. UT: Ririe Woodbury Dance Company, 1993.

Chapter 8

Aspects of Peking Opera. New York: IASTA, 1982.
Buenos Aires: The Tango—One Hundred Years. New York: Insight Media, 2007.
Classical Indian Dance. Princeton, NJ: Films for the Humanities and Sciences, 1989.
Dance Rhythms of Africa. New York: Insight Media, 2011.
Dancing. Program 2: Lord of the Dance and *Program 8: Dancing in One World.* West Long Branch, NJ: Kultur, 1993.
Kabuki for the West. New York: Insight Media, 2009.
Kumu Hula—Keepers of a Culture. New York: Winstar Home Entertainment, 1989.
Noh Theater: Dojoji. New York: Insight Media, 2012.
Of Beauty and Deities: Music and Dance of India. New York: Insight Media, 2006.
The JVC Anthology of World Music and Dance. Cambridge, MA: Rounder Records, 1990. (Also available through Multicultural Media).
The JVC Smithsonian Folkways Video Anthology of Music and Dance of Africa. Berlin, VT: Multicultural Media, 1996.
West African Dance. **www.allatantoudance.se**, 2004.

Chapter 9

All That Jazz. Columbia Pictures, 1979.
Bill Robinson: Bojangles. New York: New Video Group, 1996.
Broadway: The American Musical. New York: PBS Home Video, 2004.
Call of the Jitterbug. New York: Insight Media, 1989.
Dance Black America. Pennington, NJ: Dance Horizons, 1984.
Fosse. Chatsworth, CA: Image Entertainment, 2001.
Gene Kelly: Anatomy of a Dancer. Warner Home Video, 2002.
Jazz Changes/Daniel Nagrin. Tempe, AZ: Daniel Nagrin Theatre, Film and Dance Foundation, 1974.
Jazz Dance Jigsaw: A Video Documentary of the First Jazz Dance World Congress. Evanston, IL: Orion Enterprises, 1991.

Jazz Tap Ensemble. Pennington, NJ: Dance Horizons, 1998.
Masters of Tap. Chicago: Home Vision, 1983.
Oklahoma! 20th Century Fox Entertainment, 1998.
Spirit of Vaudeville: Black Minstrelsy. New York: ARC Videodance, 1985. Also: *Spirit of Vaudeville: Rejuvenation of the Style* and *Spirit of Vaudeville: The Heart of Vaudeville*.
Tap. Sony Pictures, 2006 (redistribution).
Tap Dance History: From Vaudeville to Film. New York: Insight Media, 2011.
That's Dancing. MGM/UA Home Video, 1985.
That's Entertainment: Part I, Part II, and *Part III*. Atlanta, GA: Turner Entertainment Company, 2004.
That's Entertainment, Treasures from the Vault. Atlanta, GA: Turner Entertainment Company, 2004.

Note: All of the musical theatre productions mentioned in this text, such as West Side Story, Singin' in the Rain *and* Kismet, *are available in most commercial video stores.*

Chapter 10

America Dances 1897–1948: A Collector's Edition of Social Dance in Film. Kentfield, CA: Dancetime Publications, 2003.
Art of Baroque Dance—Folies D' Espagne. Dallas, TX: Dancetime Publications, 2006.
Ballroom Dancing: The International Championships. New York: V.I.E.W. Video, 1991.
Burn the Floor. Hollywood, CA: Universal Studios, 2000.
Busby Berkeley Collection. Atlanta, GA: Turner Entertainment Company, 2006.
Cats. Hollywood, CA: Universal Studios, 2000.
Dancetime! Five Hundred Years of Social Dance, Part I: 15th–19th Centuries and *Dancetime! Five Hundred Years of Social Dance, Part II: 20th Century*. Kentfield, CA: Tri Valley Video, 1998.
Dancing. Program 3: Sex and Social Dance and *Program 5: New Worlds, New Forms*. West Long Branch, NJ: Kulture, 1993.
Dancing the Big Apple 1937: African Americans Inspire National Craze. Dallas, TX: Dancetime Publications, 2009.
Everybody Dance Now. New York: WNET/Dance in America, 1991.
History and Concept of Hip-Hop Dance: The Street Culture That Became a Global Expression. Dallas, TX: Dancetime Publications, 2009.
How to Dance Through Time: Volume I, The Romance of Mid 19th Century Couple Dances; Volume II, Dances of the Ragtime Era 1910–1920; Volume III, The Majesty of Renaissance Dance; Volume IV, The Elegance of Baroque Social Dance; Volume V, Victorian Era Couple Dances; Volume VI, A 19th Century Ball: The Charm of Group Dances. Dallas, TX: Dancetime Publications, 2003.
Rennie Harris Puremovement. New York: Insight Media, 1997.
Rize. Lions Gate Films, 2005.
Saturday Night Fever. Paramount Pictures, 1991.
Strictly Ballroom. Burbank, CA: Buena Vista Home Entertainment, 1992.
Tango, Our Dance. Chicago: Facets Video, 2006.
The Freshest Kids: A History of the B-Boy. Entertainment Inc. and Brotherhood Films, 2002.
The Roots of the Hip-Hop Generation. New York: Insight Media, 2004.
The Spirit Moves: The History of Black Social Dance on Film, 1900–1986: Part I, Jazz Dance from the Turn of the Century to 1950; Part II, Savoy Ballroom of Harlem 1950; Part III, Postwar Era. Dallas, TX: Dancetime Publications, 1998.

Endnotes

Chapter 1

1. Margaret H'Doubler, *Dance: A Creative Art Experience* (Madison: University of Wisconsin Press, 1940), p. xxv.
2. Ibid., p. 3.
3. Curt Sachs, *World History of the Dance* (New York: W.W. Norton and Company, 1937), p. 207.
4. Jamake Highwater, *Dance Rituals of Experience* (New York: Alfred Vander Marok Editions, 1978), p. 39.
5. Judith A. Gray, *Dance Instruction: Science Applied to the Art of Movement* (Champaign, IL: Human Kinetics Books, 1989), p. 3.
6. H'Doubler, *Dance: A Creative Art Experience,* p. 5.
7. John Nobel Wiliford, "In Dawn of Society, Dance Was Center Stage," *New York Times*, February 27, 2001 (accessed March 5, 2018).
8. Napoleon Chagnon, *Yanomamo: The Fierce People,* (third ed.) (New York: CBS College Publishing, 1983), p. 157.
9. Ibid., p. 161.
10. Planet Doc, www.planetdoc.tv/documentary-yanomami-women-dancing, October 29, 2015 (accessed February 12, 2018).
11. Highwater, *Dance Rituals of Experience,* p. 39.
12. H'Doubler, *Dance: A Creative Art Experience,* p. 8.
13. Augusto Ancillotti and Romolo Cerri, *The Tables of Iguvium* (Perugia, Italy: Edizioni Jama Perugia, 1997), pp. 61, 68, 69, 78, 82, 89, 90, 93, 95.
14. James R. Brandon, *The Cambridge Guide to Asian Theatre* (Cambridge, England: Cambridge University Press, 1993), p. 65.
15. Ibid., p. 27.
16. Betty Casey, *International Folk Dancing U.S.A.* (New York: Doubleday and Company, 1981), p. 214.
17. H'Doubler, *Dance: A Creative Art Experience,* p. 13.
18. Ibid., p. 16.
19. Ibid., p. 19.
20. Agnes de Mille, *The Book of Dance* (New York: Golden Press, 1963), p. 7.
21. Lois Ellfeldt, *Dance: From Magic to Art* (Dubuque, IA: Wm. Brown Publishers, 1976), p. 134.
22. Susanne Langer, *Problems of Art* (New York: Scribner's Publishing Co., 1957), p. 7.

Chapter 2

1. Lynne Anne Blom and L. Tarin Chaplin, *The Intimate Act of Choreography* (Pittsburgh: University of Pittsburgh Press, 1982), p. 204.
2. Alma M. Hawkins, *Creating Through Dance* (Princeton, NJ: Princeton Book Company, 1988. Revised ed.), p. 5.
3. Lois Ellfeldt, *A Primer for Choreographers* (Palo Alto, CA: Mayfield Publishing Company, 1967), p. 26.
4. Brewster Ghiselin, "Introduction," in *The Creative Process* (Ed.). Brewster Ghiselin (Berkeley: University of California, 1952), p. 12.

5. Rollo May, *The Courage to Create* (New York: W. W. Norton and Company, 1975), p. 57.
6. Blom and Chaplin, *The Intimate Act of Choreography,* p. 7.
7. Hawkins, *Creating Through Dance,* p. 42.
8. Ibid., p. 43.
9. Ibid., p. 64.
10. Blom and Chaplin, *The Intimate Act of Choreography,* p. 73.
11. Ellfeldt, *A Primer for Choreographers,* p. 83.

Chapter 3

1. Charles Engell France (Ed.), *Baryshnikov at Work* (New York: Alfred A. Knopf, 1979), p. 9.
2. Bureau of Labor Statistics, U.S. Department of Labor, *Occupational Outlook Handbook,* Dancers and Choreographers, www.bls.gov/ooh/entertainment-and-sports/dancers-and-choreographers.htm, May, 2016.
3. American Guild of Musical Artists, www.musicalartists.org, January 2010.

Chapter 4

1. Judith Lynne Hanna, *The Performer-Audience Connection* (Austin: University of Texas Press, 1983), p. 197.

Chapter 5

1. Ingrid Brainard, "Domenico da Piacenza," *The New Grove Dictionary of Music and Musicians,* Vol. 5 (London: Macmillan, 1980), pp. 332–333.
2. Anatole Chujoy and P.W. Manchester, *The Dance Encyclopedia* (New York: Simon & Schuster, 1967), p. 88.
3. Carol Lee, *Ballet in Western Culture* (Boston: Allyn and Bacon, 1999), p. 137.
4. Ibid., p. 238.

Chapter 6

1. Lois Ellfeldt, *Dance: From Magic to Art* (Dubuque, IA: Wm. Brown Publishers, 1976), p. 195.
2. Sally Banes, *Terpsichore in Sneakers* (Boston: Houghton Mifflin Co., 1979), p. 6.
3. Gorden Fancher and Gerald Meyers (Eds.), *Philosophical Essays on Dance* (New York: Dance Horizons, 1981), p. 111.
4. Banes, *Terpsichore in Sneakers,* p. 15.
5. Ibid., p. 209.
6. Nancy Reynolds and Malcolm McCormick, *Dance in the Twentieth Century* (New Haven: Yale University Press, 2003), pp. 404–405.
7. Joan Acocella, *Mark Morris* (New York: Farrar, Straus, Giroux, 1993), p. 207.
8. Susan Allene Manning, "An American Perspective on Tanztheatre," *The Drama Review,* Summer (1986), p. 62.
9. Ellfeldt, *Dance: From Magic to Art,* p. 198.

Chapter 7

1. Mary Joyce, *First Steps in Teaching Creative Dance to Children* (Mountain View, CA: Mayfield Publishing Co., 1980), p. 1.

Chapter 8

1. Joanne Keali'inohomoku, "An Anthropologist Looks at Ballet as a Form of Ethnic Dance," in *What Is Dance?* (Eds.) Roger Copeland and Marshall Cohen (New York: Oxford University Press, 1983), p. 544.
2. Ibid., p. 544.
3. Faubion Bowers, *Theatre in the East: A Survey of Asian Dance and Drama* (New York: Grove Press, 1956), pp. 325–326.
4. Ibid., p. 330.
5. Marshall Stearns and Jean Stearns, *Jazz Dance: The Story of American Vernacular Dance* (New York: Schirmer Books, 1964), pp. 14–15.
6. Robert Farris Thompson, *African Art in Motion* (Berkeley: University of California Press, 1974), p. 191.
7. Ibid.
8. Gerald Jonas, *Dancing: The Pleasure, Power and Art of Movement* (New York: Harry N. Abrams, Inc., Publishers, 1992), p. 51.
9. Kapila Vatsyayan, "Concurrent Circuits of the International Dialogue on Dance," *Journal of Physical Education, Recreation and Dance,* November–December (1991), p. 55.
10. Ibid.
11. Liza Simon, "World Hula," *Honolulu Weekly,* July 14, 1993, p. 13.
12. Sharon Māhealani. Rowe, "We Dance for Knowledge," *Dance Research Journal* 40, no. 01 (2008), p. 32.
13. Rhythm India, "Bollywood Dance," http://www.rhythm-india.com/bollywood-dance.html (accessed March 5, 2018).
14. Betty Casey, *International Folk Dancing U.S.A.* (New York: Doubleday and Company, 1981), pp. 4–5.
15. Ibid., p. 4.
16. Ibid., p. 5.
17. Ibid., p. 305.

Chapter 9

1. Lynne Fauley Emery, *Black Dance From 1619 to Today* (Princeton, NJ: Princeton Book Company, 1988), p. 80.
2. Lindsay Guarino and Wendy Oliver, Eds., *Jazz Dance: A History of the Roots and Branches* (Gainesville, FL: University Press of Florida, 2014), p. 39.
3. Marshall Stearns and Jean Stearns, *Jazz Dance: The Story of American Vernacular Dance* (New York: Shirmer Books, 1964), p. 56.
4. Richard Kislan, *Hoofing on Broadway* (New York: Prentice Hall Press, 1987), p. 19.
5. Ibid., pp. 24–25.
6. Janice LaPointe-Crump and Kimberly Staley, *Discovering Jazz Dance, America's Energy and Soul* (Dubuque, IA: Brown and Benchmark, 1992), p. 180.
7. Paul Tanner and Maurice Gerrow, *A Study of Jazz* (Dubuque, IA: Wm. Brown Publishers, 1973), pp. 3–6.
8. Dottie Horn, "Daring to Dance," *Endeavours,* Jan. 1997, p. 1. http://research.unc.edu/endeavours/win97/dance.html
9. Mike Moore and Liz Williamson, "That Eclectic, Elusive Dance Called Jazz," *Dance Magazine*, February (1978), p. 64.
10. Kislan, *Hoofing on Broadway*, p. 183.

11. April Reigh, "Broadway Black History: Shuffle Along," May, 2015, http://broadwayblack.com/shuffle-along/ (accessed March 5, 2018).
12. *Josephine Baker*, March, 2015, http://spymuseum.com/josephine-baker/ (accessed March 5, 2018).
13. Kislan, *Hoofing on Broadway*, pp. 57–59.
14. Ibid., p. 84.
15. Lois Ellfeldt, *Dance, From Magic to Art* (Dubuque, IA: Wm. Brown Publishers, 1976), p. 129.
16. Kislan, *Hoofing on Broadway*, pp. 159–160.

Chapter 10

1. History of Hip-hop, April 2014, https://historyofthehiphop.wordpress.com/hip-hop-cultures/break-dancingdance/ (accessed March 5, 2018).
2. 2015 World Records, UNLIMITED Categories, FASTEST World Record Certification Service, 2015 World Records Registration with World Record Academy, www.worldrecordacademy, August 5, 2015.
3. Improv Everywhere, www.improveverywhere.com, August 5, 2015.

Chapter 11

1. Elizabeth Stone, "There's More to Stage Lighting Than Meets the Eye," *Smithsonian*, September (1991), p. 105.
2. Burton Taylor, "Dancer's World: Dance Lighting," *Dance Magazine*, November (1983), p. 92.
3. J. Michael Gillette, *Designing with Light: An Introduction to Stage Lighting*, (fifth ed.) (New York: McGraw-Hill, 2008), p. 60.
4. W. Oren Parker, Harvey K. Smith, and R. Craig Wolf, *Scene Design and Stage Lighting*, fifth edition (New York: CBS College Publishing, 1985), p. 426.
5. Ibid.
6. Stone, "There's More to Stage Lighting Than Meets the Eye," p. 105.
7. Ibid., p. 110.
8. Martha Ullman West, "Frontier of Design: Isamu Noquchi 1904–1988," *Dance Magazine*, May (1989), p. 58.
9. TroikaTronix, *Isadora*, https://troikatronix.com (accessed March 5, 2018).
10. Molly Friedman, "Misty Copeland is Attracting New Audiences to the Ballet," *New York Daily News*, http://www.nydailynews.com/entertainment/theater-arts/misty-copeland-attracting-new-audiences-ballet-article-1.1975899, October 19, 2014 (accessed March 5, 2018).

Bibliography

Acocalla, Joan. *Mark Morris*. New York: Farrar, Straus, Giroux, 1993.

Ancillotti, Augusto, and Romolo Cerri. *The Tables of Iguvium*. Perugia, Italy: Edizioni Jama Perugia, 1997.

Au, Susan. *Ballet and Modern Dance*. New York: Thames and Hudson, 1988.

Banes, Sally. *Terpsichore in Sneakers*. Boston: Houghton Mifflin Co., 1980.

Blom, Lynne Anne, and Tarin L. Chaplin. *The Intimate Act of Choreography*. Pittsburgh: University of Pittsburgh Press, 1982.

Bowers, Faubion. *Theatre in the East: A Survey of Asian Dance and Drama*. New York: Grove Press, Inc., 1956.

Brainard, Ingrid. "Domenico da Piacenza," in *The New Grove Dictionary of Music and Musicians*, Vol. 5. London: Macmillan, 1980.

Brandon, James R. *The Cambridge Guide to Asian Theatre*. Cambridge, England: University of Cambridge Press, 1993.

Bureau of Labor Statistics, United States Government. "Dancers and Choreographers." www.bls.gov/ooh/entertainment-and-sports/dancers-and-choreographers.htm (accessed March 5, 2018).

Casey, Betty. *International Folk Dancing, U.S.A.* New York: Doubleday and Co., 1981.

Changnon, Napoleon. *Yanomamo: The Fierce People*. (third ed.) New York: CBS College Publishing, 1983.

Chujoy, Anatole, and P.W. Manchester. *The Dance Encyclopedia*. New York: Simon and Schuster, 1967.

Cohen, Marshall, and Roger Copeland (Eds.). *What is Dance?* New York: Oxford University Press, 1983.

De Mille, Agnes. *The Book of Dance*. New York: Golden Press, 1963.

Ellfeldt, Lois. *A Primer for Choreographers*. Palo Alto, CA: Mayfield Publishing Co., 1967.

_____. Lois. *Dance: From Magic to Art*. Dubuque, IA: Wm. Brown Publishers, 1976.

Emery, Lynne Fauley. *Black Dance from 1619 to Today*. (second ed.) Princeton, NJ: Princeton Book Company, 1988.

Fancher, Gorden and Gerald Meyers (Eds.). *Philosophical Essays on Dance*. New York: Dance Horizons, 1981.

France, Charles Engell (Ed.). *Baryshnikov at Work*. New York: Alfred A. Knopf, 1979.

Friedman, Molly. "Misty Copeland is Attracting New Audiences to the Ballet." *New York Daily News*, http://www.nydailynews.com/entertainment/theater-arts/misty-copeland-attracting-new-audiences-ballet-article-1.1975899 (accessed March 5, 2018).

Gerrow, Maurice and Paul Tanner. *A Study of Jazz*. Dubuque, IA: Wm. Brown Publishers, 1973.

Ghiselin, Brewster (Ed.). *The Creative Process*. Berkeley: University of California, 1952.

Gillette, J. Michael. *Designing with Light: An Introduction to Stage Lighting*. (fifth ed.) NY: McGraw-Hill, 2008.

Gray, Judith A. *Dance Instruction: Science Applied to the Art of Movement*. Champaign, IL: Human Kinetics Books, 1989.

Guarino, Lindsay and Wendy Oliver (Eds.). *Jazz Dance: A History of the Roots and Branches*. Gainesville, FL: University Press of Florida, 2014.

Hanna, Judith Lynne. *The Performer-Audience Connection*. Austin, TX: University of Texas Press, 1983.

Hawkins, Alma. *Creating Through Dance*. Revised ed. Princeton, NJ: Princeton Book Company, 1988.

H'Doubler, Margaret. *Dance: A Creative Art Experience*. Reprint: Madison: University of Wisconsin Press, 1957.

Highwater, Jamake. *Dance Rituals of Experience*. New York: Alfred Vander Marok Editions, 1985.

Jonas, Gerald. *Dancing: The Pleasure, Power and Art of Movement*. New York: Harry N. Abrams, Inc., Publishers, 1992.

Joyce, Mary. *First Steps in Teaching Creative Dance to Children*. (second ed.) Mountain View, CA: Mayfield Publishing Company, 1980.

Kislan, Richard. *Hoofing on Broadway*. New York: Prentice Hall Press, 1987.

Langer, Susanne. *Problems of Art*. New York: Scribner's Publishing Co., 1957.

La Pointe-Crump, Janice, and Kimberly Staley. *Discovering Jazz Dance: America's Energy and Soul*. Dubuque, IA: Brown and Benchmark, 1992.

Lee, Carol. *Ballet in Western Culture*. Boston: Allyn and Bacon, 1999.

Manning, Susan Allene. "An American Perspective on Tanztheatre," in *The Drama Review*. Summer, 1986.

May, Rollo. *The Courage to Create*. New York: W.W. Norton and Company, Inc., 1975.

Moore, Mike and Liz Williamson. "That Eclectic, Elusive Dance Called Jazz," in *Dance Magazine*, 1978.

Parker, Oren W., Harvey K. Smith, and Craig R. Wolf. *Scene Design and Stage Lighting* (fifth edition). New York: CBS College Publishing, 1985.

Planet Doc. www.planetdoc.tv/documentary-yanomami-women-dancing. October 29, 2015 (accessed February 12, 2018).

Reigh, April. "Broadway Black History: Shuffle Along." Broadwayblack.com http://broadwayblack.com/shuffle-along/ (accessed March 5, 2018).

Reynolds, Nancy and Malcolm McCormick. *Dance in the Twentieth Century*. New Haven: Yale University Press, 2003.

Rhythm India. "Bollywood Dance," http://www.rhythm-india.com/bollywood-dance.html (accessed March 6, 2018).

Rowe, Sharon Māhealani. "We Dance for Knowledge." *Dance Research Journal* 40, no. 01, 2008.

Sachs, Curt. *World History of the Dance*. New York: W.W. Norton and Company, Inc., 1937.

Simon, Liza. "World Hula," in *Honolulu Weekly*. July 14, 1993.

Sorell, Walter. *The Dance Throughout the Ages*. New York: Grosset and Dunlap, 1967.

Spymuseum.com. "Josephine Baker." http://spymuseum.com/josephine-baker/ (accessed March 5, 2018).

Stearns, Jean, and Marshall Stearns. *Jazz Dance*. New York: Schirmer Books, 1964.

Stone, Elizabeth. "There's More to Stage Lighting Than Meets the Eye," in *Smithsonian*. September, 1991.

Taylor, Burton. "Dancer's World: Dance Lighting," in *Dance Magazine*. November, 1993.

Thompson, Robert Farris. *African Art in Motion*. Berkeley: University of California Press, 1974.

TroikaTronix. "Isadora." https://troikatronix.com (accessed March 5, 2018).

Vatsyayan, Kapila. "Concurrent Circuits of the International Dialogue on Dance," in *Journal of Health, Physical Education, Recreation and Dance*. November–December, 1991.

West, Martha Ulman. "Frontier of Design: Isamu Noguchi 1904–1988," in *Dance Magazine*. May, 1989.

Wiliford, John Nobel. "In Dawn of Society, Dance Was Center Stage," in *New York Times*, February 27, 2001 (accessed February 12, 2018).

Index

238 Index

Terms

A

abstract, 85–90
adagio, 62
administrator, dance, 190
aerobic training, 42
aesthetic experience, 14–16
African-American musical, first, 135
African dancers, 4
AGMA. *See* American Guild of
     Musical Artists
Alexander technique, 42
alignment, 40–41
allemande, 12
American Ballet Theatre, 66–67, 74,
     75, 97
American Guild of Musical Artists, 46
amoamo ritual, 7
ancient period, 8–10, 18
arm gestures, 30
art of dance, 1–19
artistic collaborators, 171–184
artistic director, 168, 190
     duties, 168
     role of, 168
Ashikaga period, 7
assistant stage manager, 170
assistant technical director, 170
audience
     as participant, 49–50
     dynamics, 50
     props, 51
     understanding dance, 50–52
audience, the, 49–54
automated lighting instruments, 175

B

B-boys/girls, 157–159, 161
ballet, 57–78
     adagio, 62
     American Ballet Theatre, 66–67, 74,
          75
     American dance companies, 67
     ballet d'action, 59, 72
     Ballet Tech, 76
     Bolshoi Ballet, 60, 75
     China, 78

classical, 60–67, 73
contemporary, 60, 63–67
corps de ballet, 62, 64
costumes, 63–66
court ballets, 57–58, 72
early, 58–60
England, 74–75, 77
grand pas de deux, 62, 66
Harlem, 66, 76
International dance companies, 67
Israel, 76
Italy, 57, 68, 72
Joffrey Ballet, 76
Kirov Ballet, 67, 75, 76
literal gestures, 62, 66
Lyon Opera Ballet, 67
minuet, 72
National Ballet of Canada, 67
Nederlands Dans Theater, 67, 76,
     77
New York City Ballet, 66–67, 74–78
pantomime, 61–62, 64–66, 68
parallel leg position, 65
Paris Opera, 67, 73, 75, 77
pas de deux, 62, 66, 68, 75
pointe shoes, 62, 68
Renaissance period, 68
Romantic ballet, 58, 60, 73
Royal Academy of Dance, 58, 68
Royal Ballet, 77
Royal Winnipeg Ballet, 67
Russian, 73–74
San Francisco Ballet, 76
Stuttgart Ballet, 67, 76
Sun King, 58, 68, 72
Washington Ballet, 77
Zurich Ballet, 67
ballet d'action, 59, 72
ballet events timeline: 1400–2018,
     68–70
Ballet Russes, 63–66, 74
Ballet Tech, 76
ballroom dance, 4, 146, 154, 163
Bartenieff fundamentals, 42
Batsheva Dance Company, Israel, 107
beam projector, 173–174
beat, 34

Beijing Opera, 9–10
"Big Homies", 161
Black Bottom, 133, 163
Black plague, 11–12, 18
body therapies
     Alexander technique, 42
     Feldenkrais method, 42
     rolfing, 42
body therapist, 190
Bollywood, Indian dance, 124–125
Bolshoi, 60, 75
box office manager, 170
Brazilian dance rituals, 7
breakdancing (breaking), 157–158
breath, 34
breath/emotional phrasing, 34
Broadway and the movie musical,
     146
bubonic plague, 11
budget cuts, 188, 189
bugaku performance, 119–120
burlesque, 132
business manager, 170
Butoh, Japanese dance form, 92, 118

C

cakewalk, 132
captain, dance, 190
careers in dance
     administrator, 190
     artistic director, 190
     body therapist, 190
     captain, dance, 190
     company manager, 190
     costume designer, 190
     dance administrator, 190
     dance captain, 190
     dance company manager, 190
     dance historian, 190
     dance kinesiologist, 190
     dance notator, 190
     dance technology specialist, 190
     dance videographer, 190
     dance writer, 190
     fitness instructor, 190
     historian of dance, 190